WITHDRAWN
UTSA LIBRARIES

HOLOCAUST LITERATURE

Parkes–Wiener Series on Jewish Studies
Series Editors: David Cesarani and Tony Kushner
ISSN 1368-5449

The field of Jewish Studies is one of the youngest, but fastest growing and most exciting areas of scholarship in the academic world today. Named after James Parkes and Alfred Wiener and recognising the co-operative relationship between the Parkes Centre at the University of Southampton and the Wiener Library in London, this series aims to publish new research in the field and student materials for use in the seminar room, to disseminate the latest work of established scholars and to re-issue classic studies which are currently out of print.

The selection of publications reflects the international character and diversity of Jewish Studies; it ranges over Jewish history from Abraham to modern Zionism, and Jewish culture from Moses to post-modernism. The series also reflects the inter-disciplinary approach inherent in Jewish Studies and at the cutting edge of contemporary scholarship, and provides an outlet for innovative work on the interface between Judaism and ethnicity, popular culture, gender, class, space and memory.

Other Books in the Series

The Berlin Haskalah and German Religious Thought: Orphans of Knowledge
David Sorkin

Remembering Cable Street: Fascism and Anti-Fascism in British Society
edited by Tony Kushner and Nadia Valman

Sir Sidney Hamburger and Manchester Jewry: Religion, City and Community
Bill Williams

The Making of Manchester Jewry 1740–1875, Revised Edition
Bill Williams

Anglo-Jewry in Changing Times: Studies in Diversity 1840–1914
Israel Finestein

Double Jeopardy: Gender and the Holocaust
Judith Tydor Baumel

Cultures of Ambivalence and Contempt: Studies in Jewish–Non-Jewish Relations
edited by Siân Jones, Tony Kushner and Sarah Pearce

Alfred Wiener and the Making of the Wiener Library
Ben Barkow

HOLOCAUST LITERATURE

*Schulz, Levi, Spiegelman and
the Memory of the Offence*

GILLIAN BANNER

VALLENTINE MITCHELL
LONDON • PORTLAND, OR

First published in 2000 in Great Britain by
VALLENTINE MITCHELL
Newbury House, 900 Eastern Avenue
London IG2 7HH

and in the United States of America by
VALLENTINE MITCHELL
c/o ISBS
5804 N.E. Hassalo Street
Portland, Oregon 97213-3644

Website www.vmbooks.com

British Library Cataloguing in Publication Data:

Banner, Gillian
    Holocaust literature : Schulz, Levi, Spiegelman and the
    memory of the offence. – (Parkes-Wiener series on Jewish
    studies ; no. 8)
    1. Holocaust, Jewish (1939–1945), in literature
    I. Title
    809.9'3358

            ISBN 0 85303 364 1 (cloth)
            ISBN 0 85303 371 4 (paper)
            ISSN 1368-5449

Library of Congress Cataloging-in-Publication Data:

Banner, Gillian, 1956–
    Holocaust literature : Schulz, Levi, Spiegelman and the
    memory of the offence / Gillian Banner.
        p. cm. – (Parkes-Wiener series on Jewish studies,
    ISSN 1368-5449)
    Includes bibliographical references (p.) and index.
    ISBN 0-85303-364-1 (cloth). – ISBN 0-85303-371-4 (pbk.)
    1. Schulz, Bruno, 1892–1942 – Criticism and interpretation.
    2. Levi, Primo – Criticism and interpretation. 3. Spiegelman,
    Art – Criticism and interpretation. 4. Holocaust, Jewish
    (1939–1945), in literature. 5. Memory in literature. I. Title.
    II. Series.
    PG7158.S294B36 2000
    891.8'5372–dc21
                                                                99-40514
                                                                CIP

Typeset by Joanne Edwards

Printed in Great Britain by
Creative Print and Design (Wales), Ebbw Vale

In constant memory

Enid Banner (née Fox)
20 March 1926 – 20 August 1987,
and for Esmé

CONTENTS

FOREWORD

On no other subject is there so much meretricious writing and so little penetrative thinking as on the Shoah. Where thinking about the Shoah is concerned a degree of absurdity has been reached which even Bruno Schulz could not have foreseen: there are now Day Trips from England to Auschwitz. It has been said that tourism is more murderous than genocide, killing cultures, destroying what the poet David Jones called the blessed particularities, and reducing those who deal with tourists to a sort of automotive greed which obliterates all finer feeling. Holocaust tourism is the worst sort of tourism, pandering to a piety which it cannot satisfy and pretending to educate when it merely titivates. It is a substitute for hard thought and careful observation, reducing the idea of 'Being there' to 'I have been there'. Where writing about the Shoah, especially writing about the so-called literature of the Shoah, is concerned, finer feeling and acuity of observation are also rarely to be discerned; as for discernment, it has usually taken itself off elsewhere.

Gillian Banner is an exception to these strictures. Her experience of the contemporary world, as one who has worked with the abused and persecuted, has heightened her sensitivity and sharpened her intelligence. Primo Levi has seldom been written about as well as he has here. The self-destructive memories of survivors and the self-preserving memory of the perpetrator: a grasp of that fundamental dichotomy has to underpin any approach to the Shoah. It did the work of Primo Levi; it does so here. The theme of prophecy requires the most delicate handling; it gets it here. Bruno Schulz defies every classification save that of prophet. As anyone who visited the exhibition, 'Bruno Schulz Ad Memoriam 1892–1942', at the Adam Mickiewicz Museum of Literature in Warsaw in 1993, will testify, Schulz, like Mickiewicz, wore a coat of many colours. But Schulz in Drohobycz, like Joseph in Egypt, understood what to expect, that a tyrant worse even than Pharoah would arise and drive the people of God from their homes, and that this time it would be more Exit than Exodus.

All those streets of crocodiles, in Warsaw, Lodz, Krakow, Drohobycz, and every other *shtetl*, large or small, led only, ladies and gentlemen, to the Gas. Great artists, like great writers, are seismic in their reading of the universe; great poets too, as in the case of David Jones. Kurt Schwitters, artist and poet, in his 'Chor der Ordnungspolizei' warned us of what ordinary policemen would do: 'One two, one two, one two three/Very soon are finished we;/One two, one two, one two three/The police know how to deal with thee./Clear the streets and make them free,/Let's get on with the third degree.' It has taken historians 50 years *after* the event to acknowledge what Schwitters knew five years before it. Not that the Shoah can be contained in pre-Shoah categories; it broke all rules, burst all boundaries, not least of poetry and prose. Which is why Art Spiegelman's *Maus* is so enlightening. It is an anti-comic Comic Book. Gillian Banner's discussion of that work is a model of sympathetic explication. *Maus* deserves to be expounded, demands explanation; the story of a survivor and his son can never be simple; memories of the offence ensure that it will be complicated. Walter Benjamin said that anyone contemplating the wreckage of our century would have to be clear-eyed, as clear-eyed as his friend Gershom Scholem had been in removing himself from a self-destructive Europe in the 1920s. Moreover, anyone attempting to 'salvage whatever may be salvaged' has to be clear-headed as well as clear-eyed.

Gillian Banner is both. Memory is an academically fashionable subject, a more intellectually justifiable one than Trauma, which was big business under the name of Psychiatry long before there was the Memory Industry and Memory Tourism. These days we are on the brink of Holocaust Nostalgia, Holocaust Romanticism, Holocaust *shmaltz*. Take a look at the posters and postcards they sell at Birkenau, Majdanek, Treblinka, Stutthof. Gillian Banner's book is an antidote to all that. The author is as rigorous as she is imaginative. In being so she rivals Marcel Proust, the father, so to speak, of Memory Studies. No nonsense about Trauma Theory for Proust and none for Gillian Banner either. The depth of the memory is to be related to the indelibility of the offence, whether for a child that is the want of a good-night kiss or for a victim of the Shoah it is being a witness to atrocity. The victims never forget, the culprits cannot remember, and bystanders are not often as perceptive, let alone as interventionist, as Proust *père*. Is the memory of Auschwitz worse than Auschwitz? Because those who were there as prisoners continue to be there as prisoners, it has to be. And for them as they grow older, which is worse: the intensification of remembrance or the fear of forgetting? Perhaps Primo Levi could not bear to forget, could not bear the prospect of ceasing to be a witness. What will happen now that the last generations of survivors are passing away? Might we then be enabled to hear more distinctly, as Gillian Banner suggests, those voices which tell us most? Only if we are listening.

If the Shoah is still taken seriously in the twenty-first century, and 'Never Forget', a far more fitting phrase than the truthless 'Never Again', is not overwhelmed by the trivializing of a media-ridden and consumption-driven First World, the voices discussed in this book will be among those needing to be listened to. And as the guide to listening Gillian Banner's book will be indispensible.

Colin Richmond
Keele, May 1999

ACKNOWLEDGEMENTS

INTRODUCTION

SCHULZ, LEVI, SPIEGELMAN: WHY THESE THREE?

Initially, the decision to write about memory as represented and refracted through the works of Schulz, Levi and Spiegelman made itself. They were amongst the group of writers I encountered when I first began to study the literature of the Holocaust. Lasting attachments are formed in such circumstances. But this is not a sufficient reason for bringing them together now. I hope to show that this particular configuration offers a special approach to the memory of the offence.

Approaching the Holocaust through the works of these three writers presents an opportunity for encountering a revealing variety of modes and responses. Schulz, Levi and Spiegelman speak among and beyond themselves, allowing the development of quite different, though related perspectives. Textually, they employ an exciting range of writing: poetry, memoir, fiction, fantasy, realism, graphics, comic-books. Their writings and drawings encourage the apprehension and articulation of the complicated implications for the past, present and future of the memory of the Holocaust. The fact of these writers' diversity exemplifies the extent to which the Holocaust requires diverse responses.

There are perceptible differences in status accorded to works which represent the Holocaust. Often these differences depend upon the proximity of the writer or artist to that historical event. By studying these three writers and their standing in Holocaust literature I have come to recognize what seems to be a 'hierarchy' or 'genealogy' of remembrance which exists in relation to the Holocaust. This 'hierarchy of remembrance' seems to operate like the 'hierarchy of grief' which frequently appears following a death. As a spouse, child or parent might be 'allowed' or encouraged to grieve more, and more openly, for an individual than a casual acquaintance of that individual, so those writers who were closely involved in, or who lived through, the Holocaust are given more leeway in their response to the Holocaust. This becomes a question of permission: which writers are allowed to handle the memory of the offence and why are they granted that permission? Schulz's stories, though written before the Holocaust, are increasingly read as part of the literature 'about' the Holocaust. Primo Levi, by virtue of his personal experience and his shocking ability to render that experience, holds a central, almost unassailable place in the telling of the Holocaust 'story'. Art Spiegelman's engagement is not only allowed, it is deemed necessary, because of his position as the child of a survivor. Yet this too raises a question: what reception would a comic-book on the Holocaust have received had it been written and drawn by an individual without such 'credentials'? As we move on in chronological time from the historical time of the Holocaust and approach the day when the last survivor will die, the question about what will happen to the memory of the offence becomes more urgent. By dealing with three writers who form or are forming a significant part of the Holocaust canon, I hope to be able to draw some conclusions about the future of the 'genealogy of remembrance' which is being constituted. In this sense, and without being too fanciful, Schulz, Levi, Spiegelman may be characterized as grandfather, father, son. As their readers we are given unbroken access to Jewish apprehensions and experiences of the forces in twentieth-century Europe which resulted in the Holocaust.

What these three writers have in common is that they have little in common. The few characteristics they share may be quickly listed. They are all male. They are all 'Western'. They are all, at least as far as Hitler would judge, Jews. Two are dead, one survives. Only Schulz died as a direct result of German genocidal policies and actions – shot in the ghetto at Drohobycz by a German officer – during the Holocaust. Yet there is an argument to be made for suggesting that Levi also died, 40 years after the 'liberation' of Auschwitz, as an indirect result of those same policies and actions, and that Spiegelman only barely survived being the child of survivors. Two of them, Schulz and Spiegelman, are at least as concerned with graphic art as they are with words. Each writer is both historical and ahistorical. Each writer is in the grip of memory's imperative, acting upon and articulating the compulsion to remember.

Such is the extent of their features in common. Their dissimilarities are manifold. They write in different languages, employ different techniques, express different intentions.

Schulz was a Polish Jew, writing in Polish, with concerns and influences which may be characterized as twentieth-century and European. He was a modernist and surrealist, a writer and a graphic artist. He memorialized a father and a way of life which are not immediately identifiable as Jewish for it is in the barely written, the inklings, that Schulz's Jewishness is to be found. The overwhelming mood in his stories of a reality under threat may chime with an implicit Jewishness which has always had to be aware, at least, of the threats to its existence.

Schulz provides a bridge to the time before the Holocaust. He was already, in the 1930s, an established, if not in his terms successful, writer and artist. There is no evidence to suggest that Schulz was an observant Jew; like millions of other Jews in Europe he might not have recognized himself as Jewish without Hitler's antisemitic pronouncements and laws. Yet Schulz may stand here for the disappeared inhabitants of central and eastern Europe, the now-mythic heartland of European Jewry. Jews had been in Poland for hundreds of years, building a richly modulated and influential culture. They are gone. Few of those millions survived to speak to the future. Schulz's stories, whilst they never mention 'Jews' or 'Jewish', still convey essentials about the culture that was demolished. But this is not why I have chosen him. His stories are not like Singer's: his is not an explicit evocation of or longing for Jewish life before the Holocaust. I have chosen Schulz because of his relationship with memory and because his works illustrate a problematic aspect of the Holocaust in terms of our reading works written before it happened. After the Holocaust our reading of writings like Schulz's may never again be innocent or playful. For the post-Holocaust reader, it seems that in the process of remembering and inscribing the effects of a persecuted past, Schulz imagined a terrible future. His works reveal a world of loss, dispersal, desuetude. They introduce the Holocaust into European literature.[1]

In contrast to Schulz's seemingly marginal relationship with the Holocaust, it is proximity to these events which is emphasized by Levi's writings. Levi is the pivot or fulcrum of this study. His works are one of the cornerstones of the Holocaust canon. No student of the Shoah can ignore them; no student of humanity would wish to. It is a measure of their strength that his writings can bear an unparalleled scrutiny and continue to answer formidable expectations. Levi inhabited the place and time of which Schulz's stories warned. Like Schulz, Levi did not recognize himself as a Jew until Hitler's race laws impinged upon his study in Turin. A cultured Italian, a chemist and rationalist, Levi wrote in a manner which is familiar to all Western

Europeans. For this reason his works have a widespread appeal; even in insular Britain many are familiar with his texts, and year by year they sell in increasing numbers. *If This is a Man*, written shortly after his release from Auschwitz, is essential to any consideration of the 'memory of the offence' (I have borrowed the phrase from Levi) if only because it is one of the earliest, written, accounts of the death camps. The fact that Levi continued to write about his memory of the Holocaust and his memory of his memories until his death in 1987 allows an insight into the processes involved in a continuance of the act of remembrance, emphasizing the extent to which remembering is not a once-and-for-all event. Levi's willingness to engage dynamically not only with his own memories of the Holocaust but also with the problems and traps of memory *per se*, endow his perceptions with a searing and humane clarity.

Art Spiegelman's work represents the challenges and dilemmas of those born since the Holocaust. Increasingly the memory of the offence is being articulated by those who were not 'there', that is, by survivors' children, by non-survivors, by non-Jews. What does this mean for memory? Can these articulations be counted as memories of the offence? After the ephemeral oral testimony (ephemeral unless 'fixed' by recital or technology) came the book. Now, a variety of media, video-taped testimonies, films, cartoons, animation, CD-ROM, the Internet, is being used to transmit memories. These new renditions problematize our relation with the memory of the offence. As survivors die, and despite their recorded testimonies, any sense we may have of a chronological or linear proximity to the Holocaust will be challenged. The value of Spiegelman's work lies not only in the immediacy of his rendition of his father's story but also in that it encourages a timely consideration of the future which awaits Holocaust memory. As the son of an Auschwitz survivor, Vladek Spiegelman, who emigrated to America, Art Spiegelman records and represents his father's recollections whilst querying the meaning and effects those memories accrued in his own life. A consideration of Spiegelman's work allows the scrutiny of issues such as the appropriate representation of terrible events by those who did not experience them directly, the effects of memory upon survivors and survivors' children (and, by extension, anyone who comes into contact with the Shoah) and the forms that remembrance may or should take. In order to be communicable, memory has to find and adopt appropriate forms. In the case of the Shoah, there is the additional struggle to represent an event which has been characterized as unrepresentable. That Spiegelman employs the medium of the comic-book appears to be at odds with the gravity of the memory that is being conveyed. Yet, the graphic representation of memory is especially appropriate at a time when a significant proportion of the information we receive about our present reality is conveyed through images, photographs and films. By this method the memory of the Holocaust retains its particular and contemporary resonance.

The trajectory which is described by Schulz at one end, writing fantastic, elusive stories, in Polish, for a tiny readership, to Spiegelman, articulating the memory of the Holocaust via one of the twentieth century's most successful and ubiquitous media, is an image of the exponential growth of the memory of the Holocaust.

MODES, AND ESPECIALLY THE QUESTION OF FICTION

Whilst each of the three writers adopts fictional modes in his writings, only Schulz's work may be classed unequivocally as 'fiction'. Though they use narrative techniques associated with the novel, Levi's texts *If This is a Man* and *The Drowned and the Saved* are not fiction. *Maus I* and *Maus II* fall into various categories and have been classified as history, biography and autobiography.[3] They have been read by some as fiction, by others as non-fiction, and many reviewers and booksellers encountered difficulties when it came to assigning Spiegelman's texts to one genre or another. As good postmodernists, we all recognize the fictionalizing and shaping that take place in any 'true' story and would assert that no telling is free of the editing and narrating that also goes to make fiction. In this view Schulz's stories are likely to be autobiographical to the extent that Levi's memoir is fictional. I would argue that whilst these ideas are not only persuasive but also beneficial in approaches to most other literature, they do present dangers when applied to the literature of the Holocaust. The tendency to relativism which counts *Sophie's Choice* and *If This is a Man* as equally 'fictitious' or 'true' does a disservice in the case of this particular genre.[4] Levi wrote fiction, some of it, *If Not Now, When?* for example, about the Holocaust.[5] But when reading the literature of the Holocaust, the distinctions between those texts which are intended as fictions and those which are not, need to be recognized and maintained.

TERMINOLOGY

There are a number of terminological issues which I must also address here. I have found no single, unproblematic term or phrase which may be used to represent the vicious persecution and murder of Jews which took place in Europe between 1933 and 1945. *Churban* is favoured by many because it is a specifically Jewish term, has a place within Jewish beliefs and rituals, and connects with and recollects other, earlier disasters visited upon the Jews. Anthony Rudolf explains why he uses *Churban* in a note to *At an Uncertain Hour*:

> I shall use the term *Churban*, a Hebrew word for 'destruction' and one not laden with the wrong religious connotations of 'Holocaust' or even 'Shoah'.[6]

Yet these reasons also militate against the use of the term. James Young points out that:

> Its Yiddish echo (*churbm*) and explicitly religious resonances made *churban* less appealing among Labor Zionists in Palestine . . . Because they perceived events in Europe as completely unprecedented, neither secular nor religious Zionists in Palestine were content to call this merely the 'third *churban*'.[7]

That *Churban* is able to convey a powerful sense of precedent is significant but what concerns me is the extent to which it might fix those events as something specifically Jewish. Whilst it is vital to recognize the Jewishness of the victims, it must not be that these become matters *only* of Jewish concern. Also *Churban* is not yet – if it ever will be – widely used in British writing about the Holocaust and has no commonly understood meaning here.

Although what happened to the Jews of Europe between the years 1933 and 1945 was certainly genocide, I have avoided the terms 'Nazi Genocide' and 'Jewish Genocide'. I have seen both used and because of their apparent interchangeability they seem to leave room for confusion as they do not unambiguously convey who is the perpetrator, who the victim, of the genocide.

In the following discussions, I have used both 'Holocaust' and 'Shoah'. I recognize that 'Holocaust' is problematic. For many writers it is loaded with a wounding sense which turns the murder of the Jews into a sacrificial act with divine implications. It also has specifically

Christian associations which are potentially antagonistic as they invite an 'archaic Christian notion of a Jewish calvary'.⁸ Nor is 'Holocaust' an exclusive word; it is used increasingly to describe other disasters, for example, 'nuclear holocaust', and to describe other genocides, large and small, and even events not genocidal. But it is the most easily and widely recognized by those who are not students of the Holocaust and does not exclude the non-specialist.

'Shoah' probably has the most to offer as a widely acceptable term. Whilst not as familiar as 'Holocaust' to the non-specialist, it is more recognizable and less exclusive than *Churban*. It refers to Yom Ha'shoah, thus emphasizing the memorial day which gains increasing recognition as each year passes. 'Shoah' also alludes to Lanzmann's great work of memory, *Shoah*, and permits the Jewishness of the Holocaust to be recorded.⁹

I have invariably referred in the discussions which follow to 'Germans' or 'German' rather than 'Nazis'. This is deliberate. That tendency of the German population after the war to insist that 'It wasn't me. It wasn't us. We didn't know and anyway the SS made us do it' has been shown convincingly by, amongst others, Browning and Goldhagen, to be a lie.¹⁰ Similarly the anthology of shame compiled by Klee, Dressen and Riess reveals the extent to which not only were 'ordinary Germans' indifferent or permissive in their responses to Jewish persecution, they were very frequently 'Hitler's willing executioners', to the extent that many were able to characterize those days of horror as 'Schöne Zeiten'.¹¹

A final point. I am not attempting in the discussions which follow to unify the works of Bruno Schulz, Primo Levi and Art Spiegelman. On the contrary there will be elements to each writer's work which do not necessarily mesh with the observations I make about either or both of the others. It is my intention to allow anomalies and refuse any temptation to manufacture dull homogeneity out of their marvellous disparity.

NOTES

1. For a poignantly relevant example of the way in which what comes to happen colours our view of what has happened, see the chapter 'Paul Bereyter' in W. G. Sebald, *The Emigrants* (London: Harvill, 1996) and especially p. 63.
2. Primo Levi, *If This is a Man* (London: Abacus, 1987).
3. Art Spiegelman, *Maus I: A Survivor's Tale* (London: Penguin, 1987); *Maus*

II: A Survivor's Tale (London: Penguin, 1992); *The Complete Maus CD-ROM* (New York: The Voyager Company, 1994).
4. William Styron, *Sophie's Choice* (London: Cape, 1979).
5. Primo Levi, *If Not Now, When?*, trans. William Weaver (London: Abacus, 1987).
6. Anthony Rudolf, *At an Uncertain Hour: Primo Levi's War against Oblivion* (London: Menard Press, 1990).
7. James Young, *Writing and Rewriting the Holocaust: Narrative and the Consequences of Interpretation* (Bloomington: Indiana University Press, 1990).
8. Ibid., p. 87. Young's chapter 'Names of the Holocaust' is a useful introduction to the variety of arguments and qualms each term provokes.
9. Claude Lanzmann, *Shoah: An Oral History of the Holocaust – The Complete Text of the Film* (New York: Pantheon, 1985).
10. Christopher R. Browning, *Ordinary Men: Reserve Police Battalion 101 and the Final Solution in Poland* (New York: HarperCollins, 1992); Daniel Jonah Goldhagen, *Hitler's Willing Executioners: Ordinary Germans and the Holocaust* (London: Little, Brown, 1996).
11. Ernst Klee, Willi Dressen and Volker Riess, *The Good Old Days: The Holocaust as seen by its Perpetrators and Bystanders*, trans. Deborah Burnstone (New York: Macmillan, 1991).

2

MEMORY'S ATTRIBUTES

Most of the dead were poor and illiterate. But every single one of them had dreamed dreams, seen visions and had amazing experiences, even the babes in arms (perhaps especially the babes in arms) . . . If a Sigmund Freud had been listening and taking notes from the time of Adam, he would still not fully have explored even a single group, even a single person. [1]

This study is engaged in 'taking notes' from three individuals: Bruno Schulz, Primo Levi and Art Spiegelman. It is not so much concerned with literal facts as with metaphorical truths which may be discovered in the different perspectives and disparate 'memories of the offence' articulated in the works of these three writers. Before discussing the place of memory in the writings of Bruno Schulz, Primo Levi and Art Spiegelman, I wish to offer some explanation of the kinds of memory with which this study is concerned. I have not attempted to investigate the scientific, physical, chemical and cognitive processes which permit memory to operate. Nor is this study a matter of history, for memory cannot be confused with history; whilst there are considerable overlaps they obey essentially different imperatives. Memory may not be judged using the same criteria of accuracy, coherence, analysis which conventional history puts on in its attempt at objectivity, for often in the course of remembering, historical facts are metamorphosed, lost or misinterpreted. Memory offers a metaphorical approach to fact; it simultaneously represents fact whilst attempting to understand the fact it represents. It is the medium we employ to remind ourselves who we were, who we have become, who we will be. It vies with and undermines the linearity of conventional history. Whilst the Holocaust does exist in historical fact, it may not be relegated to history; for memory, there can be no 'before' and 'after' the Holocaust; the Holocaust is now. Survivor testimonies reiterate this fact. Whilst survivors are able to speak of 'before' and 'after', and are encouraged by their listeners to provide a context which relates to these markers in time, yet they regularly express the view that the Holocaust does not work in their lives like other events. It cannot be over, managed, closed. For this reason, many survivors refuse or find themselves unable to speak of the discovery of the camps by the Allies as a liberation.[2]

Memory often requires a 'fact' to be turned into a 'truth'. This process may be simply illustrated. In *Children with a Star*, Deborah Dwork presents the testimonies collected from adult survivors who experienced the Holocaust as children.[3] Many women who had been in the camps recounted that, as a result of drugs added to their food by the Germans, they did not begin to menstruate as they reached the age of puberty or, if they were already menstruating, they reverted to a state of amenorrhoea. Dwork discussed with these women the joint effects of hard labour and a starvation diet, suggesting that, as their body weight fell so their periods were prevented or ended. She reports that a significant number of women accepted this suggestion; as adult women they could see that this made sense and was the most likely explanation for their condition, especially as their periods returned once they were well again. But when she spoke with them again at a later date, their recollections had returned to their first, 'firmly held belief'; the women 'remembered' that they had ceased to have periods because the Germans put chemicals in their food. Dwork had discovered a memory which was not a fact, yet it has the status of a truth, not only for those young women, but also for those who read or hear their testimony. What they had realized was that the Germans intended to remove all Jews from existence. This meant that there must not only be no Jews left alive, but that there should no longer be any potential for Jewish life in the future. The Holocaust was an attack in the present upon both the past and the future.

> This construct rationalized their experiences: the Germans
> wanted to annihilate the Jewish people, and everything they
> did to their victims led to that end. Thus, if a girl ceased to
> menstruate she understood this phenomenon within that
> context, that was the truth. [4]

Dwork suggests that in approaching memory and testimony it is necessary 'to try to reach the "subjective" truth behind the "objective" falsehood'.[5] Similar recollections appear in *Elli*: Elli remembers that after only three weeks in Auschwitz she stopped menstruating and was told that the Germans were employing means of mass sterilization.[6]

She hardly considers that the effects of stress and hunger encountered earlier in the ghetto may have contributed to her amenorrhoea.

The change that memory enacts upon fact is not something which needs to cause alarm or wariness, nor is it something that needs to be hidden. Acknowledging memory's processes does not deny or revise facts. The history is firm, the facts are corroborated: the Holocaust happened. But it is important to allow memory its own shape and place. In *Testimony*, Dori Laub reports an account given by a woman who witnessed the Auschwitz uprising:

> All of a sudden ... we saw four chimneys going up in flames, exploding. The flames shot into the sky, people were running. It was unbelievable.[7]

In fact, only one chimney was blown up. At a later date, this videotaped testimony was presented at a conference, provoking disquiet amongst historians who felt that accuracy was vital and that the inconsistency between the woman's memory and the facts of those events called into question the veracity of her whole testimony. Believing that such fallibility of memory might aid those who seek to deny the Holocaust, that such inaccuracies may be employed as means of discrediting other testimony, it was argued that all testimony had to be historically accurate. Laub disagreed and it is the point of his disagreement which is relevant here:

> The woman was testifying ... not to the number of the chimneys blown up, but to something else, more radical, more crucial: the reality of an unimaginable occurrence. One chimney blown up in Auschwitz was as incredible as four ... She testified to the breakage of a framework. That was historical truth.[8]

This acknowledges that memory, whilst it inhabits territory which is coterminous with history, concerns itself with something other than historical accuracy. In the case of the Holocaust, memory is struggling to convey 'the reality of an unimaginable occurrence', and consequently has to employ figures and metaphors which transcend the boundaries of fact. For what use is fact alone in the communication of the unimaginable? Those soldiers who had the terrible privilege of 'liberating' the camps, saw, heard, recorded, with a military punctiliousness, the horrific extent of the evidence of atrocity which

they found. Yet their reports, whilst cataloguing the facts, often convey
their own unbelieving responses to those facts. Robert Abzug describes
this process in *Inside the Vicious Heart*:

> Less sophisticated readings of the camp were possible: ones
> that turned disbelief into an undercurrent of doubt, or at least,
> suspended judgement. On December 9, 1944, ... Colonel Paul
> Kirk and Lt. Colonel Edward J. Gully of the American Sixth
> Army Group inspected Natzwiller ... In the report they made
> to headquarters, which was eventually forwarded to the war
> crimes division, they qualified just about every observation
> that had to do with instruments of death and torture.[9]

The report uses words and phrases of uncertainty: 'what appeared
to be a disinfection unit'; 'a large pile of hair appearing and reputed to
be human female'; 'allegedly used as a lethal gas chamber'; 'the so-
called lethal gas chamber'; 'stains which appeared to be caused by
blood'.[10] Part of this hesitancy may be explained by the caution
employed by report writers in most professions but a significant factor
was their own reluctance to believe:

> Archaeologists in a modern ruin, Kirk and Gully had all the
> artifacts in place but nonetheless could not quite put together
> what they had found ... Something in them balked ... They
> believed enough to send along their report to war crime
> investigators, but retained a measure of disbelief. In this sense
> they were typical of many American officers in France.[11]

'Something in them balked.' The officers knew what they had seen,
but were unable to believe it. Again and again, in written and oral
testimonies, a resistance to belief is encountered; 'something' finds it
difficult to believe the evidence. Survivors and onlookers constantly
reiterate the difficulty of turning knowledge into belief and a halting
discourse between knowledge and belief is often heard in these matters
of memory. Even those who witness most powerfully to the memory
of the offence allow themselves to register the discrepancy between
what memory knows and what, later, seems possible. So Levi writes,
'Today, at this very moment as I sit writing at a table, I myself am not
convinced that these things really happened.'[12] And Delbo captures
this paradox:

Today I am not sure that what I wrote is true.
I am certain it is truthful.[13]

Her ambivalence is understandable because whilst we acknowledge the truth of the Holocaust, we simultaneously long for it to be untrue. As Deborah Lipstadt puts it: 'We would prefer the deniers to be right.'[14]

I insist that this matter of inaccurate or fallible memory does not need to cause alarm, wariness or the desire to erase discrepancies. Six million Jewish people were exterminated. That is irrefutable. Or at least, those who remain unconvinced in the face of monumental evidence – much of it carefully documented by the Germans themselves – will hardly be convinced by the first-hand accounts of a group of people whose numbers dwindle yearly, no matter how accurate and verifiable their memories. But there is a benefit to those of us who do not need such convincing, who are assured of 'the reality of an unimaginable occurrence' to allow disparity and plurality in the memories to which we listen and of which we read. It is in the meeting-place of discrepant memories that we will find truths which transcend the merely historical. In spite of similarities, each of the six million dead would have had a different tale to tell of his or her annihilation. Levi recognizes this in his powerful assertion, 'We the survivors are not the true witnesses.'[15] In his fictionalized, and borrowed, account of the massacre at Babi Yar, D. M. Thomas commemorated that individuality which the homogenizing machinery of the *Endlösung* had sought to deny. By looking closely at the work of three individuals, whose relationship with the Holocaust is very different, this study may offer an additional contribution to the recognition that the collective disaster which is the Holocaust was experienced individually.

THE COMPULSION TO REMEMBER

The mode of memory is *recherche* rather than recuperation.[16]

Contemporary relationships with memory and remembering are increasingly complicated and fraught with anxiety. The human tendency to look back and reminisce seems to gain pace, and memorizing media proliferate. At times it seems as if there is an ever-growing fear attached to forgetfulness. The least event must be recorded and memorialized: to not record, to be unable to recall, or replay, puts into jeopardy something essential but often intangible.

Our growing insistence upon the recording of events and our dependence upon technology to 'mind' our memories offer intriguing insights into the dynamic relationship of memory, compulsion and reliability. These tendencies imply a set of affirmations about memory: memories are made 'now'; there is a set of criteria which makes it possible to recognize the moment in which a memory is 'made'; once satisfied, it is those criteria which impart significance to memory; memory and the significant moment may be simultaneously identified and are capable of 'capture'; memories should be captured at the instant of their genesis if they are not to be 'lost'; to prevent their loss, memories should be swiftly translated into an object; it is only the attainment of materiality as photograph or video film which confirms the fixedness and transferable potential of memory. These assumptions have such potency that many social events in the West: weddings, births, christenings, retirements, babies' first birthdays, holidays, provoke recording behaviour which often contains an element of restrained frenzy.

There is one noticeable gap in this compulsion. Deaths and funerals are not subject to this intense desire to photograph or video: no one ever takes a snap in the hospice or at the graveside. To do so would provoke feelings of revulsion and disquiet in other mourners for there is an ambivalence about viewing images associated with death which sits oddly with what otherwise appears to be a widespread scopophilia associated with filmed and fantastic representations of death and violence. Such ambivalence was exemplified in the physical layout of the exhibition, 'The Dead'.[17] Museum staff were strategically posted to ensure that anyone entering understood what it was they were likely to see, unaccompanied children under the age of fourteen were not allowed to view, posters abounded warning the viewer of what was ahead.

Still, most social gatherings increasingly revolve around, and seem to depend for their significance upon, the making and fixing of memory. When the videoing of a social event fails, the response of those involved is often one of distress. It is as though, without the appropriate pictures, whether moving or still, there can be no certainty that the event took place. Memories are lost. For many, this almost-frenzied and certainly anxious relationship with the past, even, or perhaps especially, the very recent past, was intensified by the approach of the year 2000:

> As we approach the end of the twentieth century and with it the end of the millennium, our gaze turns backwards ever

more frequently in an attempt to take stock and to assess where
we stand in the course of time. Simultaneously, however, there
is a deepening sense of crisis often articulated in the reproach
that our culture is terminally ill with amnesia.[18]

We have a changing relationship with memory. We depend
increasingly upon the extrinsic, the technological and the built, rather
than intrinsic sources for memory, which results in a related
degradation of the place that ritual, repetition and story-telling play in
the reinforcement and rehearsal of memory. In the future, will memory
only be accounted memory, if it may be replayed? Or visited? This has
implications for the ways in which memories formed without the aid
of external props and evidence are 'viewed'; we are tending to believe
that there is something suspect about such memories. This approach
offers no insight into the memories of individual Holocaust survivors
which exist largely unsupported by props: in many cases all that is left
are the words of the survivor, whether written or spoken; in others, all
that is left is absence. And it is often those events which are not
captured and fixed to which memory returns obsessively.

This is not to suggest that there is any lack of physical objects,
tangible proofs, which attest to the undeniable fact of the Shoah. There
are the piles of hair, of glasses, of suitcases; the scrupulous details kept
by German officials of the numbers of 'pieces' transported; the
documents which proudly proclaim many villages, towns and
countries 'Jew-free'; the photographs and newsreels of the 'liberation'
of the camps; the filmed and written testimonies of survivors,
bystanders and perpetrators. But this study, whilst conscious of those
necessary-for-some artifacts as proof of the destruction of Jewish
people in Europe, is concerned with intangible, unfilmable memory:
the inseparable memory that resides in and becomes a part of an
individual, so that he or she may not hold up a photograph or play a
video but will be compelled to say, 'It's my skin. This is not a coat'
(Langer, *Holocaust Testimonies*, p. 205). To this extent memory becomes
the person, the person is compounded of his or her memories.

The ubiquitous employment of the camera, of the video camera, of
forms such as drama-documentary, of heritage sites which attempt,
however 'sensitively', to give some sense of what it was like to be
'there', lead to misapprehensions about memory. What is captured,
replayed, corroborated carries the status of veracity which other
memories lack so that the idea of a definitive, one-and-only memory
develops. The reconstruction of memory abounds; television and the

cinema re-present past events, often using black-and-white film which
so readily bestows authenticity, with a painstaking attention to detail –
as though assiduity may reanimate that which is in danger of being lost
or which is moribund. One effect of this may be judged by the fact that
in Kraków, tourists now visit the sites where Spielberg filmed the
scenes in *Schindler's List* which represent the liquidation of the ghetto.
The streets which are 'actually' the site of those historical scenes are
not the 'real' place of these happenings in the minds of those who come
to 'view'. Visitors to this memory are interested in standing on the
fictional sites given a factual status by the evidence of film. Similarly,
the pathway paved with reproduction Jewish gravestones for the
scenes at the entrance into the camp at Plaszów is beginning to attain
an authenticity of its own. What would it mean if these stones were
dug up and removed? By re-enacting, with a compelling attention to
detail, some of the events of the Shoah, Spielberg has brought into
being sites which for many visitors will more easily and really
represent and contain the memory of the Holocaust. Of course, these
sites are so closely related to the real sites of atrocity that there may be
little room for disquiet: presumably no street in Kraków is free of
Shoah-related associations. But what of the Polish railway car in the
Holocaust Museum in Washington? What does that object mean and
say about the Holocaust and our memory of it?

And perhaps this is the key to our determination to capture
memories. By filming events, memory is contained, managed, represented. Memory is made safe and the definitive, replayable memory
attains precedence over the untidy, frequently inaccessible, sometimes
contradictory, often disturbing, memories of individuals. The
containability, representability and transferability of memories and the
memory of the offence do not operate in comfortable proximity. The
idea that if memory, like a heritage site, is not to be lost, it must be
restored when it has fallen, like an old building, into desuetude, is at
variance with the kind of memory encountered in the recitals,
testimonies, writings of the Holocaust. For these productions testify
that memory is a dangerous matter with its own imperatives and
challenges refusing containability and closure. This type of memory is
of an altogether different kind and is characterized quite simply in the
title of Raul Hilberg's autobiography as *Unerbetene Erinnerung*, that is,
'Unsolicited Memories'.[19] Unsolicited memories do not have to be, and
may not be, re-enacted for the camera. They represent a problem as
they return unbidden 'at an uncertain hour' and constitute an
inescapable, inexorable possession of the rememberer. It is the

unsolicited element of memory, the compulsion which resists repression or returns from the place where memory has been hidden or buried to which Primo Levi was referring when he chose those particular lines from *The Ancient Mariner* as an epigraph for *The Drowned and the Saved*. The ambivalent relationship which Levi had with his memories is clear in his writing. Whilst he believed that he had a duty to witness, he was also compelled to witness; there was no fear of losing the memories. Change, decay, attrition may afflict memories but loss is not a threat. For some survivors, loss may even suggest a potential for relief from the fear which does exist: that memory will finally overwhelm and consume the rememberer.

SURVIVORS' MEMORIES: HAPPY ENDING OR MORAL VACUUM?

There are two identifiable, apparently divergent and antipathetic themes to be encountered and acknowledged in the meaning found in memories of the Holocaust whether they are oral, visual or written; factual or fictional; produced by survivors or non-survivors. On the one hand the memory of that time represents an acute attack upon hope, an absence of morality so profound that there are those who argue that the existence of this vacuum challenges the very idea of morality outside a carefully controlled, luxurious, fragile and finally dispensable series of cultural contexts.[20] This memory is the most disturbing for both the survivor and the non-survivor to encounter, for there are no brave stories; no uplifting sense of the human spirit winning through to attain nobility and sanctity; no God and nothing recognizable as civilized humanity. There is betrayal, disgrace, a shameful silence and impotence. On the other hand there is a memory that claims and upholds human kinship, which recommends a belief in the purposes of adversity and recognizes a determination to survive in order that the world should know and should benefit from that knowledge. In the first case, the 'liberation' of the camps was not a happy ending. It signalled for the survivors their entry into a time which is in many respects as onerous as that experienced during the Holocaust: the entry into the time of memory. And in the second, the conclusion of the war was a happy ending. With survival achieved, those who were left embarked upon a new life, many of them expressing the view that this was a second chance: for they had been dead and were alive.

It is not always helpful to become tangled in the search for meaning and redemption, and it is possible simply to listen to or read these testimonies and tolerate their memory of a time and a place without meaning. It is very difficult for the reader and observer simultaneously to manage these different kinds of memory for they resist each other, defying containment and assimilation so that there is a tendency to become the advocate of one or the other, to adopt either the understandable pessimism of the first or the life-affirming optimism of the second. However, the necessary task is to let both be, because both forms of memory may be metaphorically 'true'. Whilst survivors' tendencies towards one or the other are moderated according to their various experiences of the Holocaust, the meaning they have excavated from those experiences, their subsequent perceptions about what was happening during the Holocaust and the 'natural' dispositions of individual personalities, it is of no benefit to view these modes of memory as fixed or fixable. That they are not fixed is apparent from the extent to which individual survivors oscillate between expressions of hope and despair. This oscillation is further inflected by increasing age and by the tolerance, or otherwise, of the listener to listen to expressions of despair. Levi is a prime example of the difficulty encountered by survivors whenever their message tends not to fit the redemptive agenda of non-survivors but most survivors speak of the refusal of those around them to 'hear' anything other than 'survival' and 'liberation'.[21] Even in Israel, survivors encountered grave obstacles to the recital of their stories. Speaking with and listening to survivors, Segev discovered many who told him repeatedly, 'People did not want to know.' Nina Wangrove's testimony expresses her own sense of ambivalence concerning the benefits of survival:

> I've always been very closed off; my husband and I did not talk about what had been during the war. I could have made him talk about it, but I didn't want to. He's also from 'there'. I don't like to say 'Holocaust survivor'. The fact is that we did not survive, we were not saved. To this day we have not been saved . . . Other people did not understand us, cannot understand us. That is my feeling today . . .
>
> And we didn't try to understand ourselves. So one year went by and then another and another and another. Every year it became harder. Everything. The memories of the Holocaust and the memories from after the Holocaust and the memories from the Kibbutz. Every year it is harder . . .
>
> Except for my children, there is nothing that ties me here

[on the Kibbutz]. I can be here and tomorrow I can be there and the day after nowhere. This did not turn out to be a terribly important place to me. Perhaps there really are no terribly important places, or even things. Everything important died.[22]

The earliest shapes taken by survivors' memories were often influenced by a process which encouraged a statement or testimony which was 'euphoric' or 'redemptive'; this explains the existence of many 'happy ending' accounts. Also, survivor memory often took its cue from the stance of the interviewer or listener. Langer correctly emphasizes the tendency amongst interviewers who are not survivors to seek the happy ending.[23] This desire becomes insistent at times; it is as though reassurance is sought because of the interviewer's wish to discover bravery and purpose in survival. Perhaps, for non-survivors, this demand supports a necessary illusion that it was possible to maintain personality and identity. In addition, and probably of more significance in the shaping of survivor testimony, non-survivors found it difficult to listen to survivors' tales unless they were optimistic; listeners evaded knowing the worst or believed, wrongly, that the best hope for survival in the future was forgetfulness about the past. This seems to have been a common impulse: Deborah Dwork cites the example of Sara Spier who was told when she went for a job in a hospital three weeks after the war ended, having been in hiding for three years:

> The war is over now, so no word about the war. You may come, you come to work and you come to learn to be a nurse, and we won't speak about the war and you don't speak about your Jewish background. No stories.[24]

Rabbi Hugo Gryn witnessed to a similar experience:

> Actually there was very little understanding of what had happened in the Holocaust. The likes of me ... if I was asked ... where were you during the war, kind of thing, and you begin to say, well, whatever ... my story ... you could see a kind of a glazed look or an embarrassment ... an embarrassment. And there ... developed a kind of conspiracy of silence. It was also very difficult to talk about it, very painful. And who needs that?[25]

And there was also an intrinsic problem with having survived. For those who have not had to survive, there is only an unalloyed benefit in the notion of survival. For the survivor, this is different. Survival imposes its own distress and responsibilities; the survivor may easily feel that the 'I' has not survived because 'I' am not the 'me' that I was. Even outside Holocaust experience, there is a tendency to believe that it is the best, the good who die; those who survive are therefore, in their own view, the worst, the bad. Guilt is a common element of grief and Holocaust survival may be additionally tainted with the knowledge of what survival entailed or required.

Those writers who 'take sides' in the matter of memory by suggesting that memories may only express either optimistic or pessimistic perspectives, emphasize a polarized view of survivor memory which unhelpfully promotes rigidity and encourages closure. Survivors may need to hold, if not contain, both optimistic and pessimistic elements within their remembrance of what has happened and what is continuing to happen to them. In considering the representation of Holocaust memories it must be allowed that the most extreme experiences may not be assimilated, coalesced into life; individuals do not 'get over' trauma, but learn instead to live accompanied by the experience. Rememberers have to be permitted to remember and to figure their own experiences as they need; they cannot be castigated for adopting a redemptive, euphoric or pessimistic tone. It is not helpful to assume or impose a hopeful or a pessimistic message upon these representations of extremity. If a survivor says, 'This is my view', there is little justification for the non-survivor to disagree, to say, 'You don't understand your own response.' Nor is it right to privilege one form of representation over another in the belief that one is truer than the other. A survivor who consistently offers a positive rather than a negative representation should not be open to challenge.

What might be useful in approaching these memories is Delbo's use of two terms for memory – *mémoire profonde* and *mémoire ordinaire* – which Langer also discusses (Langer, *Holocaust Testimonies*, p. 5). If survivors experience at least two memory forms, the *profonde* and the *ordinaire*, this might explain the way in which they discover a spectrum of responses within themselves and express different 'versions' of their survival. These memories appear to oscillate between a redemptive or hopeful recollection which emphasizes coalescence, 'chronology and conjunction', and a despairing or dismantling recollection emphasizing 'disruption, absence and irreversible loss': one form of memory remembers meaning; the other the dismantling of meaning (Langer,

p. xi). This then is a challenge to or negation of the 'idea of continuity, and even of chronology, that testimonies from former victims *seem* to offer us by the very structure of their narratives' (Langer, p. 5). This 'seeming' is often structured or imposed by the listener; again and again there is the sense that those who hear these stories attempt to impose meaning and closure upon them and witnesses collude with this imposition.

Delbo offers the idea of there being a 'double existence' in which the normal pre- and post-Auschwitz persona ignores the Auschwitz persona or acts as though it does not exist. This way of being is coupled with an existence which contains and knows all of that very disturbing memory material, and struggles to manage it or to maintain separation from it whilst fearing that it may, at any time, burst into this new post-Holocaust world. The first persona is potentially comforting, not least for onlookers who must take responsibility for attempting to make manageable what may not be manageable. It reassures by virtue of its suggestion that extreme experience may be set aside; that it is possible to live normally after Auschwitz. The second configuration seems more persuasive though more intimidating.

After any bereavement there is often a period of time during which, whilst the bereaved experience grief and pain, there may be accompanying emotions which seem to have elements of the visionary and ecstatic. This response varies from person to person and may last for hours, days or weeks. These feelings seem to arise out of the need to discover some meaning in the loss, or, if none may be discovered, to impose meaning upon this encounter with death. At this stage, the bereaved are often strangely calm, seem to be 'taking things well', coping better than those around them might have imagined possible as they make arrangements and order their life. But alongside this positive response to death, grief continues, and this period of calm or even euphoria is superseded as the work of mourning goes on. What was needed for psychological health after the Holocaust was entry into a period of mourning on a massive scale. However, the immensity of the adjustments required, combined with the silencing impulses of non-survivors, left little room for proper mourning or proper remembering. In addition there were practical matters requiring attention which undermined any willingness to listen to survivors' stories, for example, the need for the rapid rehabilitation of and reconciliation with West Germany in the face of the Soviet threat and the reluctance to de-stabilize postwar Europe further by a vigorous tracking down of the perpetrators of war crimes. After the war, whilst struggling with the vicissitudes and uncertainties of life in that chaotic time, almost everyone could point to losses; everyone was attempting to reconcile what had happened collectively with what had happened individually. In this climate there was little space for an appropriate recognition of the magnitude of the unique loss inflicted upon Jewish people. The lack of opportunity for enacting mourning rituals is specifically referred to in survivor testimony, emphasizing the enormity of losing whole families and communities whilst having no forum for the expression of that loss. The dead cannot be left behind and they haunt in a way unknown to those of us leading more normal lives. In many cases it was years before survivors were assured that their families were not returning, and, given the continuing hostility directed towards them, that they should leave their homelands and start again elsewhere. One survivor spoke of her shock when she first attended a funeral as she realized that none of the many deaths which had been a part of her life in the camps had been properly registered or recognized (Langer, p. 99). There was no time or energy or inclination to hear, recognize or register these deaths; the tendency was to refuse the memories the Jews carried and to suppress their rehearsal of memory. It is this perhaps which led to the preference for rather uplifting tales of bravery to be the welcomed recollections of the war and of the Holocaust; tales of resistance and strength rather than surrender and despair. It is only as time passed that there has been a willingness to seek out the dark side of these memories; perhaps it is only in the last ten years that there has been a wider capacity to listen to them. This potential to hear may have arisen quite simply because those who now listen are not in competition with survivors for understanding.[26]

These changes may explain the different perception of memory which is encountered in testimony. In many respects, the memories Levi rehearsed 40 years after Auschwitz, in *The Drowned and the Saved* (1988) make that text more hope-less than *If This is a Man* (1979), written in 1947 immediately upon his return to Italy. Langer notes a similar change in Charlotte Delbo's writings. In earlier volumes she claimed that art could mitigate experience, she 'speaks of the value of literature in sustaining her during her ordeal'. Later, she refutes this claim: 'she specifically denies that reciting a poem or discussing a book or a theatrical piece while she and her fellow deportees were digging in the swamps surrounding the camp ever led to a successful "doubling" (*dédoublement*) of the self' (Langer, p. 4). This might be something like the shift that takes place between *The Truce* (1979) and *The Drowned and the Saved*. And, given that Levi deliberately identifies his work with that of the Ancient Mariner, it is illuminating briefly to remember the responses to his experience expressed by the Mariner. His initial delight at survival:

> Oh! dream of joy! is this indeed
> The lighthouse top I see?
> Is this the hill? is this the kirk?
> Is this mine own countree?
> ...
> O let me be awake, my God!
> Or let me sleep alway.

becomes the terrible, scalding imperative of memory:

> Forthwith this frame of mine was wrenched
> With a woful agony,
> Which forced me to begin my tale;
> And then it left me free.
>
> Since then, at an uncertain hour,
> That agony returns:
> And till my ghastly tale is told,
> This heart within me burns.

leaving the Wedding Guest, and those who hear the remembrances of the Shoah, 'like one that hath been stunned,/And is of sense forlorn.'

MEMORY AS PREPARATION

O Buchenwald I can't forget you
Because you are my destiny[27]

We build our expectations of the future, ... on our familiarity with the past. How could we foresee gas chambers ... when we had never heard of them? The average imagination ... perceives what it or someone else has already conceived. Death we can anticipate; but extermination. . . ? (Langer, *Holocaust Testimonies*, p. 29)

We should not come to the encounter [with survivor memory] unprepared – yet we do. (Langer, p. 20)

They expect the worst [*le pire*] – not the unthinkable [*l'inconcevable*].[28]

The idea that memory may be prepared or primed by the past is significant when considering the Holocaust. Lack of experience in common is often cited by writers and rememberers as an obstacle to really hearing the testimonies of survivors. Often, survivors speak of the worry, fear or certainty that they will not be believed and for them and their contemporaries, the issues of credibility or of legibility were different. Prior to the Holocaust, memory held no code for recognizing an event on this scale. With rare exceptions, the Jews of Europe were unable to believe that this event could be happening, even as it happened. In spite of increasingly punitive laws and brutalities, they believed at various stages that the matter would not go any further. For how could they have believed or remembered otherwise? This was a failure brought about by a gap in memory, in analogy. There was no catastrophe on this scale in their memory nor in the memory of any of their neighbours so that a perceptual difficulty arose: if such a thing has not been seen, recognized, named before, then how may it be seen, recognized, named now?

The memory of persecution and the effects of antisemitism are embedded in Jewish culture and its rituals. They shape religious and cultural observance and behaviour in a manner and to an extent which is unlike that in any other religion or culture. (It is this awareness which, I will argue, pervades Schulz's stories to the extent that they inscribe hints and inklings of impending destruction.) Yet, in spite of many instances of violence, the Jews of Europe were often settled in communities which had existed alongside their non-Jewish neighbours for hundreds of years. They could not in any real sense be considered to have been prepared or warned by the memory of ancient desolations, nor even more recent pogroms, for a modern destruction of the compass and ferocity of the Holocaust. To believe otherwise is to posit a passivity and tolerance in the face of persecution which is not feasible.

But those who come after know that the Holocaust happened. Since 1945 there has never been a time when the Holocaust has not happened; it is there, undeniably. This fact imposes an awful privilege and responsibility upon those who have come to maturity with the memory. It is possible that the Holocaust may have a different meaning for those who have grown up with the knowledge that the unimaginable and the unbelievable have happened and therefore may continue to happen. At the least, there is a different readiness to hear these stories. Increasingly, when we 'take stock' of the twentieth century as Huyssen suggests, we are encouraged to see 'a century of indescribable catastrophes and of ferocious hopes'.[29] Others put the

Shoah not only at the centre of this hellish vision but see it as a definitive event for Western consciousness:

> If anything can be concluded from the ceaseless outpourings of works in every genre and medium about the Nazi genocide, it is how central that cataclysm has become to the self-interrogation of the culture we inhabit today. Although among non-Jews the consensus evolved only very gradually, by now there is a surprisingly widespread sense that the Shoah constitutes the defining event of the Second World War, that the extermination of European Jewry was not merely one among many competing projects of the Third Reich, but rather the very essence of Nazism, and that the universe of the death camps created a decisive breach in the fabric of the modern world.[30]

The Holocaust has attained the status of a reference point for genocide and bureaucratized inhumanity: because it happened therefore it can happen. The Holocaust is the proof of its own possibility. We need no other. Even before encountering survivor testimonies we are prepared, readied, fit to hear. We believe. There is an analogy available here with other abuses which may help in understanding the way belief requires a precedent in memory, exemplifying the gap between what Langer terms 'separate narrative' and 'collective memory' (p. 21). For many, the revelations in the 1960s of domestic violence and in the 1970s of the sexual abuse of children were not at first believable. Part of the difficulty lay in the fact that general, rather than individual, memory had no reference point for such behaviour. Although women and children have always suffered from such abuses, the recognition and naming of those abuses were not widely available.

The knowledge of the Holocaust is one of the most significant changes in perception to have occurred since 1945. Before that, it was literally unthinkable for most people that notions of progress and civilization might be so illusory and fragile as to allow an event of such monumental barbarity; even, horrifically, that progress and civilization, especially as they fostered organization and bureaucracy, made the Holocaust possible. The generation which had its concept of morality and permissibility settled before 1945 does not have our 'advantages'; it believed in purpose, meaning, progress. We know nihilism and the possibilities of inhumanity without having experienced them at first hand. Many who saw the first newsreels of the camps experienced a paradox, a conundrum: how to believe in the unbelievable. For, in spite of the privations of war they were uneducated in the possibilities of such horrors.

Belief seems crucial to the procedure of sharing memory. Many writers place too much emphasis upon impossibility and unreality, allowing the reader to take refuge in impotence. It is perhaps a mark of laziness if, after 50 years, we are no more prepared now than we were then to consider the possibilities for human excess. Langer represents the Holocaust as 'impossible reality' and suggests that 'The impossibility, however, lies not in the reality but in our difficulty in perceiving it *as* reality' (p. 40). Whilst this formulation may be true, for a variety of reasons, for many observers of the memory, I would suggest that it is not true for all. Those who 'benefit' from having grown up with a perception and a memory which includes the 'impossible reality' of the Holocaust may be primed to recognize and acknowledge this reality. This group may not experience the unwillingness or difficulty identified by Langer. One detriment to his view lies in what appears to be a determination to preclude and deny the possibility that the 'impossible reality' may not be impossible for this group. This is an insistence which seems full of a desire for narrative closure not unlike the insistence which he finds culpable amongst interviewers of survivors. And this insistence takes no cognizance of those whose longing to hear matches the compulsion to tell. Understandably many writers emphasize the silence and the refusal to listen to this story which made the Holocaust possible and sentenced many survivors to a painful muteness. But what is to be made of the recent explosion of books and programmes about the Holocaust? Why is it that there are those now willing to encounter this material? I would suggest that the upsurge in memorizing activity has been enabled by a confluence of factors: those who have grown up with the recognition of the presence of the Holocaust are now in a position to demand that this material be made available; survivors, conscious of their dwindling numbers, have found that their sense of urgency is revitalized; age has released many repressed memories as survivors face new bereavements and losses; anniversaries encourage recollection so that the 50th anniversary of the end of the 1939–45 war created an opportunity for reminiscence; prepared memory makes the reception of these stories less problematic; knowledge of atrocity is more widespread and accessible, so we are better able to hear and believe Holocaust atrocities.[31]

It is the memory and knowledge of these events which make belief possible. Langer refers to the testimony of Edith P. as she remembers her arrival in Auschwitz. She recognized that this event, unlike all others, had no precedent in her life: there were no role models available to her. No one had come back from Auschwitz to tell her what to expect. And as Auschwitz was constituted as the antithesis of a memorial, as a place designed to destroy the memory of itself and what happened there, it is not surprising that she was unprepared:

> You lose the ability to think about yourself in the situation in which you find yourself ... For example ... one can say 'When I get married', or 'If I die', or 'If someone I love dies', or 'If I have a child', or 'When I get a job', or 'If I have some money', creating certain theoretical probabilities and then imagining oneself into those situations because we know how to think about them – they have precedents in our own or other people's experience. But no one before has ever said 'When I go to Auschwitz, I ... '; therefore the mind remains blank. (Langer, *Holocaust Testimonies*, p. 103)

It is only prophets, mad people or artists, those such as Moché the Beadle, Madame Schächter or Bruno Schulz, who could believe in such things before they had occurred.[32] For those who come after, the world is different; possibilities are changed and analogy is available. There has been an Auschwitz therefore there may be an Auschwitz. The memory of what has passed makes a similar future possible: memory and prophecy at last elide.

Langer's suggestion that 'we are asked to share less what is recovered than the process of recall itself' seems not to be correct (p. 40). Survivors wished us to share 'what is recovered' but found that, initially, listeners were prepared to receive only 'the process of recall itself', which presented difficulties for testimony. Survivors know that listeners may not 'share what is recovered' in any experiential sense (whilst they surely long for an imaginative sharing), yet, it seems that listeners may attempt to be completely available to the speakers by offering to share experience imaginatively. The belief that listeners will not or may not share may not be as fixed as was once assumed. So, whilst Langer speaks of the 'impossibility of its [the experience's] content' (p. 40) this seems to be a notion which is less and less useful in our engagement with Holocaust memories. For in what sense is this content impossible: in terms of plausibility or realization? This 'content' must be realized, and soon. It is the listener's duty to attempt proximity, to try to stand alongside the survivor, in a humane attempt to affirm a common humanity – which is certainly what was missing in the mechanics of the Shoah. Those who insist that survivors cannot share these memories adequately with others court a great danger, for this matter must not be permitted to remain incomprehensible and unimaginable. Almost all human experience works from analogy; it is part of the project of the imagination which ratifies our humanity. And by use of analogy and imagination we are able to draw alongside the rape victim, the terminally ill person, the abused child, to challenge the sense of impotence and isolation which might be provoked by these experiences. And, even if one has been raped, abused, or is dying, it is not possible to experience exactly what has been experienced by another; individuality dictates that some elements of uniqueness will attach to the most comparable, the most ubiquitous of events, whether good or ill. Experience can never be the same; my dying will not be as your dying. Even the Holocaust was not able to degrade human experience to that extent. Although the attempt to de-individualize persecution, dying and death appeared to have succeeded, the sense of the uniqueness of each one of the six million has not been erased. On the contrary, with each new testimony, with each name 'saved' from oblivion and added to the lists maintained by Yad Vashem and other Holocaust museums, the individuality of those destroyed millions is properly affirmed.

Contrary to the usual memory search, one which Langer characterizes as Proustian, which confers meaning, pattern and form upon the past for the present, the odyssey into memory which survivors undertake undoes any fragile meaning, pattern or form which they may have imposed or transposed upon their present lives. Survivor memory memorizes disconnectedness, not connectedness: the experiences encountered exist as distilled memory, unmediated by chronology, purpose, meaning, closure. The view expressed constantly by survivors is:

> You didn't have any choices. You just were driven to do whatever you did. So it is not things that you planned that you do; it's just whatever happened, happened. You don't think. You think on the moment what will happen *this* moment, not what the next moment will happen. (p. 177)

This is the paradoxical non-meaning of living when you knew you were dead, that it was only a matter of time: 'It is one purpose there: that is to *kill* the people, so that's the purpose there' (p. 178). Martin R. expresses perplexity at the fact that though he had been convinced that he was 'through, you're dead. You're just walking, but you're dead now', yet he remained alive (p. 190). Memory says, 'You were dead, no doubt about it', but the very fact of having a memory proves that death did not arrive. This provokes an almost impossible ambiguity for ideas about meaning and purpose to resolve.

Meaning has a tendency to disappear when considering Holocaust memory. Memories evidence disjointed, unravelled narrative: many testimonies expose the gaps and fractures which ravage narrative. How can memory make narrative sense or make sense of narratives which abolish sense? For the survivors, little or no meaning may be fashioned from the fact of being the only surviving member of a whole family or of a community. And if one may fashion meaning, what kind of meaning might this be? What positive meaning might one find in the fact of one's survival in the face of wholesale destruction? Any meaning in such circumstances can only be so compromised, tainted and distasteful as to constitute no-meaning, to negate its own meaningfulness. The idea of meaning bears with it a positive corollary, a definition which seems to contain notions of benefit and advantage. What kind of benefit or advantage may be considered to accrue from an event which requires the demolition of all those around for its achievement of meaning? A meaning which only comes into being as a result of absence, loss, destruction cannot contain those positive attributes. The only possible positive meaning to be construed from the statement: 'I am here because all around me fell', is one so arrogant – 'I was chosen' (by whom? God? or the SS? Did God mean 'selected' when He said that the Jews were His Chosen People?) – that all survivors, without exception, refuse this meaning. For what can it mean to be a chosen person amidst such demolition? And would one wish to be chosen by anything that could contemplate such destruction and do nothing more than choose?

Even a testimony like that in *Elli*, which discovers miraculous interventions and contains the most positive readings of events, recognizes finally the potential for a collapse into a meaningless void:

> How can anyone understand the aching that is Auschwitz? The compulsion to fill the void that is Auschwitz? The search, the reaching out. The futility. The irrevocable statement that is Auschwitz ... The loss of perspective. The loss. The total,

irreconcilable loss . . . I belong to this void. Nothing can change
that. Nothing . . . This is one unalterable allegiance. This is
where I belong. To Auschwitz.[33]

In memory's possibly futile search for meaning and morality in the
events of the Shoah there is the potential for a further terrible injustice
to be committed. Living now in a relatively moral society, where care
for siblings, parents, children and friends is a measure of moral
maturity, the memory of that world where all others had to be
sacrificed in order for the individual to survive, leads survivors and
non-survivors alike to form a moral judgement about behaviour which
took place in a reality that was differently structured from this one.
'Why did I/you let that happen?' becomes an insistent question which
requires of memory an explanation of the inexplicable, an explanation
for which an adequate moral and philosophical language appears to be
lacking.

The lack of language available to memory is not surprising as
silence attained an especial significance within the context of the
Holocaust. Silence was necessary in order to survive, that is, one had
to be ready at all times, not to speak up, not to challenge, not to display
care or allegiance. Yet silence was also necessary to *not* survive the
camps; the silence of camp personnel and of the complicit populace
made the system possible. Those caught up in the machinery found
themselves 'Practising the silence' like abused children (Langer,
Holocaust Testimonies, p. 71). This practice also made it difficult to speak
later; if to be silent is to survive, then to speak is to court death. (It is
this paradox in part which has fuelled the frequently partisan and
inconclusive debates over appropriate forms of response to the
Holocaust, silence or speech.) Overcoming the taboo and injunction
against speaking may be part of the difficulty for the survivor. Re-
entering a world where to speak may be essential for survival is
perhaps incomprehensible, unimaginable for the traumatized selves of
the survivors.

The re-entry into time and memory was clearly exceptionally
strenuous for survivors. They stress the futility of memory; they
cannot believe that those who have not experienced these things will
really be able to know them. The suggestion is that unless known they
cannot be believed and yet knowledge and belief are attributes which
do not necessarily confirm or disallow one another. In addition there is
the distress caused by the perception that even if memory were fully
expressible this would not necessarily render it believable or

apprehensible or imaginable. There will always be a gap between what is recollected then articulated and what is received then realized. Memory takes the survivor back to a time when he or she was dying, was dead, there could be no escape. Dying and death became reality: to live, to survive was unreal, unbelievable, unimaginable. Looking back into that memory relocates the survivors in a context which disproves their existence for they are placed in a paradoxical existence where they could not exist. To the extent that it was impossible to imagine survival so the survivor cannot have survived. This is life after death of the most macabre kind, or the life-in-death of *The Ancient Mariner*. Memory thus challenges, rather than, as more usually, assuming or reinforcing a sense of self, of aliveness. To remember is to be located again in death, to be dead again. Memory in these circumstances triggers the obverse of reincarnation.

So, troubles of a different kind begin at the point from which status as a survivor may be traced:

> Asked to describe how he felt at the moment of liberation, one surviving victim declared, 'Then I knew my troubles were *really* about to begin', inverting the order of conflict and resolution that we have learned to expect of traditional historical narrative.[34]

From the moment when memory restarts, when survivors re-enter normal existence – or at least an existence which has measure, precedent and form – survivors encounter new difficulties. Because even the return to normality has no precedent in memory; no one before has survived events like these. Until liberation, the Jews were not survivors. The achievement of this status brings difficulties unlike any encountered by non-survivors; how to survive alongside the memory of victimization, degradation, the dismantling of the identity; how to return to time, where there is not only a 'now' (which has remained throughout the experience of their victimization) but also 'before' and 'after'.

The emphasis of non-survivors upon the moment of liberation exposes the difficulties of the two different times. Reading *The Truce*, and then *The Drowned and the Saved*, one is aware that things do not get better after the liberation; they may seem to, as in *The Truce*, but then, 40 years later, the memory which prevails, the memory which attains the most substantial immediacy, is not, for Levi, the fact of liberation or the amusing recollections contained in *The Truce* but the bleak exposition of humanity depicted in *The Drowned and the Saved*. In a BBC documentary on Levi, Ruth Feldman, the translator of much of his poetry, suggested that helping a biographer had 'dredged up' difficult and possibly unmanageable memories for Levi.[35] She spoke of a letter she received one month before Levi's death in which he described a 'severe depressive crisis'. She gives further details of the letter's contents: Levi wrote that he was 'living through a period that was the worst since Auschwitz but worse still, in the next sentence he said, in a way even worse than Auschwitz, which is unthinkable'. He had signed the letter, '*de profundis*'. There is an understandable perspective, one close to a catechism, that there is, and may be, nothing worse than Auschwitz, but Levi felt that he was experiencing something worse. (Other survivors have expressed similar feelings.) If there is something worse than Auschwitz then there is still a terrible 'potential' for experience; liberation was not the end for survivors and memory engenders further horrors.

Langer points to the despair and longing of the survivor for 'someone who knows me *really*'.[36] This kind of imperative can be faintly discerned in the world when people share the experience of bereavement, illness or abuse more readily with others who have similar experience than with close friends who may not have. The greatest obstacle between the survivor and the non-survivor is not a matter of belief or knowing or memory. It is that '*really*'. The survivor can never really be known by the non-survivor, not only in terms of having experienced and witnessed things which the non-survivor has not witnessed but also because there is no one left who knew the survivor before they had survived. There may be a faint echo of this kind of feeling as one gets older and friends and family start to die; there seems to be an increasing difficulty with the notion of one's own self-identity and memory as those reference points disappear. In the same BBC documentary, Levi's friend, Jean Samuel, a survivor of Auschwitz, expresses this relationship poignantly as he talks of the loss he feels following Levi's death. 'I could always turn to him. He had such a memory. He remembered everything about himself, about others, about me. Ever since, I have felt lost.' The loss of the reference point which was Primo Levi creates a feeling of loss in Jean Samuel and it is not only that Samuel feels lost but that the 'I' is lost. The new losses of age reawaken the old losses of the Shoah.

Something happens to reality, time, identity, perception which may not be replicated to such an extent by any other experience, though it might be that the Holocaust is at the extreme end of a spectrum of experience rather than something completely other, at least in terms of its ramifications for memory and psychology. Yet, there is an element in the memory of survival that refutes any similarity or congruence with other human experience, which affirms difference, that needs the non-survivor who listens, reads or watches *not* to understand, *not* to admit consonance. For if we can understand or really know the content and form of these memories then perhaps the Holocaust experience is both trivialized and made truly uncontainable. There is pain in the isolation from normal life which survivors feel and remember, but perhaps there is potential for another kind of pain if we were to say, 'Yes, I know, I *really* know.'

To this extent the story which Holocaust memory recounts has to remain unassimilable. The survivors' need for narrative, coherence and understanding also recognizes that their memories cannot attain such form. Whilst there may be an imposed linearity, a before- and an after-Auschwitz, yet the Holocaust memory-experience remains outside, defying, whilst longing for, linearity and coherence. There is only the simulacrum of narrative, the image or representation of sequence which is overlaid upon the Holocaust memory, usually at the bidding or demand of non-survivors who have no way of reading these experiences outside of narrative. 'Narrative' and 'memory' do not appear to mix, at least, not conventional narrative which seeks and desires closure and resolution, longing for an end to ambiguity. Memory tolerates, perhaps even encourages ambiguity because it needs to be able to accommodate essentially ambiguous material concerning the dual truths 'I had been, and became again, a moral creature' and 'I was in a place where morality had no language'. We seek synthesis in memory as in tales, especially as memories come to seem increasingly to be the tales we tell ourselves about ourselves. Anyone looking back over a life has a tendency to promote the story-like, written quality of real experiences; it is inevitable that the random attains the status of the intended. The narrative function of memory is just this: the ability to tell one's story to oneself. Somehow, memory catches up with the rememberer; as time passes memories become increasingly insistent and potentially dangerous.

Memories of the Holocaust are not only owned by the survivors but may also be said to possess their rememberers. To remember whilst in the camps brought pain; to remember once out of the camps also brings pain. Terrible paradoxes of memory arise. Connections and coherence are distorted by the Holocaust experience: 'tomorrow' is suffused with the possibility of 'death', whilst to be 'alive' means to be 'alone'. In some way those who survived stand in place of the dead. Usually, when a person dies, there is a funeral or other ritual act associated with that death, but the majority of family and friends remain, only whittled at by death as the years pass. The Holocaust reversed that natural procedure, so that the survivor is in the minority; the rest may be dead but they are together. To have survived becomes the punishment for survival: the future becomes loaded with the past from which there may be no easy liberation. Paradoxically hope and despair must exist side by side in memory. The memory of the offence confirms that this is what humanity is capable of and with such a past there can be no hope for the future. And yet, the memory of that past demands that there be a future; there must be something after such a past and that something must contain hope and possibility alongside despair and the moral vacuum.

NOTES

1. D. M. Thomas, *The White Hotel* (London: Penguin, 1981), p. 220.
2. For example, Lawrence L. Langer, *Holocaust Testimonies: The Ruins of Memory* (New Haven: Yale University Press, 1991), p. 67. I have used this text frequently in this chapter as a source of survivor testimony. Further page references will be given in the text.
3. Deborah Dwork, *Children with a Star: Jewish Youth in Nazi Europe* (New Haven: Yale University Press, 1991). Further page references will be given in the text.
4. Ibid., p. xxxvi.
5. Ibid., p. xxxvi.
6. Livia E. Bitton Jackson, *Elli: Coming of Age in the Holocaust* (London: Grafton, 1984), p. 102.
7. Shoshana Felman and Dori Laub, *Testimony: Crises of Witnessing in Literature, Psychoanalysis, and History* (London: Routledge, 1992), p. 59.
8. Ibid., p. 60.
9. Robert H. Abzug, *Inside the Vicious Heart: Americans and the Liberation of Nazi Concentration Camps* (New York: Oxford University Press, 1985), p. 9.
10. Ibid., pp. 9–10.
11. Ibid., p. 10.
12. Primo Levi, *If This is a Man*, trans. Stuart Woolf (London: Abacus, 1987), p. 109.
13. Charlotte Delbo, *Auschwitz and After*, trans. Rosette C. Lamont (New York: Yale University Press, 1995), p. 1. This sense of 'unreality' about extreme events is not unique to the experience of Holocaust survivors and

can be provoked by significantly 'smaller' traumas. Speaking on BBC Radio 4's *Today* programme on 12 March 1997, the day before the first anniversary of the Dunblane shooting, the two women who were also in the gym at Dunblane when Thomas Hamilton massacred 15 children and their teacher expressed similar feelings. They used the word 'unreal' and said that they felt 'as if it hadn't happened to us'. They also spoke of their initial response to survival. At first they were 'just so grateful to be here', but that had changed since; one said 'I'm not fine' though she tells those who ask, that she is. They both spoke of their sense of 'distancing' as a technique for survival and of the significance of having had another person experience the events of that day: 'I am so grateful … that there was someone else there' and 'The two of us survived and we know exactly what we were going through that morning.' The implication is clear: no one else does.

14. Deborah Lipstadt, *Denying the Holocaust: The Growing Assault on Truth and Memory* (London: Penguin, 1994), p. xvi.
15. Primo Levi, *The Drowned and the Saved*, trans. Raymond Rosenthal (London: Abacus, 1988), p. 63.
16. Andreas Huyssen, *Twilight Memories: Marking Time in a Culture of Amnesia* (London: Routledge, 1995), p. 3.
17. 'The Dead', an exhibition of photographs at The National Museum of Photography, Film and Television, 5 October 1995 – 7 January 1996. See also the exhibition catalogue produced by The National Museum of Photography, Film and Television which includes essays by the curators Val Williams and Greg Hobson.
18. Huyssen, *Twilight Memories*, p. 1.
19. In its English translation the title of Hilberg's autobiography has become *The Politics of Memory: The Journey of a Holocaust Historian*, which suggests a very different memory project.
20. Langer for example: see his chapter 'Unheroic Memory' in *Holocaust Testimonies*, and especially pp. 198–205.
21. See Ferdinando Camon's *Conversations with Primo Levi*, trans. John Shepley (Vermont: The Marlboro Press, 1989). This insensitive and self-congratulatory book is a model of how not to conduct interviews with survivors or otherwise traumatized people.
22. Tom Segev, *The Seventh Million: The Israelis and the Holocaust*, trans. Haim Watzman (New York: Hill & Wang, 1993), pp. 452–3. See especially the chapter 'A Barrier of Blood and Silence'.
23. See especially Langer's chapter 'Anguished Memory' in *Holocaust Testimonies*.
24. Deborah Dwork, *Children with a Star*, p. 270.
25. 'Bringing the Holocaust Home', BBC2, January 1995, during the series of programmes and documentaries commemorating the 'liberation' of Auschwitz.

26. These changes are demonstrable. In *The Seventh Million*, Segev discusses the developments in Israel which made it possible at last for survivors' stories to be heard. It may be that Israeli willingness has influenced the rest of the world, especially the United States. See also David Vital, 'From Curiosity to Remorse: The Struggle to Establish the Truth about the Holocaust', *Times Literary Supplement* (7 March 1997).

27. *Buchenwaldlied*, cited in Langer, *Holocaust Testimonies*, p. 173.

28. Delbo, *Auschwitz and After*, p. 4.

29. Huyssen, *Twilight Memories*, p. 2.

30. Michael André Bernstein, 'The Lasting Injury', *Times Literary Supplement* (7 March 1997), p. 3.

31. See Huyssen, *Twilight Memories*, especially his chapters 'Time and Cultural Memory at our *Fin-de-Siècle*', pp. 1–9 and 'Monuments and Holocaust Memory in a media age', pp. 249–60.

32. Though see Segev, *The Seventh Million*, on discussions which took place in 1939 in Israel about responses to the Holocaust *before* it happened, and discussions about remembering the dead *before* they were dead.

33. Bitton Jackson, *Elli*, p. 268.

34. Langer, *Holocaust Testimonies*, p. 67. This is reminiscent of Vladek's reiteration of the phrase 'and here my troubles began': Spiegelman, *Maus II: A Survivor's Tale* (London: Penguin, 1992), pp. 75, 91. Segev also describes the almost overwhelming task faced by survivors.

35. 'The Memory of the Offence', BBC TV broadcast after the death of Levi in 1987.

36. P. 108. See also Felman's essay in *Testimony* (note 7).

3

BRUNO SCHULZ

SCHULZ AND THE HOLOCAUST: INKLINGS OF CATASTROPHE?

In the face of a catastrophe, there is an urge to surrender to the most extreme foreshadowing imaginable ... We try to make sense of a historical disaster by interpreting it, according to the strictest teleological model, as the climax of a bitter trajectory whose inevitable outcome it must be.[1]

I had a premonition that your silence had to have a serious cause, and so it turned out, poor brave Roma.[2]

The first quotation which introduces this chapter is from Bernstein's *Foregone Conclusions*. The second comes from a letter written by Bruno Schulz to a friend, Romana Halpern, on 10 March 1938. In this chapter I discuss the extent to which Schulz's writings may contain inklings of the Shoah. This entails some general, contextualizing comments about Schulz, his mode of expression and the critical responses of other commentators to his life and work; some thoughts on the difficulties provoked by the idea of prophecy, especially in relation to the Holocaust; and an analysis of some of Schulz's stories to illustrate my employment of this approach to Schulz's work.

Schulz's writings have no direct, explicit relationship with the Holocaust, nor with memories of the Holocaust. It is safe to assume that his stories, collected under the titles *Cinnamon Shops* (1934) and *Sanatorium Under the Sign of the Hourglass* (1937), were written long before the political changes which took place in Germany in 1933 could have taken on any sufficiently worrying or threatening aspects to make them generally registerable by the Jewish communities of Poland. It was clearly possible at that time to propose that the appearance of the author of *Mein Kampf* as Führer in Germany would have some repercussions for the Jews of Germany. But not even the most sophisticated or pessimistic of political observers would have plotted the particularly 'bitter trajectory' Hitler's leadership would

describe, nor its awful consequences for Jewish communities across
Europe. In such circumstances to suggest that Schulz 'foresaw' the
Holocaust in any conscious manner would be wrong.

What I am suggesting is that whilst engaged in the process of trying
to recollect and render a domestic, mundane and not explicitly
threatened past, Schulz produced representations of a shocking,
fearful, violent, dislocated future. It is those elements of Schulz's work
which, in memorializing the past, offer inklings and insights into the
future, with which this chapter is concerned.

The devastation that engulfed Europe between 1939 and 1945 did
not allow the survival of detailed biographical evidence of Schulz's life
and only remnants of his work are left. And yet, year by year, his
reputation and the claims for his work grow, in some cases as
fantastically as the vegetation in his lushest depictions. His story 'The
Street of Crocodiles' has served as the inspiration for an animated film
and a stage play. Cynthia Ozick has not only written about Bruno
Schulz in her capacity as critic, but also set herself the task, nearly
accomplished in her novel *The Messiah of Stockholm* (1987), of bringing
back into the world Schulz's lost manuscript *The Messiah*.[3] Schulz also
makes an appearance as a significant character in David Grossman's *See
Under: Love*.[4] Though only one amongst the millions of Jews and the
thousands of artists who were annihilated by the machinery of Nazi
Germany, Schulz's position of relative obscurity in a relatively obscure
part of Europe has taken on, or been endowed with, a special kind of
significance. Increasingly he seems to represent something about a
whole world which was lost.

Schulz was born in Drohobycz in 1892. In 1942 he was killed there,
inside the Jewish ghetto, by an SS officer.[5] He spent most of his life in
Drohobycz. In spite of occasional forays to Warsaw and Paris, Schulz
showed little inclination to leave his home town permanently in order
to inhabit the cultural centres of Europe. Even when a possibility of
escaping on false identity papers presented itself, Schulz stayed in
Drohobycz.

His written output was not large: it included what may have been
a significant quantity of correspondence; some essays; two books of
short stories; and two novels *Homecoming* and *The Messiah*, which have
never been found. The short stories were published during his lifetime
– letters and essays have been published since. He taught at a local
school and worked as a graphic artist leaving many drawings of a
surreal nature which did survive the war. For many of those who have

written about him, Schulz seems to represent the cliché of a provincial existence. He is frequently attributed with having experienced a life of unexpressed desires, of unfulfilled ambitions.

These few biographical facts tend to be recycled in most of the essays on Schulz; they are constantly rearranged and reinterpreted. Where facts fail, imagination and conjecture mend the gaps. Many essays offer paradoxical and fantastic views of Schulz. They betray an uneasy, and at times unpleasant, combination of idealization and of voyeurism. Some writers display an almost lascivious delight in the frequency with which they are able to refer to Schulz's sexual attributes and inclinations. Clichés abound concerning his appearance; his sexual proclivities; his shyness; his provincialism. Descriptions such as 'One of the great solitaries of literature';[6] 'morbidly shy';[7] 'sickly, neurotic, sexually abnormal (Schulz was a self-admitted masochist)'[8] emphasize Schulz's peculiarities, his difference and his separateness from us. Oddly, in the majority of reviews and critical approaches to Schulz's work, there is little explicit reference to Schulz's Jewishness. This may merely reflect the fact that in Schulz's work itself, Jewishness remains undisclosed, or at least, coded. (Such codedness may be compared with the protective mannerisms adopted in the works of gay writers writing before explicit, gendered reference to lovers became acceptable.) But it is possible to detect in some articles implicit and uneasy allusions to Schulz's Jewishness. It is as though his alien status must be represented covertly. For example, Baranczak suggests that photographs of Schulz:

> show his face invariably at a peculiar angle, strangely foreshortened, as if he were glancing coyly upward from some humble, kneeling position ... His sunken eyes hide uneasily under his prominent, almost simian eyebrows. He looks like the facial epitome of an inferiority complex, of introversion. (p. 28)

This seems to be a caricature of the supplicant Jew who, with his 'sunken eyes' and 'almost simian eyebrows', may not be quite human. This stereotype is intensified by hints of sexual abnormality as Baranczak continues, in reference to Schulz's drawings: '[they] show him more revealingly. And more shockingly. Even by today's standards, Schulz's way of portraying himself is sometimes disturbingly "indecent"' (p. 28).

Alongside these insistences upon Schulz's difference and separateness there are frequent allusions to the backwater status of Drohobycz. So 'the little Galician town',[9] as Brown puts it, also becomes part of the myth-making that surrounds Schulz, who has been described variously as 'a volcano, smouldering silently in the isolation of a sleepy provincial town'[10] and 'A humble, shy homunculus … from Drohobycz, a quaint town in the foothills of the Carpathian Mountains'.[11] There is as much contradiction and ambiguity in these evocations of Drohobycz as the reader is likely to find in Schulz's stories: for Budurowycz the 'somnolent Drohobycz' is a 'quaint town'; 'oddly picturesque'; 'pervaded with old-fashioned charm', and a 'unique city'; 'the capital of the "Galician California"' which 'acquired some garish, even vulgar – in Schulz's own words "pseudo American" – characteristics'; 'a boom town'.[12]

In much of the critical writing on Schulz there appears a dangerous conflation of the writer with his creations comparable to the difficulties which arise in discussions of Plath and her poetry. This slippage is 'dangerous' because it protects the reader from the full force of the concerns being expressed by Schulz. As long as he may be represented as a self-centred individual imaginatively estranged or distinct from his social and political context, then his Jewishness and his relationship to the persecution of Jews are not at issue. An additional problem with Schulz's Jewishness may be located in a development which gained momentum after the war as the full impact of the Holocaust began to be revealed. For some, Schulz represents another stereotype – that of the despised Jew of the Diaspora. Assimilated into his surroundings, seeking to be a Polish or European, rather than Yiddish or Jewish writer, Schulz is apparently estranged from his Jewish persona. Bernstein points to the way in which the Holocaust has been used by some Zionists as proof of

> the untenability of the Diaspora, and the self-destructive absurdity of the attempts by European and, more specifically, by Austro-German Jewry to assimilate to a society that only waited for its chance to exterminate them.[13]

In this context, Schulz's works may be read as being ahistorical, exclusively autobiographical and expressive of a tendency towards a self-indulgence which bordered on the autoerotic. Brown provides a typical example of such readings. Referring to Schulz's influence upon Danilo Kis, Brown makes a critical mistake: when he is not reading

Schulz surreally, he reads him literally. He does not employ the skills of reading between the lines familiar to feminist or psychoanalytic criticism. Consequently, Brown draws a fallacious distinction between the works of Kis and Schulz in terms of their representations of the realities of Jewish existence in Eastern Europe. He writes:

> *Garden, Ashes* [Kis's novel], for example, is set in recognizable modern history, however surrealistic, while Schulz's Drohobych is a timeless locale. The Scham family flees from the persecution of an anti-semitic Fascist mob, which is trying to break into their home, while the Jewishness of Joseph's family [Joseph is Schulz's ubiquitous narrator] is not that of a persecuted minority; indeed, no one around them is even specifically non-Jewish. *In Schulz the anti-semitism, pogroms, and wars of the twentieth century are simply invisible.* [my italics][14]

I will argue that, far from being invisible, Schulz's recognition of the 'persecuted minority' and the 'anti-semitism, pogroms, and wars of the twentieth century' is central to his imaginative world; that his writings do not, as Brown suggests, '[operate] largely outside of history',[15] nor are they an escape from reality. It seems to me that they offer a complete engagement with the past which provides inklings of the future.

The notion of 'inklings' employed in these readings has developed from an earlier characterization of Schulz's writings as 'prophetic'.[16] Whilst the looser and less emphatic word, 'inklings' is to be preferred, issues concerning the idea of prophecy remain to be considered in relation to Schulz's writings. To the reader with an awareness of the Shoah, Schulz may be characterized as an elegiac prophet. This phrase represents the back-to-backness of elegy and prophecy, the relationship between Schulz's work and of his status 'on the edge'. Schulz's work, the time and the place he inhabited, were both marginal (back to the idea of 'somnolent Drohobycz') and central: he lived in the vortex which was the Holocaust. Whilst looking back into the life of Jews in Poland, he could not avoid seeing forward. If Schulz were to be represented as a mythical figure, Janus would be the most appropriate. The liminality of the Roman god of doorways, passages and bridges, who provides the name for the month when the old year and the new are viewed simultaneously, depicts exactly Schulz's own threshold status. It was this that led me to think of Schulz in prophetic terms, for perhaps it is in the nature of prophecy that in order to envision the future a prophet must re-vision the past. The writings of Schulz occupy just such an ambiguous position: psychologically, historically, culturally, emotionally, they seem to embody elegy and prophecy simultaneously, in different proportions. His work looks back and lingers with pleasure, sorrow and an acute sense of loss over the shape and meaning of the past and its memories whilst, in the process, producing an imaginary, surreal, but possible future. Schulz seems to have been determined to render his experience of experiences.

Almost all his stories are concerned with the past; those stories which deal with a father and a family have a wistful, longing note of recollection and nostalgia. It is this element that has encouraged critics to see him as Proustian. But Schulz's rendering of the past is constantly being subverted and disrupted, as the future insists on being acknowledged, so that Schulz rarely achieves what appears to be his intention. At some point in almost all of the stories his narrative leaves the realms of what-was, to enter the realms of what-might-be and the what-might-be is usually very odd, ashen, cracked, broken, certainly not Proustian. For these reasons, prophecy seemed an appropriate term. In the threat of a featureless, grey present and future, Schulz seemed to have represented something related to the approaching Holocaust.

However, there are also significant problems with the idea of prophecy. The disadvantage, at least, of this word is that it implies an inevitability which sits uneasily alongside the fact of the Holocaust. For, whilst we may see how the Holocaust happened, we must resist any sense of its inevitability. Modernity and its bureaucracies made the Holocaust possible, but surely not inevitable, for there is always a distinction to be drawn between possible and inevitable outcomes.[17] The idea that Schulz's stories display prophetic aspects highlights some of the problems associated with reading literature, and especially this kind of literature, in the light of historical knowledge. As Bernstein reminds us in *Foregone Conclusions*:

> Danger signals obviously existed in significant quantities, but so did countless contradictory and, in the main, reassuring ones, and there is nothing inherently surprising that it should have been the latter that most people chose to believe. (p. 30)

> Thus, when new waves of what initially seemed like the same madness broke out, they [the Jews] naturally turned to history and communal memory for guidance and found sufficient reason to think that this latest episode would also pass without jeopardizing their survival. (p. 33)

For these reasons, I do not suggest that there is in Schulz's writings anything as crudely definitive as an explicit prophecy of the events which constituted the Shoah. Those events could not in any simple sense have been foreseen and it is only with the terrible benefit of hindsight that we may trace the route that led to the demolition of a longstanding culture and the near-extinction of the Jews in Europe. What I am suggesting is present in Schulz's writings is a hint, impossible to read or recognize except in the light of later events, of a surreal dismembering and reconstitution of matter; a sense of sickening foreboding; a depiction of a world gone mad. The menace which Schulz inscribed in his recollections and imaginings contains inklings of a terrible future. Without the Holocaust these hints would have remained unattached and unassimilated, slightly at odds with the rest of the world, to be explained as an individual and feverish response to a particular, lived experience. Reading them with the Holocaust in mind, Schulz's writings assume a different resonance.

NARRATIVE AND CONTINGENCY

Schulz's stories may be characterized by a phrase from Langer's *Holocaust Testimonies*: 'The absence of sequence in his narrative reflects an absence of consequence too' (p. 119). Langer is commenting upon the testimony of a survivor, Moses S., which contained numerous odd revelations. One of these described a bizarre occasion when, after the barracks had been fumigated against lice, the SS camp official, expecting that all lice would be dead, announced that in return for the discovery of a living louse, an extra portion of soup would be distributed. Moses S. went outside, searched around, and found a living louse. 'I looked after it [he says] like somebody looks after gold.' He returns to the barracks and, in a farcical scene, is ordered, as 'a dead louse is worthless', to prove to the officer that the louse is alive by making it walk. 'Moses S. then paraded his louse on his shoulder – and the officer sends him for an extra portion of soup' (p. 116). This tale is Schulzian in its surrealism, in its undermining of logic, in its exposition of ludicrous (but deadly) human behaviour. That so much sense could seem to be invested in the discovery of a louse and the demonstration of its abilities disturbs any coherence which might be attached to Holocaust narratives. Langer's point is that much of the testimony of Moses S. displayed, with 'gleeful cynicism', this extreme dislocation and refusal of narrative 'sense'; that Moses S. seemed almost to delight in confounding his listeners with the juxtaposition of the oddities which composed his camp experience.

Langer again provides a phrase which usefully links the reading of survivor testimony with Schulz's narratives of incoherence: 'One could rarely anticipate the consequences of an action (or an inaction)' (p. 122). Meaning, predictability, certainty, are rarely found in survivor testimony or in Schulz's work. Notions of 'learned helplessness' (p. 138) which Langer refers to as a part of the fragmented identity of survivors and is a result of the moral disarray and chaos imposed upon people during their camp experience is something which appears constantly in Schulz's writings. Randomness and a profound challenge to meaning enter the world: or their presence in the world is revealed. The growing emphasis in literature since the end of the war upon entropy, decay and chaos, is prefigured in Schulz.

Schulzian memory remembers disconnectedness, not, as usual, connectedness: the experiences encountered exist as distilled memory, unmediated by chronology, purpose, meaning or closure. The view, again reported by Langer and expressed constantly by survivors, is:

> You didn't have any choices. You just were driven to do whatever you did. So it is not things that you planned that you do; it's just whatever happened, happened. You don't think. You think on the moment what will happen *this* moment, not what the next moment will happen. (p. 177)

This notion of contingency, of 'it's just whatever happened, happened' is to be found throughout Schulz's work.

'AUGUST'

'August', the opening story of the collection, *The Street of Crocodiles*, immediately confounds any conventional expectations the reader may have of a story with such a title.[18] Schulz at once brings the reader into contact with an acutely paradoxical, unnerving and threatening world. This is not a benign or gentle representation of the recollection of summer days: 'In July my father went to take the waters and left me, with my mother and elder brother, a prey to the blinding white heat of the summer days' (p. 15). The narrator's father disappears; the family is left behind to be preyed upon by intense heat and light, a massive conflagration which is represented as a threat to the family, rather than a blessing. The monstrous heat and light result in disturbing transformations:

> Passers-by, bathed in melting gold, had their eyes half closed against the glare ... Upper lips were drawn back, exposing the teeth. Everyone in this golden day wore that grimace of heat – as if the sun had forced his worshippers to wear identical masks of gold ... [they] greeted each other with these masks ... they smiled at each other's pagan faces – the barbaric smiles of Bacchus. (p. 16)

The inhabitants of that place have to adopt an outward expression of uniformity which belies their difference. This masquerade also requires them to deny their proper religious identity in favour of the pagan. The phrase 'golden day' apparently represents a menace, whilst the heat and light also conjure the possibilities of a technological or mechanistic process. That same heat and light seem to have destroyed, cleansed or scoured, so that the natural gathering-place, the Market Square, which should be full of people, 'was empty and white-hot, swept by hot winds like a biblical desert' (p. 16). Yet, in spite of the enforced assumption of pagan identity, biblical images remain present:

> One expected that, at any minute, the Samaritan's donkey, led by the bridle, would stop in front of the wine merchant's vaulted doorway and that two servants would carefully ease a sick man from the red-hot saddle and carry him slowly up the cool stairs to the floor above, already redolent of the Sabbath. (p. 16)

Schulz juxtaposes images in this passage which, in the context of his stories, are antithetical and produce a dichotomy between the idea of an outside which is burning, pagan, threatening, and an inside which is cool, biblical, healing. And buried in his reference to the Good Samaritan, a Christian parable of extending help to the despised and outcast, is a Jewish resonance in his use of the word 'Sabbath'. There is potential in this story for a rescuing and healing human presence based on a belief in ethics and a strictly ordered code. But that potential is overshadowed by the more frequent images of loss and destruction, of the emptiness and nothingness which are to be found in the midst of the overwhelming heat and light: 'The squares of the paving stones slowly filed past – some the pale pink of human skin, some golden, some blue-grey, all flat, ... trodden to the point of obliteration, into blessed nothingness' (p. 17). It is difficult, reading these lines, to avoid the image of the desecration of Jewish memorial stones, graveyards and other sacred texts, as part of the process of the destruction. It might also be that these numerous paving stone squares are representative of the almost countless market squares throughout Poland where it was not stones but people who were 'trodden to the point of obliteration'.

The second part of 'August', as usual in Schulz's stories, intensifies this sense of oddness and threat. It takes the familiar motifs discovered in recollections of the past, but re-presents them in a threatening way. In common with many of the stories, matter seems not to be kept within its usual or recognizable boundaries. Insect and plant life become synonymous, so stubble becomes 'a tawny cloud of locusts' and 'seed pods exploded softly like grasshoppers' (p. 17). The lushness associated more conventionally with an abundance of midsummer life is represented here as corrupt, overblown and with a tendency to decay. This memory of the past seems Edenic and prelapsarian initially, but also contains bizarre and inexplicable occurrences and a disturbing sense of a potential for corruption. Into the stillness of the hot day there is the sudden intrusion of a bewildering event as the narrator describes the appearance of the girl, Touya. The narrator offers no explanations for this presence. The reader is left bewildered by Touya's sudden outbreak of madness and rage and with a complex feeling: the desire both to read and yet not to read. These scenes are like the intermittent flashbacks of a disturbed memory and the reader experiences a fear of the unknown in the face of such narrative uncertainty.

Part three of 'August' is equally disturbing as it describes the poignant fragility of the future, alongside an evocation of the past:

> Coming through the garden to visit her [Aunt Agatha], we passed numerous coloured glass balls stuck on flimsy poles. In these pink, green, and violet balls were enclosed bright shining worlds, like the ideally happy pictures contained in the peerless perfection of soap bubbles.
>
> In the gloom of the hall, with its old lithographs, rotten with mildew and blind with age, we discovered a well-known smell. In that old familiar smell was contained a marvellously simple synthesis of the life of those people, the distillation of their race, the quality of their blood, and the secret of their fate. (p. 19)

The narrator is emphatic about the word 'their', seeming to deny any connection between himself and the people he visits. Yet he is unable entirely to refute the existence of a relationship, even if he wishes to:

> They were sitting as if in the shadow of their own destiny and did not fight against it; with their first clumsy gestures they revealed their secret to us. Besides, were we not related to them by blood and by fate? (p. 19)

Fate and a doomed existence attain great significance in the narrator's perception and representation of this world. His 'Uncle Mark, small and hunched ... sat in his grey bankruptcy, reconciled to his fate' (p. 20). Aunt Agatha displays a sense of acute fearfulness associated with the future of her children and generation. The narrator says:

> There was something tragic in that immoderate fertility, the misery of a creature fighting on the borders of nothingness and death, the heroism of womanhood triumphing by fertility over the shortcomings of nature, over the insufficiency of the male. But their offspring showed justification for that panic of maternity, of a passion for child-bearing which became exhausted in ill-starred pregnancies, in an ephemeral generation of phantoms without blood or face. (p. 20)

Any idea of a secure future is frustrated or disturbed by the image of 'an ephemeral generation of phantoms without blood or face'. The use of the word 'generation' focuses attention on two aspects of the future. It describes not only the reproductive capacity for child-bearing, but also the children and grandchildren to come. Prophetically, the phrase depicts a future generation which is identified by its disappearance, its effacement.

Emil, the son of Agatha and Mark, is described in similarly disappearing terms:

> His pale flabby face seemed from day to day to lose its outline to become a white blank wall with a pale network of veins, like lines on an old map occasionally stirred by the fading memories of a stormy and wasted life. (p. 21)

This is very like the map in 'The Street of Crocodiles' and also the maps of concentration and death camps with their blank areas committed to erasure. Emil's potential for disappearance and invisibility is not confined to his features but affects his behaviour too: 'With his gaze wandering over old memories, he told curious stories, which at some point would suddenly stop, disintegrate, and blow away' (p. 21). The narrator says 'My eyes followed him nostalgically', which is odd; what has provoked this nostalgia for Emil's presence when he is not yet absent?

Throughout this and many of the other stories such ideas of emptiness are reiterated; objects, especially clothes, are frequently used as substitutes for the human or to mark where the human has been. They attain a talismanic intensity: 'In a straw-filled chest lay the foolish Maria, white as a wafer and motionless like a glove from which a hand had been withdrawn' (p. 19). Emil's physical presence in a sofa 'seemed as if it were only his clothes that had been thrown, crumpled and empty, over a chair' (p. 21). This loss of the human presence from the material world is emphasized by references to absence, erasure, dissipation, which the narrator continues to note particularly in relation to Emil: 'His face seemed like the breath of a face – a smudge which an unknown passer-by had left in the air'; 'From the mist of his face, the protruding white of a pale eye emerged with difficulty'; 'that ghost of a smile'; 'his face receded into indifference and became absent and finally faded away altogether' (pp. 21–2).

'VISITATION'

This smudginess or mistiness, the ephemerality of human presence and existence, is referred to again and again in the stories. The opening paragraph of 'Visitation' (p. 23) depicts a disturbing affliction which has come upon the town. It is clear that the town is losing its place in the world. There is a sense that this is not accidental but is the result of deliberate activity on the part of some external agency. The second paragraph makes a failed attempt to normalize this scene, to offset this sense of menace, with the suggestion that this affliction is autumnal, the result of approaching winter. But this attempt does not succeed and the reader is left with an impression of foreboding.

This foreboding is enhanced by the descriptions of the square where the narrator lives, 'in one of those dark houses with empty blind looks, so difficult to distinguish one from the other' (p. 23). The image of the labyrinth, with its deathly and mythical connotations, is applied to something as mundane as embarking upon an errand. The labyrinth is an integral part of the world inhabited by the narrator, a world which results in 'endless possibilities for mistakes' (p. 23). The idea of the labyrinth, coupled with other images which are used in 'Visitation' of 'endless mistakes', 'the wrong doorway', 'the wrong staircase', 'unexpected doors opening on to strange empty courtyards' may announce the presence of a dangerous potential for being in the wrong place at the wrong time. The only mitigating element is that, so far at least, the narrator is able to return to his home. But even at home, the sense of safety is compromised, although the narrator seems able to explain the strange disappearances which are also taking place there.

> No one ever knew exactly how many rooms we had in our apartment, because no one ever remembered how many of them were let to strangers. Often one would by chance open the door to one of these forgotten rooms and find it empty; the lodger had moved out a long time ago. In the drawers, untouched for months, one would make unexpected discoveries. (pp. 23–4)

The narrator's father diminishes, 'slowly fading, wilting before our eyes', whilst his dislocation from reality becomes more acute (p. 27). This dislocation is accepted and tolerated by his family to the extent that they cease to show any concern and he becomes marginalized:

> We did not count him as one of us any more, so very remote had he become from everything that was human and real . . . What still remained of him – the small shroud of his body and the handful of nonsensical oddities – would finally disappear one day, as unremarked as the grey heap of rubbish swept into a corner, waiting to be taken by Adela to the rubbish dump. (pp. 28–9)

'PAN'

This kind of disturbed logic and compromised sense of security is also found in the story 'Pan' (p. 53). As with so many of Schulz's stories, the reader starts in one place and ends in another, apparently unrelated, place. Whilst it is possible to look back and trace the narrative that brings both the narrator and reader to this particular end, it still remains a shock.

This tale begins in a place which might be a representation of a ghetto. It is inhospitable and displays an antipathy to all life but especially the human: 'a blind alley'; 'ultimate cul-de-sac'; 'a dismal spot'; 'the land's end'. At first this place seems to be without any exit; it is surrounded by fencing which '[encloses] that little world with finality' only 'a rivulet of black stinking water, a vein of rotting greasy mud' escapes, forming 'the only road which led across the border of the fence into the wider world' (p. 53). This is a sinister image, which recalls the recognition and frequent assertion made by the inhabitants of concentration and death camps that it was only once they had become something else, something likely to be 'black', 'stinking', 'rotting' that they could expect 'escape' via the chimneys.

And yet, the narrator and a group of his contemporaries, identified specifically as 'prisoner[s] of the courtyard', do escape via a breach made in the fence into a heavenly, Edenic domain, 'a large, overgrown garden'. This place, in contrast to the alley they have left behind, seems brimful of life and expectation; the grass is 'never cut' and fruit, herbs and seeds are left to fulfil their potential. Exquisitely lovely and unfettered, full of air and light, and endless possibilities, the garden becomes for the narrator a simulacrum of the world: 'When you lay in the grass you were under the azure map of clouds and sailing continents, you inhaled the whole geography of the sky'; the garden has 'various zones and climates' (p. 54).

But this vision does not continue to represent a pure place of escape; the narrator is drawn, or driven, into an area of hellish dimensions:

> Where the ground extended into a low-lying isthmus and dropped into the shadow of the back wall of a deserted soda factory, it became grimmer, overgrown and wild with neglect, ... until, at the very end between the walls, in an open rectangular bay, it lost all moderation and became insane. (p. 54)

This brief description contains many of the elements of the concentration camp. The 'low-lying isthmus' seems to be somewhere which, though clearly connected with the world represented by the rest of the orchard, is also apart and different. This area is 'low-lying' and 'dropped into the shadow'; in hierarchical terms this place must be descended into, whilst the light that might properly expose its horrors has been intercepted, dimmed, perhaps extinguished, by the factory wall. The 'deserted soda factory' looms over the scene imparting a sense of menace; its presence is evidence of an approach to life which seems antithetical to the rest of the garden-world. The fact that it was soda, some forms of which have a benign use as a domestic aid to cleanliness or a refreshing drink, that was produced in the factory is also revealing. In its very ordinariness, and banality, soda seems to offer little threat. Yet, as caustic soda, it puts on the aspect of a scouring, burning purgative, an almost hellish substance, which intensifies the sense of menace. 'At the very end' suggests not only a place, but also a state of being or not-being; the 'very end', the true end, met with in the gas chamber or on the killing ground. 'Between the walls' recapitulates the sense of imprisonment with which the tale begins, but whilst the alley-ghetto, though disturbing and vindictive, could be escaped, there is a sense that at this 'very end between the walls' all potential for escape has gone. This place, 'at the very end between the walls', in spite of remaining close by, and having access to, the garden-world, still 'lost all moderation and became insane' (p. 54).

The descent into the shade inflicts upon the vegetable inhabitants of this place a corresponding descent into madness: 'There, it was an orchard no more, but a paroxysm of madness, an outbreak of fury, of cynical shamelessness and lust' (p. 54). The conditions in which these 'inhabitants' exist provoke their excessive behaviour. Elsewhere in the garden-world, the plants grow in full light and fresh air and they adopt the most pleasing aspect: 'From one side [the garden] was open to the sky and air, and there it offered the softest, most delicate bed of fluffy green' (p. 54). But where the plants have to grow on the 'low-lying isthmus', it is only opportunists and survivors, the thistles, nettles and 'a rash of weeds', which have any chance of existence. These plants are described in the most extreme terms, evoking a plethora of contradictory associations. In order to survive in such adverse conditions, the plants have to become degraded:

> There, bestially liberated, giving full rein to their passion, ruled the empty, overgrown, cabbage heads of burs – enormous witches, shedding their voluminous skirts in broad daylight, throwing them down, one by one, until their swollen, rustling, hole-riddled rags buried the whole quarrelsome, bastard breed under their crazy expanse. And still the skirts swelled and pushed, piling up one on top of another, spreading and growing all the time. (p. 54)

This depiction of a swelling mass may be seen as an extreme representation of the camp population. It is not an evocation which is easy to tolerate, but there is something here which is reminiscent of certain descriptions of concentration and death camp existence, for example Borowski's stories and memoirs which recall the tribulations of ghetto life. The revulsion provoked is appropriate; it signals the likely revulsion and horror which must attend even the most compassionate observer of the results of the camp system, of the effects upon a humiliated and degraded population which had 'dropped into the shadow of the back wall of a deserted soda factory'. Such a composite and complicated tone of sympathy and disgust, fascination and revulsion, affection and loathing, pervades many of Schulz's stories.

'CINNAMON SHOPS'

'Cinnamon Shops' (p. 59) enacts a series of thwarted intentions and oscillates between a sense of intense threat and a magical, fairy-tale relief of that threat. It has a surreal, dream-like quality. Each event or 'set' within the story seems to possess an internal logic and sense which bears little relation to the event which comes before or follows after. This results in a serial, but disjointed, logic. Each component of this bizarre story, which, in a work barely ten pages long, is fragmented into at least 13 distinct and almost unrelated narratives, seems rational but when strung together the whole has little normal coherence or narrative and there is an overall lack of logic. These are shards of logic and coherence and the whole offers no more than a series of *non sequiturs*. It is very difficult to say what this story is about. It seems like the narrative of a quest, a *Bildungsroman*. But the nature and purpose of the quest is never made clear. In each small section a purpose or meaning is identified only to be set aside, trivialized or forgotten when the next 'purpose' is revealed.

Like many of Schulz's stories, 'Cinnamon Shops' begins in a 'dusky' indeterminacy and relates the bizarre behaviour of the narrator's father: 'my father was already lost, sold and surrendered to the other sphere' (p. 59). The terms used to describe his father's status in relation to 'the other sphere' are not positive. There is no suggestion here that his engagement with 'the other sphere' is one of fulfilment, nor does it appear to be the result of intellectual or spiritual endeavour, a beneficial withdrawal from the mundane into the transcendent. To be lost mimics the vulnerability of a child; to be sold, the slave's lack of autonomy and metamorphosis into an object (*Stück?*); to be surrendered, the betrayal of a victim or hostage. Three processes of dissolution, rather than one, are employed in the father's removal from the world.

Again, as in 'August', there is a proliferation of bizarre growth. As a reaction perhaps to his being 'lost, sold, and surrendered' the narrator's father becomes other than human so that his features and characteristics take on animal attributes:

> His face and head became overgrown with a wild and recalcitrant shock of grey hair, bristling in irregular tufts and spikes, shooting out from warts, from his eyebrows, from the openings of his nostrils and giving him the appearance of an old ill-tempered fox. (p. 59)

And, in his new fox-like persona, the father also becomes wary:

> His sense of smell and his hearing sharpened extraordinarily and one could see from the expression of his tense silent face that through the intermediary of these two senses he remained in permanent contact with the unseen world of mouseholes, dark corners, chimney vents, and dusty spaces under the floor. (p. 59)

This might be the depiction of a hunted animal, conscious of every change, sensitive to every threat and aware, in every fibre of its being, of all possible hiding places. Whilst these traits may be no more than an expression of the father's dislocation and are out of place and bizarre in the context of a sane life, he actually develops the skills he would need if he were to have any chance of survival in the camps. This is like Vladek Spiegelman only in reverse: the father develops and practises survival skills in advance of their necessity. Just as Vladek's skills become less relevant and an embarrassment after Auschwitz, the narrator's father's skills are out of place and inappropriate before.

> He was a vigilant and attentive observer, a prying fellow conspirator, of the rustlings, the nightly creakings, the secret gnawing life of the floor. He was so engrossed in it that he became completely submerged in an inaccessible sphere and one which he did not even attempt to discuss with us. (p. 59)

That the father is a 'fellow conspirator' makes clear where his allegiance resides and suggests sympathy or empathy with the creatures which hide themselves. The father is prepared to consider any and all potential hiding places, and in his alliance with 'the secret gnawing life of the floor' there is perhaps a conflation of the human and the animal which mimics the representation of the Jew as vermin. His willingness to consider any hideaway also resonates with the stories of survivors who lived beneath floorboards, behind cupboards, in sewers; there is a sympathy for the exigencies of the hunted, trammelled existence of the persecuted.

The father's knowledge of such an existence enables him to '[exchange] knowing looks with our cat' (p. 59). Whilst this seems to suggest complicity with the hunter which is at odds with the father's allegiances, it seems more likely that this recognizes a common knowledge of the 'real world' which exists between cat and mouse. Of course, the cat is not a fellow conspirator with the father. The cat, 'also initiated in these mysteries', is on the side of the hunters and persecutors, and can afford, with its privileged not-mouse status and in common with human killers, to display 'its cynical cold striped face... with an air of indifference and boredom' (p. 59). There is a further reference to this apparent collaboration when the father leaves the dinner table 'with a feline movement' (p. 59), but this might also display the necessity of adopting 'skills' and 'behaviours' which more properly reside with the hunters in order to avoid them successfully. The family's response to the father's disturbed and distressed behaviour is shaped by the narrator's mother: 'To provide some distraction for him and to tear him away from these morbid speculations, my mother would force him to go out for a walk in the evenings' (p. 60).

As so often in Schulz's stories, the narrator assumes that the reader has access to greater knowledge than is the case; this frequently leaves the reader perplexed and given to re-reading the text to discover when, if at all, this or that piece of information was conveyed or explained. So, although the narrator has described his father's unusual activities, the precise nature of 'these morbid speculations' has not been made clear. The reader is presented with a puzzle – the first of many – as the question is raised: what is the content of the father's speculations? Does he fear a plot or entrapment and with whom, or what, is he conducting his 'interior monologue'? The narrator's mother represents the need and the impulse to carry on as normal; the father appears to sane people to have gone mad but there is little evidence that the provocation for his state is investigated.

Just as the reader is settling down to read the story of the narrator's father's 'madness', Schulz interposes the first of the narrative's changes. The transition seems arbitrary, a surreal and irrelevant movement to a new 'setting'. What, at first sight, appear to be clumsy shifts in the plot, in Schulz's work act as de-familiarizing and de-stabilizing techniques to unsettle the reader and challenge his or her complacency in relation to the narrative. Schulz seems determined to confound expectation, and his narratives take unexpected and unexplained (inexplicable?) routes which force the reader to re-read and reassess everything that has gone before. This technique is disorienting and very like the lack of sequence and the menace to linear coherence which is often discovered in survivor testimony. The reader is left again and again with a feeling of disjunction and alienation, for, in spite of their lyricism, there is nothing aesthetically reassuring about Schulz's stories.[19]

It is ironic that it is the theatre, epitome of illusion, which the mother chooses to recover and distract the father from what she considers to be his 'speculations'. The theatre may not offer any mitigation of his disturbed perceptions for it merely proposes its own illusory reality; once again, things are not what they seem. The theatre also acts as an area of acute ambiguity; whilst not overtly malign, it is at least disconcerting with its own 'vibration of reality' (p. 60). This 'vibration', however, is also related to 'the glimmer of revelation' which recalls the potential for a correspondence between madness and prophecy. Whatever expectation of spectacle the word 'theatre' conjures is undermined by its first representation: 'that large, badly lit, dirty hall, full of somnolent human chatter and aimless confusion' (p. 60). These elements may be threatening; along with the 'fictitious floodlit world' and the 'echoing scaffolding of the stage' they represent ambiguous purposes which, like the soda in 'Pan', may contain benign and malign connotations. The ordinary in Schulz always contains the potential for malignity.

The theatre's spectacle seems to the narrator to offer an opportunity for a transcendent experience, a revelation of powerful eventfulness. But his expectations are thwarted; once again the narrative moves away from what the reader has assumed to be its course and the meaning that is about to be revealed is frustrated: 'I was not allowed to experience that moment, because in the meantime my father had begun to betray a certain anxiety' (p. 60).

This anxiety is connected not only with the imminence of the theatrical revelation but is provoked by a discovery: 'He was feeling in

all his pockets and at last declared that he had left behind at home a
wallet containing money and certain most important documents'
(p. 60). As usual in Schulz, the meaning of this discovery is
compromised, for the 'true' status and significance of this wallet is
unclear. On the one hand, the narrator's father may be displaying the
tendency to obsessional behaviour sometimes experienced by those
considered to be mad, in which case his desire to take money and 'most
important documents' on a theatre visit may be explained by
eccentricity. It may also be the case that the money is in danger as there
seem to be qualms about Adela's honesty. And there is clearly no need
for the wallet in order for them to gain admittance to the theatre; they
are already seated and ready to watch the performance. Yet, the
father's anxiety may contain prophetic elements, the indication of a
present perception, an inkling, of a future need. There even seems to
be a hint of this in the phrase 'certain anxiety' for 'certain' may as easily
mean 'the absence of doubt', 'convinced' or 'confirmed' as 'a kind of'.

Certainly, as the knowing reader reads, there is an inescapable
recognition that there will come a time, for the narrator, his father, his
mother, when to be caught away from home with neither money nor
'most important documents' would present a challenge to any chance
of survival. And that the result might be that one would be taken to a
'large, badly lit, dirty hall, full of somnolent human chatter and aimless
confusion'. This emphasizes the circularity, rather than linearity, of
Schulz's stories: places and events are constantly revisited and they
refer to, yet are invariably unrecognizable as, themselves.

So, the narrator is sent off on the third event of this eventful,
pointless narrative. His lack of volition becomes more noticeable and
disturbing in the course of the story, when every intention is hindered
or subverted. Partly his lack of volition is explicable as characteristic of
the narrator's youth: it is natural for children to be required to carry
out their parents' wishes. But there is a disturbing sense to this lack;
the reader comes to fear for the narrator and almost wishes not to look,
not to read, as there seems to be a growing sense of threat implicit in
the lack of control. That potential seems to be too intense for the
apparent context which is merely a matter of collecting a wallet and
returning to the theatre in time to witness the performance. This is
surely not a matter of life and death. Yet, again, for the knowing reader,
the moment when the narrator is sent, by his family, from the theatre
to retrieve the wallet recalls and bears a likeness with those myriad of
moments of 'luck' recounted by Holocaust survivors when, for one
reason or another, they were not present when 'the curtain rose'.

The narrator leaves on his quest, and finds that, like the theatre, the night outside is full of illusions. He steps into the marvellous. For a brief time, the description of the night is fabulous and there is something reassuring in its beauty. It seems as though the immanence which was about to burst upon the boy in the theatre is actually waiting for him outside. But after a brief respite from the sense of menace and unease, the potential for anxiety, at least, returns. The streets are dangerous in their plurality and their ambiguity. They resist fixedness and instead display a disturbing reflexivity and doubling which bewilders the boy and the reader alike.

> It is exceedingly thoughtless to send a young boy out on an urgent and important errand into a night like that, because in its semi-obscurity the streets multiply, becoming confused and interchanged. There open up, deep inside a city, reflected streets, streets which are doubles, makebelieve streets. One's imagination, bewitched and misled, creates illusory maps of the apparently familiar districts, maps in which streets have their proper places and usual names but are provided with new and fictitious configurations by the inexhaustible inventiveness of the night. (p. 61)

The image of the map that cannot function as a map because it is 'illusory', where places 'are provided with new and fictitious configurations', was a compelling one for Schulz, and he deployed it to disorienting effect in 'The Street of Crocodiles'. The status given in Schulz's prose to the significance of maps and their bewildering tendency to be non-records of places or records of absence and erasure will be discussed at greater length in my analysis of 'The Street of Crocodiles'. Intriguingly, Ficowski employs the map motif in his description of Schulz's life: 'It [Schulz's biography] remains incomplete, the map of his life is strewn with blank spots and lacunae. We don't even know how many blanks there are or where to try to fill them in with conjectures.'[20] The act of moving out of the theatre and into the night metamorphoses the narrator. No longer merely the observer of theatrical illusion, he becomes part of and overtaken by 'real' illusion. The doubling and trebling of the streets is reflected in the sky: 'The moon was doubled and trebled, showing all its phases and positions at once' (p. 61). The consequence of this must be that linear time is compromised. In this condition which is outside of conventional time and space and more like his father's surrender to the 'other spheres', the narrator recalls the cinnamon shops. It is as if the narrator is released from one mode of being and ushered into another which recollects and reveres the presence of a different and perhaps more exotic state.

> On such a night, it was impossible to walk along Rampart Street, or any of the other of the dark streets which are the obverse, the lining as it were, of the four sides of Market Square, and not to remember that at that late hour the strange and most attractive shops were sometimes open, the shops which on ordinary days one tended to overlook. (p. 61)

The cinnamon shops are filled with exotica and many of their esoteric objects seem to be the necessary ingredients and tools for magical activities: unlike the objects to be found in other shops, they are old or specialized and imbued with rare significance.

> These truly noble shops, open late at night, have always been the objects of my ardent interest. Dimly lit, their dark and solemn interiors were redolent with the smell of paint, varnish, and incense; of the aroma of distant countries and rare commodities. (p. 61)

Their otherness is not malign; their depiction is both fabulous and poignant. The shops seem to be museums, the repositories of the last remnants of dislocated and lost cultures, the final resting places of the fragile signs of extinct societies. Certainly they no longer have any place in the prosaic world of 'ordinary days'. They are objects from an Other world. The shopkeepers too seem to be people from another time and place:

> I remember those old dignified merchants who served their customers with downcast eyes, in discreet silence, and who were full of wisdom and tolerance for their customers' most secret whims. (p. 62)

There is an oscillation here, which dislocates the time which the narrator is inhabiting. It seems odd that, whilst in narrative terms he is on his way to the cinnamon shops, yet he speaks of them with a wistfulness and longing more usually associated with something that is long gone and never to be recovered. It is as if briefly there are two voices: the voice of the narrator as boy and of the narrator as adult. The adult recollects the cinnamon shops which the boy was able to visit. There seems to be an unconscious hint that the cinnamon shops are gone. The narrator never identifies the cultural context out of which these shops have grown but the reader cannot avoid the assumption that these merchants are Jewish, and likely to be scholars of the gematria and kabbala, alchemy and hasidism:

> But most of all, I remember a bookshop in which I once glanced at some rare and forbidden pamphlets, the publications of secret societies lifting the veil on tantalizing and unknown mysteries. (p. 62)

In spite of the fact that he has been entrusted with retrieving his father's wallet, the narrator decides that he cannot surrender the opportunity to visit the cinnamon shops, and turns from his appointed course to find them. The reader is at least as eager as the boy to 'see' the shops and both are disappointed when it becomes clear that the shops are elusive. He has visited them on previous occasions yet he finds himself in unrecognizable territory. Again the oscillation between threat and security is evident as the excited anticipation of a visit to the cinnamon shops is frustrated and the narrator enters a place of menace: 'the appearance of the street was different from what I had expected' (p. 62).

He finds himself in a labyrinth with no sign of escape or even of human habitation whilst the moon, so recently a source of wonder, has become antipathetic:

> I was in a street of houses with no doors and of which the tightly shut windows were blind from reflected moonlight ...
> I was walking faster now, rather disturbed, beginning to give up the idea of visiting the cinnamon shops. All I wanted now was to get out of there quickly into some part of the city I knew better. (p. 62)

The area provokes a feeling of being lost, trapped and confused. The cinnamon shops and all they represent of a culture on the edge of destruction, may or may not be nearby, but the boy, overwhelmed by a sudden panic of alienation and displacement, fears to seek them. Were they always only figments of the boy's imagination? Or have they already been swept aside and their treasures lost forever? Certainly the difficulty of the transition from, and the recognition of the gulf between, the narrator's consciously ordinary, daily life to the moonlit unconscious represented by the cinnamon shops is made quite explicit. Looking for or associating with a (or his?) lost culture provokes acute anxiety and a sense of danger in the boy. Yet, almost as soon as he gives up his dangerous behaviour and decides not to look for the cinnamon shops, the boy is restored to safer, more recognizable territory and the feeling of entrapment dissipates: 'I felt on me the breath of a wide open space' (p. 62). In spite of the fabulous treasures which they display, the cinnamon shops represent a world that could exist, almost invisibly, alongside the affluent gardens and orchards, the 'picturesque villas' and 'the private houses of the rich' (p. 62). It is not surprising that the narrator recollects the merchants serving their customers 'with downcast eyes, in discreet silence'. In common with many 'aliens', their discretion and silence may have been born of wariness and a recognition of their precarious status.

The boy though is safe again. He finds that he is at 'the back of the high school which I had never seen from that side' (p. 63). This matter of sides not only expresses the way in which physical realities can display different, usually hidden, aspects which are rarely revealed but also conveys a sense of where the boy is coming from. He is approaching his school from the 'side' of the cinnamon shops, the place of the 'strange and rare'.

The reader quickly loses all sense of time in this story; the events could be taking place over days and could be in the past or the present. The narrator often narrates almost simultaneous representations of the same event, one seen 'now', the other viewed from a time in the future and looking back at the episode.

The narrator goes in to his school, recalling as he does that Professor Arendt might be holding one of his classes. There is an odd shift which takes place between the paragraph beginning 'I remembered' and the one beginning 'A small group'. In the first, the classes 'to which we all flocked, fired by the enthusiasm for art which that excellent teacher had awakened in us' (p. 63) are described in the most positive terms. In the second, the narrator admits, 'To be truthful, we did not draw very much during these classes and the professor was not very exacting' (p. 63). These two versions of 'reality' may both be 'true' but it is unclear why the narrator changes his 'story'. Are these 'official' and 'unofficial' versions? Is the narrator still conscious of the way in which events may be seen and reported from different 'sides'? Or is he only emphasizing his capacity to be truthful and untruthful by turns?

The boys wait for the professor; when he arrives he seems to have a lot in common with the merchants of the cinnamon shops. He is 'short, bearded, given to esoteric smiles and discreet silences and exuding an aroma of secrecy' (p. 63). Possibly Professor Arendt, who seems to have scholarly, or rabbinic, tendencies, is an assimilated Jew. Yet he is no less wary than the merchants; both he and they employ the technique of maintaining 'discreet silences'. In his room he keeps the plaster heads of Greek mythology and culture but there is no pride in this display of Hellenism:

> We could see over his head a crowd of plaster shadows, the classical fragments of suffering. Niobides, Danaides, and Tantalides, the whole sad and sterile Olympus, wilting for years on end in that plastercast museum. The light in his room was opaque even in daytime, thick from the dreams of plastercast heads, from empty looks, ashen profiles, and meditations dissolving into nothingness. (p. 63)

The contents of the professor's room are reminiscent of the contents of the cinnamon shops so that there seems to be little difference between the two, and both places have the air of a last resting place. But the objects in the cinnamon shops have infinitely more vitality and potency than these 'crumbling gods withering in the boredom and monotony of their twilight' (p. 63). It is clear that classical society and culture have little to offer to the narrator, and though he was endangered by his search for the cinnamon shops that association had more potential.

In another dislocating sequence the narrator describes the nightly drawing classes which he and his peers enjoy. These memories seem at first to be a description of something that is part of the chronological sequence of this narrative; the realization that they are the imaginative recollection and recapitulation of past events comes as a surprise. Whilst the whole story relies very heavily upon language which articulates a variety of absences, this emphasis is especially noticeable in this part of the narrative. There are 'half-empty benches', some of the students sleep, 'the candles were burning low', time devours 'whole empty periods'. This is a monochrome world composed of black-and-white illustrations, colour has fled, all that remains are shades of grey. The professor shows the boys 'unfashionable engravings, woodcuts and prints' and 'old lithographs of night landscapes, of tree clumps in moonlight, of avenues in wintry parks outlined in black on the white moonlit background' (p. 64). It is as if the professor is showing the boys representations of their absent selves; the scenes the narrator describes seem to be 'copied' from images of erasure and of loss which have yet to be made. The repetition of paper and line, of black and white, of engraving and illustrating becomes monotonous, literally monotone and is a feature of many of Schulz's stories. These attributes do not privilege the written over the drawn and there is in this descriptive mode a recognition of the visual world which the narrator and reader inhabit. They also remind the reader that Schulz was an accomplished graphic artist; many of his engravings, crayon and ink drawings – which have survived the Shoah – have similar repetitive, self-referring copying elements. Again and again the landscapes, real and imagined, which he depicted in words also appear in his drawings and engravings. There is a connection here too with photography.[21]

> The diffuse whiteness of light filtered by the snow, by the pale air, by the milky space, was like the grey paper of an engraving on which the thick bushes corresponded to the deep black lines of decoration. The night was copying now, at that late hour, the nightly landscapes of Professor Arendt's engravings, re-enacting his fantasies. (p. 64)

As the boys leave the school and enter into the landscape of darkness, night and 'milky space' they seek out hiding places:

> In the black thickets of the park, in the hairy coat of bushes, in the mass of crusty twigs there were nooks, niches, nests of deepest fluffy blackness, full of confusion, secret gestures, conniving looks. (p. 64)

They sit 'cracking hazelnuts' and animals come out from the trees and into the moonlight. Yet there is little Edenic about this scene. The reader wonders at the need for the 'nooks, niches, nests' and the 'confusion, secret gestures, conniving looks' which fill them. Nor are the animals wholesome. They are

> Furry, ferreting elongated animals, on short legs, stinking of sheepskin. We suspected that among them were the exhibits from the school cabinets which, although degutted and moulting, felt on that white night in their empty bowels, the voice of the eternal instinct, the mating urge, and returned to the thickets for short moments of illusory life. (p. 64)

This image of 'illusory life', of death in life may be read positively; the animals' reanimation may be an expression of the potency of existence. But this kind of reading is difficult to sustain in the face of phrases like 'stinking of sheepskin', 'degutted and moulting', 'empty bowels' which do not attribute any recognizable or tolerable vitality to the animals. Their return is in such a state of compromised liveliness that it is not to be encouraged. That the boys are able to see them is also disturbing. Boys and animals seem to share a twilight world of the barely live; in that ghostly, liminal landscape they are all wraiths, frail shadows and hints of their former selves. The attributes of 'illusory' life seem to depend upon the animals' reproductive incapacity. Not only are they dead, they cannot live on through the generations which should come after. (This connects with the lost generations of 'August'.) This incapacity is reinforced by the fact that they were once 'exhibits from the school cabinets'. As with the goods in the cinnamon shops, the idea of a cultural remnant arises. In this case it is the culture of the animals which has been destroyed; only remnants survive to be displayed as reminders to the curious or objects of study for the scholar.

Suddenly, as though rousing himself from reverie, the narrator recalls himself and the reader to the fact that he is not actually taking part in one of these 'nightly drawing sessions' (p. 64) but is reminiscing about them. These sudden reversals and changes in time, space, knowledge may be explicable as evidence of the narrator's dream landscape. It is as though he falls into and out of a fantasy world. The form of this narration and its challenge to chronology and established knowledge is very bewildering and results in a bizarre dislocation for the reader. Repeatedly, dislocation is made experiential for the reader so that the narrator's own confusions infest the reader's perceptions. It becomes apparent that the descriptions of the drawing classes, which seemed to have the force of contemporaneous reporting, were in fact the recital of memories. For the narrator the lived present and the remembered past overlap and become coterminous, they inhabit or compete for the same space, each taking turns to interrupt the other, until they seem one and the same.

Having gone to great lengths to depict what is usually (though the kind of 'usually' which exists in this narrator's world is entirely negotiable) to be found in the school and attracted by the possibility that there might be such a drawing class in progress, the narrator goes into the school – and finds the unusual: 'I was in a wing of the school building completely unknown to me' (p. 65).

He finds himself in a silent, empty, magnificent apartment. The inhabitants, who might be expected to be present at this late hour, are absent. The narrator is awestruck and curious. Aware that he would have to explain his presence, he considers withdrawing but decides that 'To retreat halfway, not having carried through the plan I had, would be cowardly' (p. 65). This is the first that the reader knows of any 'plan'; the idea that the narrator has a plan seems like a joke, for most of his actions seem to be motivated by contingency. The narrator crosses the floor of the apartment and, without any clear demarcation between 'inside' and 'outside', makes the transition from the rooms and into 'a city square' where 'some of the garden furniture stood directly on the pavement' (p. 66).

Schulz describes a world of contingency and non-sequence. In the course of this story the narrator's purposes are constantly exchanged, compromised or set aside. His father's madness, the theatre, his errand to collect his father's wallet, the cinnamon shops, the drawing class are all surrendered when necessary and with apparent ease, though they are not forgotten. And, as the narrative draws to its end, although anything like conventional closure is rare in Schulz's stories, the story sheds or escapes entirely from coherence, becoming increasingly non-sequential.

Once out in the street and again under the influence of the stars and moon, the narrator finds a cab. As if in a fairy-tale, one cabbie in particular seems to identify the narrator as the person for whom he has been waiting:

> 'Shall we go, master?' he asked . . .
> But who would entrust oneself on such a night to the whims of an unpredictable cabbie? . . . I could not agree with him on my destination. He nodded indulgently at everything I said and sang to himself. We drove in a circle around the city. (p. 66)

The 'unpredictable cabbie' compounds the narrator's aimlessness and finally gives up all pretence of directing the drive when he jumps down and leaves the narrator in the care of the cab-horse. Fortunately 'that horse inspired confidence – it seemed smarter than its driver' (p. 66). Together, the horse and the narrator leave the city and enter into another fantastic landscape which seems almost to be a vision of heaven; it is certainly not an earthly landscape. The narrative becomes blissful and transcendent as the horse draws the cab and the narrator further away from the city until, hindered by a bank of snow, the horse can go no further. It is only then that the narrator discovers the sacrifice the horse has made to bring him so far:

> The horse was panting, hanging its head. I hugged its head to my breast and saw that there were tears in its large eyes. I noticed a round black wound on its belly. 'Why did you not tell me?' I whispered, crying. 'My dearest, I did it for you,' the horse said and became very small, like a wooden toy. (p. 67)

The horse's martyrdom releases the narrator: 'I left him and felt wonderfully light and happy' (p. 67). His return to the city is accomplished swiftly and easily; for the first time in the story he seems to have superhuman control of his movements and intentions, but there is no explanation for leaving behind the blissful landscape outside the city which he discovered in the horse's company. The air of heightened consequence which had been conjured by his journey with the horse remains but the source of its significance is either obscured or absent. This part of the story is imbued with a frustrating and contradictory mood of meaningless meaning.

Back in the city the endless, marvellous night continues. Its presence demands a response; people are out walking and exulting in its magic. The narrator is so moved by the night's display that he 'completely stopped worrying about my father's wallet' (p. 67). As with the 'plan' in the headmaster's apartment, there has been no evidence that the narrator has been worrying; he experienced no real qualms about seeking out the cinnamon shops before fulfilling his 'mission'. Like all the other people, he is also affected by the night and becomes 'full of ideas and projects' (p. 67) so that he wishes to return to his home. This half-formed intention is thwarted almost instantly when he meets his friends 'on their way to school already, having been wakened by the brightness of that night that would not end' (p. 68).

The story 'ends' in acute uncertainty. The narrator and his friends are unsure 'whether it was the magic of the night which lay like silver on the snow or whether it was the light of dawn . . .' (p. 68). Oddly, in this context, the dawn, in an inversion of its usual symbolic sense of relief or release from danger, seems to represent a threat and an end to the relative safety of the night. This dawn's approach implies a question: what will come with the new day? Its image is shaped by the knowledge of other, more terrible dawns to come: 'Dawn came on us like a betrayer; it seemed as though the new sun rose as an ally of our enemies to assist in our destruction.'[22]

'THE STREET OF CROCODILES'

Of all Schulz's stories 'The Street of Crocodiles' (p. 69) is likely to have
had the widest audience. As well as providing the title for the
publication in English of the collection of stories which Schulz had
published as *Cinnamon Shops*, 'The Street of Crocodiles' has been the
inspiration for a play and an award-winning animation made by the
Quay Brothers in 1986.[23] Whilst I have concentrated here upon the text
of Schulz's story, I have also discussed this animated version.

In many respects 'The Street of Crocodiles' and 'Cinnamon Shops'
may be read as companion pieces. Whilst they differ significantly in
terms of their narrator, 'plot' and 'conclusions', they share many themes
and images. There is the same emphasis upon a very visual
representation of the world: drawing, engraving, photography are much
in evidence as creative media, though they are often characterized as
'copying'. Connected with this focus is the recapitulation of a world
endangered by its lack of colour, which is only capable of expressing
itself in black-and-white and shades of grey. The area which is defined
by 'The Street of Crocodiles', although not exactly the place of
'Cinnamon Shops', is very similar in its labyrinthine and unpredictable
attributes. And there is the same focus upon theatricality and pretence,
the sham and manufactured nature of 'reality'. There is a view of reality
expressed in 'The Street of Crocodiles' which seems to describe the
realities with which all Schulz's stories concern themselves. This view
is concentrated in one sentence: 'Reality is as thin as paper and betrays
with all its cracks its imitative character' (p. 73).

Both the short story and the film of 'The Street of Crocodiles' work
with and through the unspoken and the repressed. Like the 'grey areas'
of the map, meaning is construed by implication; as in painting, it is
what happens in the 'gaps' which provides the most resonance. Like a
thesaurus of ambiguity the story repeats certain words: 'dubious,
intermingling, suspect, equivocal, double meaning'. 'The Street of
Crocodiles' represents everything that antisemitic Polish and German
society could not tolerate. Though the word 'Jew' is never used, it is
implicit in the story's language so that other words, phrases and
attributes are 'read' in its place. In the animation, words are
remarkably important, in spite of the fact that there are so few spoken,
because multiple meanings hang on the words and phrases suggested
by the images. Within both versions there is an acute and disturbing
oscillation of meaning, an unfixed, impressionistic, kaleidoscopic
'reality'. This movement is not confined within the boundaries of

either version, but spills over, so that watching the one changes and comments upon the reading of the other, in a seemingly endless manner. The animated version of 'The Street of Crocodiles' presents an exceptionally disturbing depiction of the demolition and depersonalization of the individual. It is suffused with a bizarre malevolence and a gothic threat, with the expression of a marginal and trammelled existence in the hunted and bewildered look of the main 'character'. It also enacts a terrible disintegration and dismemberment of the body which is associated with the unravelling of reality.

The father introduced at the beginning of 'The Street of Crocodiles' is not the paranoid man of 'Cinnamon Shops'. This father is a keeper, the curator of 'an old and beautiful map' (p. 69). The map is not ordinary and is presented as having great value and rarity. This opening seduces and lulls the reader into thinking that the story is going to be a lush evocation of the narrator's childhood, a Polish *A la recherche du temps perdu*. And yet, the map that is described has an odd, oscillating appearance, with almost magical properties. It is so finely detailed that looking at it seems to be almost the same as looking at the landscape it depicts as it has three-dimensional attributes which allow the viewer a perception of the landscape which contains perspective. It is somewhere between a map, a painting, an exquisitely detailed etching and a computer-generated, infinitely movable, possibly interactive graphic. The land beyond the city is described with an affectionate lyricism:

> The map ... opened a wide view of the valley of the River Tysmienica, which wound itself like a wavy ribbon of pale gold, on the maze of widely spreading ponds and marshes, on the high ground rising towards the south, gently at first, then in ever tighter ranges, in a chessboard of rounded hills, smaller and paler as they receded towards the misty yellow fog of the horizon. (p. 69)

This world has colour, mostly gold and yellow, colours associated with warmth, vitality and wealth. In this context the city does not seem to be an unambiguously attractive place at first, its 'undifferentiated mass' and 'dense complex' seem opposed to the 'wide view' of the land beyond. Yet it has its own beauties, very conscious, man-made beauties of form and architecture:

> In that section of the map, the engraver concentrated on the

complicated and manifold profusion of streets and alleyways, the sharp lines of cornices, architraves, archivolts, and pilasters, lit by the dark gold of a late and cloudy afternoon which steeped all corners and recesses in the deep sepia of shade. (p. 69)

The narrator emphasizes the drawing skills involved in the cartographer's process, and almost all of the city is rendered with an exquisite, precise detail. There is a real sense of wholeness and wholesomeness about this depiction and no hint that the narrator is being ironic. His final reflection upon the map and therefore upon the city which it represents suggests a completeness of creativity: 'The solids and prisms of that shade ... dramatized and orchestrated in a bleak romantic chiaroscuro the complex architectural polyphony' (p. 69). This sentence expresses the diversity of artistic and cultural riches in the area surrounding the Street of Crocodiles. It brings together terms associated with a variety of creative arts: music, theatre, drawing, painting and architecture are all represented in the space of a few words, whilst writing is represented by its own presence. The narrator's tone, up to this point in the story, is precise, educated, calm with distinct poetic tendencies in the choice of language. There is little sense of threat or cynicism about these opening paragraphs, and the reader is lulled into expecting the story to continue in this cultured mode. But, whilst this place is exceptionally beautiful, there is a hint of danger. The recurrent use of words like 'maze, chessboard, complex, canyons, recesses, honeycombed', creates a convoluted territory in which it would be easy to become completely lost; whoever enters these streets must be certain of the way out. As the Street of Crocodiles is introduced, these inklings proliferate. Because of the 'empty whiteness' of the Street of Crocodiles the narrator is not able to leave the map to speak for itself. Whilst the rest of the city may be apprehended easily, safely, and at a distance, by studying the map's detailed representations, the narrator must venture into that area in person in order to convey its nature to the reader. Alongside the rest of the city's 'baroque panoramas', the paucity of detail which characterizes the Street of Crocodiles seems unfortunate, perhaps even culpable. In amongst all that light, colour, texture and structure, amongst all that gives form and substance to reality, the Street of Crocodiles is no colour, no place. That the Street of Crocodiles' 'empty whiteness' is also like 'polar regions' or 'unexplored countries' suggests a comparison with alien cultures and hostile or uninhabitable places.

That it is a ghetto is implicit in the phrase 'grey areas'. Those who occupy this space and those who live outside struggle to ignore or refuse to acknowledge the nature of its existence.

The 'simple unadorned lettering' used on the map in the area around the Street of Crocodiles seems opposed or judged in relation to the 'noble script' used elsewhere (p. 69). There is a sophisticated recognition on the part of the narrator about the way in which the prejudices of a map-maker, historian or other recorder direct the kind of representations permitted so determining what is written in, and what is written out: 'The cartographer must have been loath to include that district in the city and his reservations found expression in the typographical treatment' (pp. 69–70). The use of the word 'reservations' alerts the reader: 'reservations' is hardly strong enough to permit a professional to leave out a whole section of the map. There is an acknowledgement of euphemism here, the first hints of the irony which pervades 'The Street of Crocodiles', for 'reservations' are really 'prejudices'. The Street of Crocodiles which the narrator proceeds to describe is an ironic representation of the Street of Crocodiles which the cartographer believes exists; at the end of the story the narrator, wearily, points out that this place is neither better nor worse than any other. The Street of Crocodiles is ordinary. The narrator is challenging the inaccurate conceptions and unfounded fears which attach themselves to areas which are considered alien or beyond the pale: 'In order to understand these reservations, we must draw attention to the equivocal and doubtful character of that peculiar area, so unlike the rest of the city' (p. 70). This is surely ironic. The whole story is a fantastic representation of the ideas about the area rather than the 'true' nature of that area. The tailor's shop and its assistants provide the strongest example of that prejudice.

The Street of Crocodiles which the narrator then describes is like a stage-set, a site of pretence and pastiche. Everything is shaky, fake, cheap. The glass in the windows is cracked and wavy, so that views are distorted and misrepresented; it is impossible to understand where 'reality' ends and 'reflections' begin. The whole area is composed of organic, corruptible material which is decomposing, turning to a thick dust which covers every surface. The 'dull, dirty and faulty glass panes in which dark pictures of the street were wavily reflected' (p. 70) assume a different meaning which includes more than the merely descriptive. This shaky staginess is given visual expression in the animation which also emphasizes that this is a world in a state of terminal decay; there is dust, peeling plaster, rust, an organic,

elemental chaos everywhere. The animation also dramatizes the acute
reflectiveness of the text; there are so many mirrors, oblique angles and
panes of glass that the point of view becomes disturbed. This provokes
consternation and questions for the viewer: where am I watching
from? Am I seeing the real thing or is this a reflection or a fantasy?
Whose side am I on? These questions have a particular resonance in
creative work produced since the Shoah because they problematize the
stance of the onlooker by making the viewer into a bystander. The type
of seeing that takes place within the animated version is disturbing.
Mainly covert and voyeuristic, it displays a fascination with the
forbidden. As well as being oblique, vision is often 'smeared', greasy
and there is a frequent suggestion that something is happening just
out of sight, at the edge of vision. This way of seeing suggests that
a hidden or ignored violence is taking place to which the viewer
responds warily. This violence seems to be explicit in the scene with
the watch. It is ticking, in spite of the fact that its mechanism is set out
around it in an orderly fashion. These screws and cogs are unlike any
of the other mechanisms; they are shiny, clean and properly inanimate,
but not performing their function. Three large 'screws' (thugs, prison
officers) appear, the kind that have been 'coming out of the woodwork'.
They screw themselves into the watch ('screw up the works') in an
unnecessary act of vandalism, for the watch presents no threat. As a
result of this attack, the watch bursts open, revealing unidentifiable
viscera and the thug screws roll away. This action takes place with
neither provocation nor retribution; the viewer watches, puzzled and
impotent, but vaguely implicated in the attack.

As the story's narrator begins to describe the Street of Crocodiles
he employs language and images which are familiar from other stories.
As in 'Pan', the area displays an unnatural and prolific growth, a 'rich
but empty and colourless vegetation' (p. 70), without any value or
merit. The theatrical and imitative nature of the area is apparent: 'One
could see there cheap jerrybuilt houses with grotesque façades,
covered with a monstrous stucco of cracked plaster' (p. 70). As in
'Cinnamon Shops', copying recurs as a motif though its significance is
shrouded. It is unclear why this narrator, like others, is obsessed by the
idea of copying, by seeming to be or attempting to look like something
else. On the one hand this preoccupation may be simply explained;
copying may be just one amongst a range of symbols employed, so that
it is not problematic in a context which uses the disciplines of drawing,
engraving and photography so frequently to supply metaphors. But
there is the suspicion, too, that to copy may be to mask one's identity

or 'true' nature. In the context of narratives which speak silently of Jewishness, copying becomes a necessary element of a protective masquerade. This also explains the frequency of images of façades and ideas about identity being only paper-thin. For many Jews, identity, whether as Jew or non-Jew, was paper-thin. Jewishness was imposed upon those who did not necessarily consider themselves to be Jewish, by legislation, by the initial J marked on documents for example. For others, the 'escape' from their 'dangerous' Jewish identity was made possible by the possession of forged documents, always copies of real documents, that provided a non-Jewish façade. This idea of copying, of one individual or group being able to seem like another is very disturbing to the status quo and is often treated as a provocation by those in authority. Authenticity is all, though who sets the criteria for authenticity and what is constituted by authenticity are always subject to disagreement. The idea of the Other 'passing for' the legitimate subject provokes great anxieties, on both sides. In Hitler's regime and as a consequence of German propaganda this anxiety regarding the Jews reached murderous proportions. Distinguishing between the 'true' and the 'copy' became an obsession. The recurrent emphasis upon reflectivity in 'The Street of Crocodiles' and in other Schulz stories may have a similar resonance. The ability to reflect what is around and therefore to offer back a representation of the 'true' or 'real' which confirms to the reflected a sense of its own truthfulness and reality whilst masking the otherness of the reflector is a vital part of the 'passing for' which permits assimilation. This would also explain the vehemence with which the people of Germany acceded to the categorizations imposed upon music, art, writing, culture, politics, all the attributes which go to compose identity generally. If a person could 'pass for' a non-Jew by escaping the racist stereotypes of physical characteristics, other tests of identity had to be applied so that to approve of certain forms of artistic expression or political philosophy could be seen as evidence of otherness.

The written text makes it clear that there are two worlds: one inhabited by the established city-dwellers who, it is implied, have a right to be where they are, and that of the inhabitants of the area round the Street. There is a system of apartheid in operation. The narrator never assigns a name to the people who inhabit the Street of Crocodiles just as Schulz never uses the word 'Jew' in any of his stories. But it is implicit in the stories that Jewish life, the 'real' life as well as the version promoted by propagandists, is being represented. The language of prejudice pervades and shapes the story. What is represented is a place and a community which, because of its lack of proper human attributes, deserves neither compassion nor recognition. For any non-Jew, that is, any one of the 'old established inhabitants of the city', to go into the Street of Crocodiles and fraternize with the people who live and work there is, by extension, a sign of their own moral decay and weakness.

> The old-established inhabitants of the city kept away from that area where the scum, the lowest orders had settled – creatures without character, without background, moral dregs, that inferior species of human being which is born in such ephemeral communities. But on days of defeat, in hours of moral weakness, it would happen that one or another of the city dwellers would venture half by chance into that dubious district. The best among them were not entirely free from the temptation of voluntary degradation, of breaking down the barriers of hierarchy, of immersion in that shallow mud of companionship, of easy intimacy, of dirty intermingling. (p. 70)

These tones, phrases and modes of expression remind the reader of the German exhortations to guard against any possibilities of 'dirty intermingling'. The narrator repeats and reports these phrases in a rhetorical manner reminiscent of the declamations of the racist and the antisemite, nor does he seem, at this point in the story, to challenge, except by the use of an implied irony, the truth of these declarations. It is only in the final paragraphs of the story that the truth of these assertions is problematized by the narrator's 'admission'.

The 'lack of colour' from which the Street suffers is alluded to again and again, and it applies equally to the inhabitants, who are also represented as colourless. Why 'lack of colour' should be 'fatal' is not clear. As with the idea of copying there may be a number of connotations which are significant. For human beings to lack colour may indicate illness, weakness, a compromised vitality or anaemia, maybe in this case the kind of moral anaemia of which they would be accused by their detractors. The phrase suggests references to 'blood' but here the ideas of 'dirty intermingling' which fuel racist fears for the purity of 'blood' give rise to paradox. The inhabitants of the area are less than human because they are colourless, lacking in blood, whilst the women who work in the tailor's shop, who are, after all, inhabitants of the area, are also less than human because they have too much colour, that is they have too much 'thick' blood.

The animation alludes to the 'fatal lack of colour' of the text by using sepia tones, as well as black and white with some greenish tones and red. Colour, when it appears inside the shop, is shocking. The texture and lighting make the film appear much older than it is, perhaps locating it with newsreels. The animation opens with an old man entering a large room, maybe a lecture hall or projection room, filled with seats. He is whistling, calmly going about his work, performing his duties or acting under orders. He approaches a contraption, looks down into it and sees a mechanism, which seems to have fallen out of use, covered in dust and a gluey redness, which may be blood. This mechanism may be related to a sewing machine, there seem to be pulleys, spools and needles. Throughout the animation, there is a particular emphasis upon sewing and tailoring, which not only calls up one of the characteristic stereotypes of Jews as tailors, but also legitimizes access to images of cutting, dissecting, dismemberment. The man gathers sputum in his mouth and spits into the machine, with deliberation but without disgust, as though he knows that this will free the mechanism and set in motion the machine's process. At first sight his behaviour is acceptable, but it becomes increasingly inexplicable. This is a bizarre, disconnected event; throughout the animation and the text there is a focus upon ritual and ritualized behaviour which, under scrutiny, becomes meaningless.

Inside the mechanism, which is also the Street of Crocodiles, a white-faced man has his hand trapped inside what seems to be a glass lantern. It is tied with cord and as the mechanism moves it flutters with impotent frenzy. The mechanism is full of pulleys, pistons, wheels, wire, but its purpose is unclear. Because it looks like a machine the assumption is that it will have meaning; the purpose of machines is to have a purpose, but this machine's meaning is hidden. The white-faced man is tied by his wrist (pulse?) to a system of pulleys and the omnipotent man outside the machine uses a pair of scissors to cut through the string/wire/cord. The white-faced man is freed, but it is not clear whether this is good or bad, something to be desired or shunned. This freeing is threatening, especially as the scissors seem old and odd, like the tools used for ritual emasculation, for cutting the umbilical cord, or for circumcision. There is so much potential for meaning that meaning collapses. Needles, cotton, scissors proliferate like weapons. They hang in the air, reinforcing the connections with sewing and tailoring. As the white-faced man reaches to loosen a knot in front of him, another pair of scissors threatens or offers to cut the string, but the knot is loosed before this can happen. As a consequence, a large sheet of smeared glass is raised and he is able to walk under it. Again, this action is ambiguous and it is not clear whether this passing over or through is beneficial or detrimental.

The place depicted in the animation is a place of brokenness and desuetude. It is difficult to discover where is inside or outside, up or down; what is good or bad. It is a place of oppositions, but ones which are continually in flux. The circularity of events and repetition of movement without progress heighten this disturbance. Strange mechanisms are visible through glass, they seem to have perpetual motion, constantly drawing together then springing apart, enacting repulsion and attraction, tension and release. The white-faced man looks around, watching some hands that seem to be reaching towards the breast of a dummy behind glass, exhibiting a bizarre commodification of desire. It is very difficult in this sequence to discover the point of view, there is so much glass and so many mirrors; there is obfuscation and revelation in equal amounts and it is almost impossible to distinguish one from the other. This is a voyeuristic and hermetic system. Another reflection from an open window high up in a building catches the attention of the white-faced man. But it may be the reflection of a reflection of a reflection . . .

The white-faced man comes like a wary spider out of his hiding place, watching the turning pulleys on the floor. They lead off like a tram-track into darkness, into obscurity. Cogs and mechanisms are stopped or set in motion without apparent reason or effect. There is the vague murmur of disembodied voices, as if a radio had been left on, with other, oddly disturbing sounds like trains in the distance or a foundry working or a processing factory. Conscious effort is required on the part of the viewer to ignore these troubling signs of what may be a malevolent potential. Dandelion clocks which have dispersed, reform; a melted ice cube becomes ice, melts and becomes ice again. Time is turned around, the clocks are turned back, anything can happen. There is a sense that many of these effects are conjuring tricks, though for whose benefit they are performed is unclear. There are strange appearances and disappearances. There is also a feeling of yearning, of longing and of displacement, though this may be because of the context of the film.

As the viewer watches the white-faced man, it is unclear where he is located. It is like being in a hall of mirrors which presents a threat because something might appear, but it will not be clear where it is coming from. Repetition and obsession lurk, there is a recurrent and powerful sense of threat and repression, of oppression. The white-

faced man suddenly flees towards and bangs upon the glass. Glancing
fearfully behind him into the darkness in the direction where the
pulleys run, he seems to be watching a figure engaged in rolling up the
wire from the pulleys; there is so much wire, it is dangerous. Then it
is revealed that the white-faced man has in fact run towards the thing
from which he had appeared to be fleeing; he has embraced or faced
what appeared to be the threat. And the being who is winding up the
wire now appears benign and welcoming, is inside the shop inviting
him to enter.

The short story's description of the tailor's shop places emphasis
upon a bureaucracy which is out of control. It is difficult to believe that
this was not written as a response to the experience of Jews in the
Holocaust, prefiguring, as it does, a deranged officialdom with a vision
of 'enormous shelves', 'storerooms stacked high with boxes and crates',
the 'enormous filing cabinet rising to the attic to disintegrate into the
geometry of emptiness' (p. 71). The windows are like ledgers, resonant
with a murderous attention to bureaucratic detail. No daylight
penetrates but there is a strange light in the shop, which can only be
generated from within the room; a sort of internal 'sense' which has no
correlation with the 'outside'.

As the narrator describes the tailor's shop, the language and
contradictions of prejudice gather force. All the sexual accusations
directed against Jews are here. The 'slender young salesman' is
described critically with a focus upon his behaviour and manner which
are represented as inappropriate for a 'proper' man. He is
'astonishingly servile, agile and compliant', he 'pranced and simpered
like a transvestite', he displays a 'pale powdered cheek', is 'effeminate
and corrupted' (pp. 71, 72). Later:

> Exhausted by his eager importuning, [he] slowly withdrew
> into feminine passivity. He now lay on one of the many sofas
> ... wearing a pair of deeply-cut silk pyjamas. (p. 72)

In contrast to the languor of the salesman, the salesgirls display an
inappropriate degree of sexually charged energy. They attract more
vehement and explicit accusations; their fertility and appetite present a
greater threat to the purity of blood than the salesman's lack of virility.
His passivity is represented as sordid but his kind of 'corruption'
implodes whereas their potential for fecundity (as in 'August')
explodes.[24] Their hirsuteness implies a gross sexual appetite and an
animal desire, it 'betrayed their thick, black blood' (p. 72) which

suggests the menstrual, the vampire. They stain and smudge the things they touch; the stain is both revolting and fascinating and conjures an animal, or other, sexuality, not 'normal' or manageable but perverse. Their darkness is so intense that it colours the air around them and gives off its own smell, like sex. They are not named as Jews, but they are clearly the foreign, the Other. They are depicted as being like prostitutes as they parade; their sexuality is disturbing in its intensity and potential for rapacity. They are not passive like the salesman, and their vigour is seen as an attack and a provocation. Perhaps there is implicit in this disparagement the fear of 'the temptation of voluntary degradation' (p. 70) so that the salesgirls attract a stronger hostility to the extent that they are seen as significantly more likely to invite a fraternization which would be difficult for all but the strongest to resist. They have no individuality and may be spoken of and described as one being. They are 'tall dark salesgirls, each with a flaw in her beauty'; as the narrator remarks, the 'flaw' is '[appropriate] for that district of remaindered goods' (p. 71). It is also 'appropriate' if they are Jewish for, naturally, they cannot be perfect, which is a state of grace reserved for the Aryan. This recognizes the impossibility of any individual from the Street of Crocodiles being permitted acknowledgment as wholly beautiful. For, in spite of appearances to the contrary, even the most beautiful will always be 'scum' (p. 70) and no amount of beauty can eradicate or compensate for this unavoidable taint.

The salesgirls are associated very closely with the 'collection of highly questionable books' (p. 72) which have been shown to the customer; they stain the books, the books stain them. They 'walked up and down between the rows of books' as though parading the living embodiment of the 'licentiousness' the books describe. The conflation of the women with the books is completed when they are represented as having 'faces, like grey parchment', something to be written on or read, something with as great a potential for corruption as the books. The detailed description of the salesgirls which follows is a stunning example of an implicit construction of The Jew:

> The salesgirls now walked up and down between the rows of
> books, their faces, like grey parchment, marked with the dark
> greasy pigment spots of brunettes, their shiny dark eyes
> shooting out sudden zigzag cockroachy looks. But even their
> dark blushes, the piquant beauty spots, the traces of down on
> their upper lips betrayed their thick, black blood. Their

overintense colouring, like that of an aromatic coffee, seemed
to stain the books which they took into their olive hands, their
touch seemed to run on the pages and leave in the air a dark
trail of freckles, a smudge of tobacco, as does a truffle with its
exciting, animal smell. (p. 72)

Not a word is wasted here; every one counts as indictment against the
beautiful young women. It is all a matter of looking and seeing, of
revulsion and fascination. This is the language of xenophobia which
displays an acute fear of blood and of the Other, which depicts that
Other as animal. This kind of construction, which severs or denies the
humanity of the subject, ends in the representation of that subject as
vermin or parasites, to be destroyed. The salesgirls' faults are
numerous. These women are too intense, they are not cool, blonde,
Aryan; they are 'greasy'; insect-like, therefore parasitical; their blood is
'thick, black'; contact with them leaves a 'stain'. And their most
damning flaw is that they fascinate. For, as this paragraph inscribes
intense loathing, it also inscribes desire, the lure of the exotic and
taboo. The women are available for consumption, they are costly
commodities which whet the appetite: they are 'coffee', 'olive',
'tobacco', 'truffle', the props of seduction, of the brothel, or of the
boudoir. These attributes are not confined to the salesgirls. All the
women in the Street of Crocodiles are similarly polluted:

> Showily dressed in long lace-trimmed gowns, prostitutes have
> begun to circulate. They might even be the wives of
> hairdressers or restaurant bandleaders. They advance with a
> brisk, rapacious step, each with some small flaw in her evil
> corrupted face; their eyes have a black, crooked squint, or they
> have harelips, or the tips of their noses are missing.
>
> The inhabitants of the city are quite proud of the odour of
> corruption emanating from the Street of Crocodiles ... They
> maintain that every woman in that district is a tart. In fact, it
> is enough to stare at any of them, and at once you meet an
> insistent clinging look which freezes you with the certainty of
> fulfilment. Even the schoolgirls wear their hair ribbons in a
> characteristic way and walk on their slim legs with a peculiar
> step, an impure expression in their eyes that foreshadows their
> future corruption. (p. 75)

The animation emphasizes the erotic content of the transactions in the shop. There are four doll assistants, their eyes are empty yet a burning light spills out which might be fanaticism, desire or obsession. They have no tops to their heads, which are empty. Like a magician, the male doll displays his command of the needles which perform by 'walking' up and then back down his arm. He orchestrates and conducts the movement of the others. A sudden and shocking catalogue of colour is presented in the form of a 'list' of braids. One is chosen, then a long swathe of gorgeously coloured cloth is dragged from a shirt rack. There is a sudden cut to a map. A pair of scissors and a cotton bobbin lie on the map, pins are stuck in it. The strange, clawed hands of the boss doll point out and seem to encircle the boundaries of Poland. There are stitches along the boundary, as though holding the country in place, it is 'all stitched/sewn up'. There might be a correlation between the choice of the braid, a militaristic ornament and the sewing/stitching up of a country, a people. The boss doll, in its role as magician, conjures a huge piece of liver from nowhere and this completely covers the map and is then covered in dressmaking tissue, normally used for making patterns. Meanwhile the white-faced man is still being 'attended to' by the doll assistants. He has been swathed in the bolt of gorgeous cloth, his own head has been removed and replaced with one of the empty china doll heads. As the boss doll smoothes and pins the dressmaking tissue to the liver on the map, the assistants smooth and pin tissue to the torso of the white-faced man, so that there seems to be a correlation between him and the liver; he becomes another piece of meat, of offal, the meat that is often rejected. The cavity in his skull is filled with cotton wool which is then pulled out through the eyes, ears and mouth, preventing him from seeing or hearing whilst enforcing silence. For hair he has been given a dandelion clock. The boss doll caresses the bodiless head with affection or possessiveness. The scene describes a derangement of cause and effect, of rationality; there is meaning and purpose but it is hidden, bizarre, elusive.

The short story emphasizes that in the tailor's shop, 'lasciviousness had become general'. The salesgirls ignore the narrator/customer. Instead they

> demonstrated to one another the poses and postures of the drawings on the book jackets ... they adopted arrogant poses, shifting their weight from foot to foot, making play with their frivolous footwear, abandoning their slim bodies to the serpentine movements of their limbs and thus laid siege to the

> excited onlooker whom they pretended to ignore behind a
> show of assumed indifference. (p. 72)

The narrator/customer, clearly not considering himself to be an
'excited onlooker', takes this opportunity to leave the shop. 'No one
stops us', he says, but does not explain why they might. Once back into
the Street of Crocodiles, the narrator returns to the colourless world it
represents:

> It is, as usual in that district, a grey day, and the whole scene
> seems at times like a photograph in an illustrated magazine, so
> grey, so one-dimensional are the houses, the people, the
> vehicles. (p. 73)

Looking at the photographs in Roman Vishniac's book, the reader
sees what Schulz and the narrator imagined.[25] All that world, so live
once, is now only available in black and white photographs: 'Reality is
as thin as paper.' Reality in Schulz's work, and maybe in reality, is
always vulnerable to disintegration. It is the narrator's expectations
which form reality, beyond is only chaos. There is something acutely
pathetic, and now poignant, about this representation of a reality which
was/is only ever a matter of theatre and contingency. Nothing here may
be trusted, there is no room for reliability or security. That reality is
depicted as a matter of theatre does not hide the fact that there is
something dangerous in the destruction of that façade. If civilization is a
matter of veneer only, an agreement in common about what is or is not
permissible which is no more than skin deep, then civilization and its
'realities' are easily torn to reveal the incivilities which lie behind the
façade.

The narrator's descriptions of the city are ambiguous and express a
subtle oscillation between approval and disapproval. The city is full of
contradictions. The street into which the narrator steps 'is as broad as
a city boulevard, but the roadway is made, like village squares, of
beaten clay, full of puddles and overgrown with grass' (p. 73). The
crowd is 'eager to live up to its metropolitan aspirations' yet 'despite
the bustle and sense of purpose, one has the impression of a
monotonous aimless wandering, of a sleepy procession of puppets'
(p. 73). And 'the crowd flows lazily by and, strange to say, one can see
it only indistinctly', though

> at times . . . we catch among the turmoil of many heads, a dark
> vivacious look, a black bowler hat worn at an angle, half a face

split by a smile formed by lips which had just finished
speaking, a foot thrust forward to take a step and fixed forever
in that position. (p. 74)

The people of the Street of Crocodiles almost seem not to be there,
most pass without making any impression, only occasionally does a
smile or foot or a 'dark vivacious look' stand out from the crowd. Read
after the Shoah, these descriptions are coloured by our knowledge of
the mechanics and effects of its depersonalizations. The vast numbers
of those Jews who went to the gas chambers remain unknown,
unrecognized, they are a part of the 'sleepy procession of puppets'.
There are few who survived, who retained their individual delineation
'among the turmoil of many heads'. These descriptions are poignant
when read in the light of what happened to streets like the Street of
Crocodiles. They recall the reader again to the photographs which
survived the Shoah, the paper realities which exist even after the three-
dimensional ones have been torn apart.[26]

Having depicted the features of the area, the narrator, like a tour
guide, proceeds to discuss its transport system. The street traffic is the
pride of the area's inhabitants; yet it is strangely formless, ghostly,
hazy, indistinct and undefined. The transport system is strange: the
railway station is unfinished, offering no way out of the area; the
cabmen have abandoned their cabs and wander along the streets; the
trams are papier-mâché and have to be pushed along by porters; they
are without self-motivation. None of the modes of transport to which
the narrator refers guarantees any certainty of arriving safely at one's
intended destination.

The cabs, as in 'Cinnamon Shops', are driverless; the drivers
abdicate their responsibilities and leave their customers in the care of
the cab-horses. The trams are

> papier-mâché with warped sides dented from the misuses of
> many years. They often have no fronts, so that in passing one
> can see the passengers, sitting stiffly and behaving with great
> decorum. These trams are pushed by the town porters. (p. 74)

The passengers make the best of a very bad job and their behaviour
is used as an image of civilized behaviour deployed to ridiculous effect.
Why should the passengers behave with decorum in such
circumstances? The Badenheim-esque tone is intensified by the
narrator's statement about the city councillors: 'In them [the trams] the

ambition of the city councillors has achieved its greatest triumph'
(p. 74). What is there to be triumphant about?

But it is the trains which attain most significance in the Street of
Crocodiles, and which provoke most disquiet in the reader, if not,
apparently, in the narrator. Logic, rationality and sanity are entirely
disrupted. No one knows when the trains will come or where or
whether they will stop, so people wait in different places and there is a
noticeable absence of consensus about the best course to be adopted.
There seems to be something horrible and demeaning about the way
in which prospective passengers wait patiently for something which
may or may not happen. The train, like the shop women, is deformed
or tainted and the 'buildings of the railway station' are 'as yet
unfinished' (p. 73).

There is so much misplaced pride in this place; in the street which
is no street, in the transport system which does not function, in the
smell of corruption. The people who inhabit this area are a broken
people, not rational or thinking but forced to follow a terrifying
'pattern' which has been 'cut out' for them. No object is used for its
proper or usual purpose, all things are divorced from conventional
humanity. There are no reassuring elements in the written or the
animated versions of 'The Street of Crocodiles'. Nothing is as it seems,
expectations are constantly overturned and it is disturbing, especially
in the animated version, to see the evidence of anything that is, or has
been, alive inhabiting this 'grey area'.

The 'sin' of The Street of Crocodiles seems to be the way in which
impulse is thwarted; there is an awful failure of communication, a
sense of terrible loss and the absence of the desired thing. But, meaning
and ending remain elusive. The narrator says that the suspicious
appearance of the tailor's shop was a sham, that the shamminess was
fake and that 'really' the shop was ordinary, the women were not as
depraved as they were represented to be, there were no possibilities for
'dark and unusual passions'. In the animated version, a disembodied
voice recites the last lines of the written story and the words
'Obviously, we were unable to afford anything better' are repeated
three times, like a stuck record, each time more slowly, as if the
'machine' is winding down. The most striking element about both the
short story and the film is the way in which they correspond with one
another.

'The Street of Crocodiles' does not offer or permit the reader to
adopt a fixed position in relation to this world, nor is it clear whether
the reader is to be shocked, disapproving, excited or disturbed by this

material. It demands of the reader a close attention to his or her own responses and prejudices but more than this, leaves the reader in a condition of acute anxiety and uncertainty. Although 'The Street of Crocodiles' was written before the machinery of the Shoah was in place, the text seems full of allusion to, commentary upon and analysis of the Holocaust. It 'speaks' of the Shoah. It seems likely that as Schulz was inscribing his experience of antisemitism, many of the elements which went to the construction of his circumscribed world would necessarily reappear, though in larger and more terrible forms, in the literature of the Holocaust. The post-Shoah reader cannot prevent knowledge of the Shoah from leaking out and informing the reading of Jewish texts made prior to the Holocaust. 'The Street of Crocodiles', as story and as animation, dramatizes the installation and mechanism of prejudice and the terrible consequences which occur at its extremities. 'Read' together they provide a comprehensive 'mapping' of the arbitrariness and malleability of 'reality'.

Schulz was not a prophet. There is no evidence that he was adopting a Cassandra role or seeking to warn his people. The threats, fears, disappearances and desolations of which he writes were intended as fiction. Yet they were realized, not only for Schulz but for all those around him. From the first days of the German invasion of Poland in 1939 until his death, Schulz will have lived with the daily realization of his wildest dreams – or nightmares. We know that Schulz was not killed by Einsatzgruppe D which carried out executions in Drohobycz on 14 July and 28 July 1941.[27] Nor was he amongst any of the three deportations which took place in March, between 6 and 8 August, and on 17 August 1942 of over 9,000 Jews from Drohobycz. Along with other Jews from the towns and villages of Eastern Galicia, the lives of the deportees from Drohobycz were ended at Belzec. Nor was Schulz amongst the 200 old and sick Jews who were murdered on the streets of Drohobycz as a preliminary to a further deportation of 2,300 people to Belzec some time between 15 and 31 October 1942.[28] However, by the time the remaining Jews of Drohobycz were murdered on 27 August 1943, Schulz was dead.[29]

In the midst of so much anonymous and mass slaughter, the place and mode of Schulz's death was witnessed and later recounted by another inhabitant, Izydor Friedman.[30]

> On a day I don't recall in 1942, known as Black Thursday in
> Drohobycz, the Gestapo carried out a massacre in the ghetto.
> We happened to be in the ghetto to buy food [instead of at

work outside]. When we heard shooting and saw Jews run for their lives we too took to flight. Schulz, physically the weaker, was caught by a Gestapo agent called Guenther, who stopped him, put a revolver to his head, and fired twice. During the night I found his body, searched his pockets, and gave his documents and some notes I found there to his nephew Hoffman – who lost his life a month later. Toward morning I buried him in the Jewish cemetery. I was unable to identify his grave site after the liberation of Drohobycz in 1944.

Friedman, who survived the German occupation by masquerading as a non-Jewish Pole, gave information about the almost congenial library work upon which he and Schulz were employed during the war. In the course of their friendship, Schulz also told Friedman that 'he had deposited all his papers, notes, and correspondence files with a Catholic outside the ghetto'.[31] In spite of attempts after the war by Friedman and others to find this anonymous Catholic friend, Schulz's cache of papers was never discovered.

Schulz's last surviving letter, written to his friend Ania Plockier and dated a year before his death, is also his last communication with the future. Having learned that Ania was leaving for Warsaw, Schulz wrote:

November 19, 1941

How sad to think that at 30 Mazeppa Street, where I spent so many lovely hours, no one will be left, all of it will become mere legend. I don't know why I feel guilty toward myself, as if I had lost something and it was my own fault.[32]

In these few lines Schulz encapsulates many of the characteristics of his writings. There is his poignant sense of loss and regret; his nostalgia for the beautiful past; his recognition of the ashen and empty future; his emphasis upon the legendary in the quotidian. As in his stories, the universal is to be discovered in the particular; the apparently trivial marks the ineluctably significant; what is marginal becomes central. The loss of a Jewish presence at 30 Mazeppa Street might stand at this point in Schulz's life and perceptions for the loss of a Jewish presence in Drohobycz and, by extension, for the loss of a Jewish presence in Poland. Of course, in such circumstances his guilt was terribly misplaced: he was not in any measure responsible for Ania's departure. Yet even in his expressions of unfounded self blame there is something real, a perception which also gives inklings of the future for, in a very similar manner, survivors often echo his words when they speak of their own overwhelming and misplaced sense of guilt, 'as if I had lost something and it was my own fault'.

NOTES

1. Michael André Bernstein, *Foregone Conclusions: Against Apocalyptic History* (Los Angeles: University of California Press, 1994), p. 9.
2. Jerzy Ficowski, *Letters and Drawings of Bruno Schulz with Selected Prose*, trans. Walter Arndt (New York: Fromm, 1990), p. 176.
3. Cynthia Ozick, *The Messiah of Stockholm* (London: André Deutsch, 1987).
4. David Grossman, *See Under: Love*, trans. Betsy Rosenberg (London: Cape, 1990). Russell Brown in 'Bruno Schulz and World Literature', *The Slavic and East European Journal*, 34: 2 (1990), p. 234 suggests that Danilo Kis and Bohumil Hrabal have also been influenced to a noticeable degree by Schulz's work and life.
5. There are slightly differing versions of Schulz's death: for examples see Friedman's testimony recounted in Jerzy Ficowski, *Letters and Drawings of Bruno Schulz*, p. 248; Celina Wieniewska's Preface to *The Fictions of Bruno Schulz: The Street of Crocodiles and Sanatorium Under the Sign of the Hourglass*, trans. Celina Wieniewska (London: Picador, 1988), p. 11; Stanislaw Baranczak, 'The Faces of Mastery', *The New Republic* (2 January 1989), p. 32.
6. Russell Brown, 'Bruno Schulz and World Literature', p. 224.
7. Baranczak, 'The Faces of Mastery', p. 28.
8. Colleen M. Taylor, 'Childhood Revisited: The Writings of Bruno Schulz', *The Slavic and East European Journal*, 13: 4 (1969), p. 456.
9. Russell Brown, 'Bruno Schulz and World Literature', p. 224.
10. *The Fictions of Bruno Schulz*, trans. Celina Wieniewska, p. 12.
11. Bohdan Budurowycz, 'Galicia in the Works of Bruno Schulz', *Canadian Slavonic Papers*, 28: 4 (December 1986), pp. 360–1.
12. Ibid. In contrast to the descriptions of Drohobycz which represent it as a sleepy backwater, Martin Gilbert's, *The Dent Atlas of the Holocaust: The Complete History* (London: Dent, 1993), map 28, shows that, on the eve of the war, Drohobycz had 17,000 Jewish inhabitants who comprised 44 per cent of the total population of approximately 38,600 people. The Jewish community had been in Drohobycz since the fifteenth century. By comparison, in 1999, Buxton had slightly less than 20,000 inhabitants and was little more than a leisure centre for the Dukes of Devonshire until the mid-eighteenth century.
13. Bernstein, *Foregone Conclusions*, p. 13.
14. Russell Brown, 'Bruno Schulz and World Literature', p. 235; Danilo Kis, *Garden, Ashes* (London: Faber & Faber, 1985) (United States: Harcourt

Brace, Jovanovich, 1978).

15. Russell Brown, 'Bruno Schulz and World Literature', p. 234.

16. Schulz's stories are not the only ones to display 'prophetic' tendencies arising out of perceptions of the past: see also Isaac Babel, 'The Story of my Dovecot' in *The Penguin Book of Jewish Short Stories*, ed. Emanuel Litvinoff (London: Penguin, 1979).

17. See Zygmunt Bauman, *Modernity and the Holocaust* (Oxford: Basil Blackwell, 1989).

18. *The Fictions of Bruno Schulz*, trans. Celina Wieniewska, p. 15.

19. This kind of alienated mode appears repeatedly in survivor testimony, and Langer draws attention to it on a number of occasions, for example: 'Defamiliarized reality is the dismissal of a whole lexicon of safeguards for the security of the integrated self: choice, will, power of deliberation, confidence in predictive certainty,' Langer, *Holocaust Testimonies: The Ruins of Memory* (New Haven: Yale University Press, 1991), p. 177.

20. Jerzy Ficowsi, *Letters and Drawings of Bruno Schulz with Selected Prose*, p. 26.

21. For examples of Schulz's drawings and engravings, see the illustrations which accompany Schulz's stories in *The Fictions of Bruno Schulz*, especially 'Sanatorium under the Sign of the Hourglass', p. 237; Ficowski, *Letters and Drawings of Bruno Schulz*; Ficowski, *Le Livre Idolâtre* (Varsovie: Editions Interpress, n.d.) and Bruno Schulz, *Ilustracje*, ed. Jerzy Ficowski (Warsaw: Wydawnictwo Reprint, 1992). Also see Quay Brothers (1986), *The Street of Crocodiles*, which 'animates' Schulz's menacing, illusory cityscapes. Schulz is rarely referred to as an artist, for example he is not mentioned in Avram Kampf, *Chagall to Kitaj: Jewish Experience in 20th-Century Art* (London: Lund Humphries, 1990). There are elements to Schulz's drawings which, as with his stories, have inklings of the drawings to come out of the Shoah. See for example, Monica Bohm-Duchen, *After Auschwitz: Responses to the Holocaust in Contemporary Art* (London: Lund Humphries, 1995) and especially the drawings on pp. 28–31, 37, 43.

22. Primo Levi, *If This is a Man*, trans. Stuart Woolf (London: Abacus, 1987), p. 22.

23. Quay Brothers, *The Street of Crocodiles* (1986).

24. This also reminds the reader of the ferocity with which Jewish mothers and children were destroyed by the Germans. A significant threat to the success of the 'Final Solution' was fertility.

25. Roman Vishniac, *A Vanished World* (London: Penguin, 1986).

26. This is not unlike the much-maligned scene in *Schindler's List* (1993) when, during an *Aktion* to clear the ghetto, a small girl is identified by the coat she wears. Though the film is shot in black and white, she wears a bright red coat, the only colour used in the film until its end. She seems to escape but later a small red bundle is visible on a pile of bodies.

27. SS Sergeant Felix Landau's testimony in Martin Gilbert, *The Holocaust: The Jewish Tragedy* (London: Collins, 1986), pp. 170–1; 173–4. See also map

73 in Martin Gilbert, *The Dent Atlas of the Holocaust: The Complete History* (London: Dent, 1993).

28. Ibid., map 165. And see maps 207 and 223.
29. Martin Gilbert, *The Holocaust*, p. 605.
30. Friedman's testimony is recounted in Jerzy Ficowski, *Letters and Drawings of Bruno Schulz*, p. 248. Clearly, he was later able to confirm the date satisfactorily.
31. Ibid., p. 248.
32. Ibid., p. 213.

4

PRIMO LEVI

LEVI AND MEMORY

Of my two years of life outside the law I have not forgotten a single thing. Without any deliberate effort, memory continues to restore to me events, faces, words, sensations, as if at that time my mind had gone through a period of exalted receptivity during which not a detail was lost. I remember, for example, as they would be remembered by a tape recorder or a parrot, whole sentences in languages I did not know then, and don't know now ... It seems to me obvious that this attention of mine at that time, turned to the world and to the human beings around me, was not only a symptom but also an important factor of spiritual and physical salvation.[1]

If This is a Man and *The Drowned and the Saved*, Levi's two great works, stand separated by 40 years of survival, at the beginning and end of his writing life.[2] They represent a central aspect of Holocaust literature in their analysis of and struggle with the experiences of being a survivor. This chapter is concerned with Levi's memory of that survival and his study of what memory meant in 1947 and came to mean towards the end of his life. As well as considering chapters from *If This is a Man* and *The Drowned and the Saved* I have given some attention to 'The Thaw' (p. 9) and 'Force Majeure' (p. 62) as examples of my thesis that the memory of the offence is not containable and may surface in writing which is not explicitly about the Holocaust.[3] The introductory remarks which follow are intended to provide a context for the closer reading of these texts. They constitute a series of loosely connected observations about Levi's representations of memory and survival which will underpin my readings.

RICORDATI: 'CARRIED IN THE HEART'

What you carry inside you, they can't take away from you.[4]
He had no document but his memory; the training he had acquired
with each added hexameter gave him a discipline unsuspected by those
who set down and forget temporary, incomplete paragraphs.[5]

If This is a Man is valued and valuable for the intensity and
determination with which Levi inscribes his memories of Auschwitz.
One of the most compelling elements of those recollections is the extent
to which the text makes clear that recollection itself had a significant
role in Auschwitz. There are at least two aspects to this. There is the
task of memorizing Auschwitz which Levi says he engaged in to ensure
that 'not a detail was lost'. There is also the recognition that, for survival
to be possible, memories of life 'before' and 'outside' Auschwitz were
vital, recollection was life-giving. In Auschwitz, it was imperative that
Auschwitz form only part of memory's matter. To attempt survival, the
recollection of the person and the life that had been was a necessary if
painful act. That remembering oneself was an act of resistance is
emphasized by the bureaucratic and brutal techniques which the camp
system employed to discourage that remembrance. Those who 'forgot'
themselves, those unable to maintain any sense of their humanity,
certainly could not survive. They were vulnerable and succumbed
rapidly to the degradations designed to demolish identity. Yet, too much
remembering of the 'before' and the 'outside' could leave the prisoner
demoralized and unfit to respond to the terrible exigencies of life inside
Auschwitz. Two incidents described by Levi convey this paradox and
the urgent need for a balance to be found. Both occurred soon after his
arrival in Auschwitz.

> We Italians had decided to meet every Sunday evening in a
> corner of the Lager, but we stopped it at once, because it was
> too sad to count our numbers and find fewer each time, and to
> see each other ever more deformed and more squalid. And it
> was so tiring to walk those few steps and then, meeting each
> other, to remember and to think. It was better not to think. (*If
> This is a Man*, p. 43)

Before they realize the nature of the place to which they have come,
Levi and his compatriots initiate a ritual which they believe will help
them maintain contact with one another. Perhaps they had imagined
they would reminisce, speak Italian without misunderstanding or
interruption, strengthen and emphasize their common bonds. It is a

benign suggestion, one which in almost any other situation would offer many benefits. However, the ritual fails 'at once', it becomes a paradox, an unpractised ritual to be repeated only by the reader each time the lines are read and the scene which might have been is imagined. The losses and grave injury to which the Italians had been exposed are intensified by the poignancy and swiftness of their recognition that memory is a problem, that to be reminded of the people they once were might only damage them further.

The second incident reveals that this view was not universally held. Levi's meeting with Steinlauf revolves around the assertion that survival is absolutely dependent upon remembering oneself, 'that precisely because the Lager was a great machine to reduce us to beasts, we must not become beasts' (*If This is a Man*, p. 47). Steinlauf is not a naïve man, he knows that survival is never assured and is prey to the capricious behaviour of those in power. But he insists that the only possibility for survival is to treat oneself as human and to remember the shape that humanity takes: 'one must want to survive, to tell the story ... to survive we must force ourselves to save at least the skeleton, the scaffolding, the form of civilization'. It is significant that Steinlauf, or the Steinlauf whom Levi remembers, elides the future with the past, asserting that in order to be fit 'to tell the story', they must remember and rehearse what they were before Auschwitz.

One part of the method which Steinlauf employs to remind himself of his identity seems to Levi, after only a week in the Lager, to be 'a mechanical habit, or worse, a dismal repetition of an extinct rite'.

> In this place it is practically pointless to wash every day in the turbid water of the filthy washbasins for purposes of cleanliness and health ...
> I must confess it: after only one week of prison, the instinct for cleanliness disappeared in me. (p. 46)

Washing belongs to the old order, the prehistoric times of a week earlier when to wash was meaningful. The ritual, so unconsciously repetitive that Levi the scientist characterizes it as 'instinct', is devoid of sense. The likeness here with any religious or cultural practice which develops within a particular context only to be followed more or less slavishly in entirely different, and hostile, circumstances cannot be avoided. Just as many secular writers have expressed amazement at the determination of Orthodox Jews to pursue dietary laws and to observe the prescribed fasts whilst in the camps, so Levi registers a similar astonishment at Steinlauf's behaviour. Yet, even as he recognizes the power of this ritual to help Steinlauf manage the days in which he finds himself, Levi is not able to put on this 'religious' demeanour, even if it could save him.

> Nothing is of greater vanity than to force oneself to swallow whole a moral system elaborated by others, under another sky. No, the wisdom and virtue of Steinlauf, certainly good for him, is not enough for me. (p. 47)[6]

Levi refuses to take Steinlauf's route to remembrance, but he is not without his own identity-affirming rituals which will remind him of himself. The memory of his life outside and before Auschwitz has to find some means of expression if Levi is to survive. And though religious observance is not available to Levi as a means of keeping his identity intact yet the method which comes to his aid does have recognizable religious elements.

> Intimately connected with the custom of reading and repeating aloud was the practice of reading the written Torah and repeating the oral with a rhythmical melody ... Rhythm and cantillation certainly did not originate for pedagogical reasons, but they fulfil *de facto* a pedagogical function: the texts which are learned in this way are memorized and transmitted more faithfully and more exactly than those learned in other ways. Folk-lore provides many examples of the tenacity with which archaic wording lives on in cantillated traditional texts, long after the meaning of the texts has been forgotten.[7]

Levi comes to a very similar conclusion in 'Rhyming on the Counterattack' though he places his emphasis upon rhyme rather than rhythm:

> Whoever reads good verses wants to take them along with him, remember them, possess them ... Now for recording by memory, rhyme is a fundamental help: one verse line pulls along another or the others, the forgotten verse can be reconstructed, at least approximately. The effect is so strong that, in the mysterious but limited storehouse of our memory, poetry without rhyme often makes room for rhymed poetry, even if the latter is not as noble. From this follows a pragmatic consequence: poets who wish to be remembered (in Italian

ricordati, 'carried in the heart': and in many languages, memorizing is called learning 'by heart') should not neglect this virtue of rhyme. (*The Mirror Maker*, p. 113)

Levi asserts that one of the most significant aspects of rhyme, significant to the extent of supplying a deeply felt human need, is that rhyme aids remembrance. Whoever has memorized a poem has something that cannot be destroyed or stolen.[8] In Auschwitz some of the aids to Levi's survival were the memory, rhythms and rhymes of poetry, which demanded his attention and brought him to himself. Other writers recognized similar imperatives and benefits:

> Since Auschwitz, I always feared losing my memory. To lose one's memory is to lose oneself, to no longer be oneself. I had invented all kinds of exercises to put my memory to work: memorize all the telephone numbers I used to know, all the metro stations along one line, all the boutiques along the rue Caumartin between the Athénée theater and the Havre-Caumartin metro station. I had succeeded, at the price of infinite efforts, in recalling fifty-seven poems. I was so afraid they might escape my mind that I recited them to myself every day, all of them, one after the other, during roll call. It had been so difficult to reconstruct them! Sometimes it took days for a single line, a word, which simply would not come back. And now, all of a sudden, I had a whole book I could memorize, a whole text.
>
> I learned *Le Misanthrope* by heart, a fragment each evening ... And until departure, I kept the play within my throat.[9]

MEMORY AND *IF THIS IS A MAN*

The views Levi expressed in 'Rhyming on the Counterattack' shed light upon this project of remembrance; the significance of learning by heart and of remembering or being remembered by others are central to *If This is a Man*. This section will refer to *If This is a Man* in general terms and then discuss three chapters, 'On the Bottom', 'Chemical Examination' and 'The Canto of Ulysses' in greater detail.

Levi opens with a characteristically undramatic assertion:

> As an account of atrocities, therefore, this book of mine adds nothing to what is already known to readers throughout the

world on the disturbing question of the death camps. It has not
been written in order to formulate new accusations; it should
be able, rather, to furnish documentation for a quiet study of
certain aspects of the human mind. (p. 15)

As a representation of what follows, Levi's stated intention seems
inadequate. Anything less likely to promote 'quiet study' than a
contemplation of the events of the Shoah is difficult to imagine. The
brutalities and inhumanities which Levi catalogues rightly demand
vehement accusation. Yet Levi eschews this approach for one
apparently more dispassionate and renders the world that was
Auschwitz with a deliberate intent to query all our assumptions. His
assertion that he is not writing 'in order to formulate new accusations'
is apparently borne out as he depicts the world that was Auschwitz in
the careful prose of a rational man, and his text does 'furnish
documentation for a quiet study of certain aspects of the human mind'
in abundance. Yet, belying what would seem to be a distinct lack of
emotional engagement, Levi's writings are amongst the most moving
and most bitter expositions of the Lager world. This discrepancy
between his stated intentions and their outcome may or may not itself
have been intentional. What is clear is that his rationality served Levi
just as well as, or better than, any emotional plea to the reader, in his
determination to convey his memory of the offence.

The first words encountered in *If This is a Man* are a shock to the
reader; they act as a sign that he or she must be prepared to read
carefully and without preconceived ideas: 'It was my good fortune to
be deported to Auschwitz only in 1944' (p. 15). The shock lies in the
fact that these two apparently antithetical phrases, 'my good fortune'
and 'deported to Auschwitz', appear together in one sentence, though
Levi is able to support his assertion. In the process the reader becomes
aware of a response which marks out a pattern for what follows. The
reader will be shocked again and again, not so much by Levi's
descriptions of the inhumanities perpetrated in Auschwitz, but by his
insistence upon approaching and rendering those experiences with an
honesty which results in unexpected conclusions. When Levi says, 'it
was my good fortune' his determination to be as truthful and as
objective as possible means that the reader's own assumptions and
hypotheses are tested. Whatever we think we know of or understand
about Auschwitz is challenged by Levi.

The refusal of anger and blame which forms *If This is a Man* leaves
the reader impressed by the sense that there is a kind of judicious

neutrality at work in Levi's indictments. It is clear from the language Levi employs that he believes that there is an argument to be undertaken about the camps. Words and phrases indicate an approach which owes a great deal to Levi's education as a scientist; 'formulate, documentation, study, system, reason, premiss, syllogism, at the end of the chain, logical, conclusion', all suggest that these are matters of cause and effect. Levi examines his experiences, then extracts and condenses whatever is essential and useful to those of us fortunate enough not to have been part of what he called 'a gigantic biological and social experiment' (p. 93).

In the 'Preface', Levi also draws attention to and apologizes for 'the structural defects of the book' (p. 15). His discussion here gives a valuable insight into the creative process involved in writing *If This is a Man*. Levi emphasizes not only that he had formed his intention to 'tell our story' whilst still in Auschwitz but also that this 'need'

> had taken on for us, before our liberation and after, the character of an immediate and violent impulse, to the point of competing with our other elementary needs. The book has been written to satisfy this need: first and foremost, therefore, as an interior liberation. Hence its fragmentary character: the chapters have been written not in logical succession, but in order of urgency. (pp. 15–16)

This draws the reader's attention to two impulses driving the writing of the text. On the one hand, Levi's intention is 'to furnish documentation for a quiet study of certain aspects of the human mind'. On the other 'the book has been written ... first and foremost, therefore, as an interior liberation'. *If This is a Man* is written with a scientist's attention to detail and concern with objectivity and yet it speaks with passion and 'urgency' of the offence. The 'structural defects' to which Levi alludes are not 'defects' at all, and what Levi calls its 'fragmentary character' is one of this text's strengths. The conjunction of Levi's seemingly incompatible impulses and his willingness to set aside chronology in order to accommodate more urgent demands offer considerable benefits to the reader.

The tone of this preface is reassuring as it introduces the reader to the text with something like a promise that what follows is going to be manageable, that although there is 'urgency', that urgency will be governed by 'documentation'. Instantly, this mood of reassurance and calm is disturbed. Immediately following the 'Preface' is the poem, here titled 'If This is a Man' but elsewhere it is 'Shemá'.[10] Levi's poem, his most widely quoted and anthologized, offers no comfort to the reader and shatters all the promises of 'quiet study'. Its presence here draws attention to a mode which becomes increasingly apparent in Levi's writings. His assertions of intent cohere around ideas and principles connected with objectivity, rationality and the refusal of blame and anger. Yet, frequently, the reader comes across the kind of 'outburst' which is represented with such power and authority in 'Shemá'. It is as though, in spite of his wishes, Levi cannot always adequately control his material or himself.

Levi's journey into memory begins quite properly, with a date. 'I was captured by the Fascist Militia, on 13 December 1943' (p. 19). Dates are rare in this text, not only because they are a luxurious part of the civilization which rapidly disappeared in the camps but also because, as Levi makes clear, chronology was not often his main concern. Dates belong to the ordinary world outside the camps. They disappear as Levi descends into that other world, and reappear in the final chapter of *If This is a Man* in 'The Story of Ten Days' as he 'ascends' back out of it. They attain significance there both as aids to his return and as markers of his recovering humanity. In the body of the text, the closest Levi comes to dates is to name months, so there are references to 'October', or 'November'. For the rest of the time there are only 'days', 'nights' and 'events', undifferentiated yet unforgettable tracts of barely manageable time which Levi discusses in chapters titled 'Our Nights', 'A Good Day', 'The Events of the Summer'. The specificity of '13 December 1943' is not shocking to the reader who has not yet learnt the significance and pleasure of being able to name dates with such accuracy and defiance. It becomes shocking in 'The Story of Ten Days' when Levi is able to name the days which led up to the Russians' entry into Auschwitz. Levi is constantly reminding the reader, often in this oblique manner, of the privilege of naming which is given to free people.

It is a measure of Levi's determination to speak the truth that he reveals how, when he was captured, he admitted his Jewish status out of fear rather than pride, believing that punishment for a politically motivated partisan might be worse than for a Jew. He carefully records the events which led up to his deportation, with 649 other *Stücke*, to Auschwitz on 22 February 1944, but this chapter is not only concerned with factual detail. Levi displays immediately the extent to which his concerns will encompass both the matter-of-fact and the conclusions which might be drawn from the evidence of those facts. The first hint that memory is not always beneficial and that there are times when memory itself should be erased appears in this opening chapter.

> The time for meditation, the time for decision was over, and all reason dissolved into a tumult, across which flashed the happy memories of our homes, still so near in time and space, as painful as the thrusts of a sword.
>
> Many things were then said and done among us; but of these it is better that there remain no memory. (p. 22)

'ON THE BOTTOM'

Levi's insistence upon the necessity of remembrance often masks from readers the numerous occasions when he asserts that it is better to forget. Survival, psychological as well as physical, depends on a ready perception of the necessity of recognizing when to remember, when to forget. Memory is represented as acutely painful; to remember homes whilst in the process of being taken from them bestows little benefit. Yet, in the camp, there are occasions when Levi recollects his home and family and discovers that the process helps him to recollect himself. There was a balance to be attempted between remembering and forgetting which was difficult to achieve but vital for survival. Remembering in the camps acted as an antidote to the poisonous attack upon identity which began as soon as Levi entered Auschwitz. Levi realized too that we are constituted not only of what we remember, but of what we have control over and are able to own. In Auschwitz this applied as much to the abstract and conceptual as to the physical and tangible. In 'On the Bottom' Levi makes his first lengthy statement describing the intimacy between memory and identity.

> Then for the first time we became aware that our language lacks words to express this offence, the demolition of a man. In a moment, with almost prophetic intuition, the reality was revealed to us: we had reached the bottom. It is not possible to sink lower than this; no human condition is more miserable than this, nor could it conceivably be so. Nothing belongs to us any more; they have taken away our clothes, our shoes, even our hair; if we speak they will not listen to us, and if they listen, they will not understand. They will even take away our name: and if we want to keep it, we will have to find ourselves the strength to do so, to manage somehow so that behind the name something of us, of us as we were, still remains.

We know that we will have difficulty in being understood, and this is as it should be. But consider what value, what meaning is enclosed even in the smallest of our daily habits, in the hundred possessions which even the poorest beggar owns: a handkerchief, an old letter, the photo of a cherished person. These things are part of us, almost like limbs of our body; nor is it conceivable that we can be deprived of them in our world, for we immediately find others to substitute the old ones, other objects which are ours in their personification and evocation of our memories. (p. 33)

This passage is typical of Levi's writing, of the confluence of objective argument and of urgency. The argument, though carefully delivered, resounds with a passionate intensity which demands not only an intellectual but also an emotional response from the reader. The passage exemplifies too the way in which identity and memory are so intricately tangled that undoing one, unravels the other. Levi quickly understood the difference between physical attacks upon the body which, damaging as they were, did not necessarily compromise the integrity of identity in the way that attacks upon selfhood did. So broken limbs were one thing, but the shaving of hair, the theft of an old letter, the denial of a name, were quite another. The accuracy of this insight is borne out again and again in Levi's writing as the desperate fragility of the self is revealed. This theme, the ease with which humanity is undone, is one which literature has found compelling; to find it corroborated and to know that it is not only an idea but a fact makes Levi's vision almost intolerable.

This passage is also very significant when read alongside Levi's later assertion in *The Drowned and the Saved*, 'We the survivors are not the true witnesses' (p. 63). There seems to have been a change in his memory of the nature of the 'demolition' to which he had been subjected. In 1947 Levi wrote, and presumably believed, that, 'It is not possible to sink lower than this; no human condition is more miserable than this, nor could it conceivably be so.' But the passage of almost 40 years shifted this perception and led him to conclude that he and his fellow prisoners had not known the worst and therefore could not truly be witness to the worst. Perhaps the discrepancy between his 1947 view that he had touched bottom and his later view expressed in *The Drowned and the Saved* that he had not, signals the shock to the self which such treatment constitutes. The young Levi found these events so unexpected, so unknown to his experience, that he could not believe that there was anything worse. The mature, and possibly despairing, Levi knew that there had been.

The relationship between having a name and having a self, an important theme for Levi and one to which he frequently returned, is also introduced in this passage.

> They will even take away our name: and if we want to keep it, we will have to find ourselves the strength to do so, to manage somehow so that behind the name something of us, of us as we were, still remains. (p. 33)

Keeping one's name, like remembering, required strength and determination; it required a decision. Only the remembrance of 'us as we were' offered any hope of survival. Levi exposes the danger of being unnamed, or of allowing one's name to slip away from one's self, in his description of Null Achtzehn. 'Everyone' calls this boy by

> the last three figures of his entry name; as if everyone was aware that only a man is worthy of a name, and that Null Achtzehn is no longer a man. I think that even he has forgotten his name, certainly he acts as if this were so. (p. 48)

'Everyone' uses this no-name, that is, not only those whom one would expect to be engaged upon the demolition of Null Achtzehn, but also others like Levi who are clinging on to their own ragged identities. There is an implicit equation here; in order for some to survive in the Lager, it is necessary that others will die. Levi's characterization of Null Achtzehn and his suggestion that Null Achtzehn is incapable of the deliberate act of will which is needed in order to remember himself is tinged with disapproval. This kind of disapproval is absent from *The Drowned and the Saved* so that the reader is again drawn to the conclusion that the benefit of hindsight resulted in Levi's developing different perceptions, in this case about *Musselmänner*. What becomes a cornerstone for Levi's understanding of the nature of survival in *The Drowned and the Saved* is rudimentary here, and Levi came to recognize that it was the presence of a mass of 'indifferent' individuals like Null Achtzehn which contributed positively toward the possibility of survival for those like Levi. Zero Eighteen, Null Achtzehn might represent those others, even less nameable than Null Achtzehn, who enabled Levi's survival. By remembering this unmemorable boy, Levi memorializes them all.

Null Achtzehn has other emblematic qualities. He represents a type of man who is not a Pikolo and therefore seems not to be as valuable to Levi in assisting Levi to remember.[11] In a moment of enforced delay, of which Pikolo would certainly have taken advantage to communicate with Levi, Levi and Null Achtzehn stand as a train passes in front of them. The sickening and repetitive litany of German names *'Deutsche Reichsbahn. Deutsche Reichsbahn'*, ends with the appearance of 'Two huge Russian goods wagons' (p. 49). A flourish of Italian names, beautiful in their variety, appears, *'Cavalli 8, Uomini 40, Tara, Portata'*. Levi boards the train in his imagination and memory and is transported back, via the 'rhythm of the wheels',

> until, at a certain moment [the antithesis of an 'uncertain hour'?], the train would stop and I would feel the warm air and the smell of hay and I would get out into the sun; then I would lie down on the ground to kiss the earth, as you read in books, with my face in the grass. (p. 49)

This moment of revelation fades as 'the last wagon passed' (p. 50) and the dream which is sparked by the sight of the Italian names evaporates. With Pikolo, Levi's reverie might have developed into a feat of memory comparable with that in 'The Canto of Ulysses'. But Levi is not with a person, he is with Null Achtzehn. There is no possibility of sharing his experience, so that the moment remains inexpressible, elusive and debilitating; it only serves to reinforce Levi's idea of his beast-like status. Null Achtzehn seems to have nothing to offer Levi; unlike Pikolo, with whom Levi is delighted to work, Null Achtzehn is 'a dangerous companion' (p. 49). Still, Levi has to acknowledge how like Null Achtzehn Levi himself is:

> no one wants to work with him; and as, on the other hand, no one wants to work with me, because I am weak and clumsy, it often happens that we find ourselves paired together. (p. 49)

Yet even Null Achtzehn's state of nonentity becomes significant for, of course, Null Achtzehn does have a name, one which neither Levi nor the reader may forget. He is Null Achtzehn. This no-name is imbued with significance too, for eighteen is *'chai*, the Hebrew number of life'.[12] So, Null Achtzehn is No Life, Levi's alter ego, who makes Levi's survival possible. Null Achtzehn is surely going to die, but before he does, his lethargy assists Levi's survival. By dropping the iron support which wounds Levi, badly enough to give him time in Ka-Be, but not so badly that Levi becomes dangerously ill, Null Achtzehn gives Levi that breathing space at the start of his time at Auschwitz which, perhaps, made the difference to his survival. Once in Ka-Be, Levi was able to take stock and to recoup his strength, to the extent possible in such circumstances.

'CHEMICAL EXAMINATION'

This intricate correlation between the maintenance of identity and the need actively to remember oneself is also exemplified in 'Chemical Examination' and 'The Canto of Ulysses'. Like 'The Canto of Ulysses', 'Chemical Examination' (p. 107) 'commences' in Auschwitz, goes back via Levi's act of memory to a place and time before and outside the Lager, then returns to Auschwitz. Levi's recollections have no ameliorating effect upon the circumstances to which he returns; his brief and exhilarating restoration to selfhood is easily undone by the Kapo's inability to recognize that this is a man standing before him. Again, Levi emphasizes the connection between memory and identity. Whilst he is only Häftling 174517 he finds it almost impossible to believe that he is also 'the B.Sc. of Turin' (p. 112); if he has difficulty with what amounts to an act of faith it is hardly surprising that his examiners have similar difficulties. In order to pass the chemical examination Levi must first remember who he is; it is this, more than the recital of formulae, which is the test he faces and which requires an audacity and bravery which would be unnecessary outside Auschwitz.

His surroundings do nothing to enhance his chance of success. His first disappointment is to find that the Kapo, Alex, is 'a professional delinquent' (p. 107); the Chemical Kommando has insufficient status to merit a Kapo with a knowledge of chemistry. Alex undermines the candidates' fragile sense of self still further by making it clear that being chemists, 'Intelligenten' (p. 107), is no cause for pride. It is Alex who tells them that all those who have applied to join the Chemical Kommando must take a test and it is clear from his speech that he expects this announcement to flush out the imposters.

Levi perceives the test as an impossibility for his compromised self:

> At last we can speak, and to each one of us what Alex said seems a madman's dream.
>
> With these empty faces of ours, with these sheared craniums, with these shameful clothes, to take a chemical examination. (p. 108)

The particular test of memory which Levi must face seems inappropriate when he considers the person he has become, or the non-person he has been made to resemble. His first thoughts about the examination express fears which are not familiar to most students:

> We will have to go in front of some blond Aryan doctor hoping that we do not have to blow our noses, because perhaps he will not know that we do not have handkerchiefs ... And we will have our old comrade hunger with us, and we will hardly be able to stand still on our feet, and he will certainly smell our odour, to which we are by now accustomed, but which persecuted us during the first days, the odour of turnips and cabbages, raw, cooked and digested. (pp. 108–9)

This emphasis upon their corporeality suggests that Alex's description of the prospective candidates as *'Intelligenten'* was intended to be ironic. Is it possible for such detritus to be *'Intelligenten'*, or is it that their status as filth and as *'Intelligenten'* are related? Levi acknowledges that to anyone other than his fellows, he is merely an unpleasant coalescence of bodily fluids, smells and indignities, reduced to something like a walking corpse. Maybe this acknowledgement contains positive signs, for as long as Levi is aware of the discrepancy between what he was and what he has been formed into, the possibility exists of reclaiming something like his prior self. This potential is emphasized when Levi questions one of the other prisoners, Clausner, about the likelihood of the chemical examination being another 'joke' at the expense of the Jews.

> Clausner shows me the bottom of his bowl. Where others have carved their numbers, and Alberto and I our names, Clausner has written: *'Ne pas chercher à comprendre.'* (p. 109)

In what is almost an aside, Levi affirms again the absolute imperative of remembering one's name, of identifying oneself not as a number but as a person with a memory and a history. To carve the number assigned by the Lager upon the bowl which represents almost the extent of one's possessions is to acquiesce in the dehumanizing bureaucracy of the camp. To carve one's name is to refuse to be a 'piece' and it is in similar small but necessary acts of defiance that a modicum of integrity might be retained. Clausner has adopted a different strategy altogether and his response, *'Ne pas chercher à comprendre'*, reflects the view that to attempt to understand is a waste of time for *'Hier ist kein warum'* (p. 35).

Levi, unlike Null Achtzehn with whom he has compared himself, has somehow preserved the will to live, though he is very conscious of the dangers he faces as a consequence of his traits: 'I know that I am not made of the stuff of those who resist, I am too civilized, I still think too much, I use myself up at work' (p. 109). Yet he realizes that those very attributes which threaten him may offer him the means of survival: 'And now I also know that I can save myself if I become a Specialist, and that I will become a Specialist if I pass a chemistry examination' (p. 109). This saving of himself means more than not dying, it represents an affirmation of his Primo Levi-ness, an aware self-consciousness which had been destroyed in people like Null Achtzehn. In the camp a most significant aspect of that self had been denied or erased; the chemistry examination offered an opportunity of restoration. Restoration may be constituted of very slight elements or components but they are essential to the individual that is Levi. When Levi describes the examinees' discovery that, 'Balla has a pencil and we all crowd round him. We are not sure if we still know how to write, we want to try' (p. 110), he is reminding the reader that it is those parts of the self which are often taken for granted which may most easily be forgotten – how to write, how to eat, how to be the person that was.

'Here is Alex. I am a chemist' (p. 110). These simply constructed sentences are reminiscent of those found in a child's first reading book, as though Levi is having to read and remember himself from scratch. There is also in those two sentences a vivid expression of the difference between Alex and Levi. It is an almost chemical difference, a matter of opposites, of matter and anti-matter, action and reaction. And, though Levi is trying to convince himself of his chemist-ness, he veers between the extremes of 'chemist', which here represents personhood for Levi, and *Zugang*, which is no-person. Within himself Levi is a mass of conflicting impulses and memories and the outcome of his struggle to remember and persuade himself that he is a chemist, rather than a *Zugang* or *Muselmann*, will determine whether or not he will survive.

Levi is introduced in disparaging terms by Alex to Doktor Pannwitz as 'an Italian, has been here only three months, already half kaputt . . . *Er sagt er ist Chemiker* . . .' (p. 111). The reader is shocked that only three months have passed, for already Levi's time in the Lager has seemed interminable. This reflects Levi's own expressions of astonishment at the ways in which time passes in the Lager. Alex's scepticism over the matter of Levi's *Chemiker* status is opposed to Jean's eagerness to engage with Levi and encourage his feat of memory when he recalls the Canto of Ulysses. Alex is indifferent to Levi's metamorphosis yet Levi is about to perform a feat more astonishing than his recital of Dante. He is going to make himself into a chemist by remembering that he is one. Something like this kind of metamorphosis occurs at different points throughout this text, and especially in 'The Story of Ten Days' when Levi and his fellows begin to remember that they are men by remembering that men share bread (pp. 165–6).

Once alone in front of Pannwitz, Levi quails and almost loses the will to be what he needs to be: 'I am aware even at this moment that the position at stake is important; yet I feel a mad desire to disappear, not to take the test' (p. 111). The insults and injuries which have been inflicted quite systematically upon Levi's self and sense of integrity almost succeed at this point. The desire to give up and 'to disappear' reflects the demolition which has taken place since his entry into Auschwitz and the compromised nature of his belief in himself. Again, this frailty is represented by a set of oppositions. Pannwitz is

> tall, thin, blond; he has eyes, hair and nose as all Germans ought to have them, and sits formidably behind a complicated writing table. I, Häftling 174517, stand in his office, which is a real office, shining, clean and ordered, and I feel that I would leave a dirty stain whatever I touched. (p. 111)

Standing before Pannwitz, Levi becomes intensely aware that Pannwitz does not see a man when he looks at Levi, but only a 'something . . . which it is obviously opportune to suppress' (p. 112): 'That look was not one between two men [it] came as if across the glass window of an aquarium between two beings who live in different worlds' (p. 111). Pannwitz's gaze has nothing to offer Levi in his attempt to remember himself because that gaze is not prepared to construct a man. On the contrary, Pannwitz's gaze is engaged upon and complicit with what Levi calls the 'demolition of a man' (p. 32); Pannwitz does not wish and may not permit himself to remember that what stands before him is a man. As Levi recollects this moment and, remembering it, makes it available to the reader, he reveals how significant that look was and remained even in the years after Auschwitz. This represents the essence of the survivor–perpetrator dyad. Levi never forgot Pannwitz and the look which did not recognize him as a man. For Pannwitz there will have been thousands of identical non-persons who stood before him in Auschwitz; it is unlikely that he recollected any one of them. For Levi, the memory of that gaze was fixed at the moment it occurred; for Pannwitz, there may be no memory of that moment because it had no meaning. He would be as likely to distinguish one frog amongst thousands of its fellows, as Levi from the mass of other prisoners.

To have any hope of surviving this attack, Levi's response to Pannwitz's demolishing gaze had to be one of insistent self-fashioning, a repetition of himself as though he had learned himself by heart: 'I am a specialist in mine chemistry. I am a specialist in organic syntheses. I am a specialist . . .' (p. 112). Levi had to act as his own advocate in this 'interrogation'; only by representing himself to himself is he able to discover the necessary temerity to answer Pannwitz's questions. As Pannwitz questions him, Levi finds himself amazed by the person he is claiming to be, but the act of claiming to be, restores him to himself:

> I took my degree at Turin in 1941, *summa cum laude* – and while I say it I have the definite sensation of not being believed, of not even believing it myself; it is enough to look at my dirty hands covered with sores, my convict's trousers encrusted with mud. Yet I am he, the B.Sc. of Turin, in fact, at this particular moment it is impossible to doubt my identity with him, as my reservoir of knowledge of organic chemistry . . . responds at request with unexpected docility. And even more, this sense of lucid elation, this excitement which I feel warm in my veins, I recognize it, it is the fever of examinations, *my* fever of *my* examinations. (p. 112)

That italicized, repeated 'my' constitutes a challenge to Pannwitz and all that he represents of the Lager's mechanisms. This is a moment of triumph, not only for Levi, but for the reader as he or she wills Levi to remember and to reoccupy himself. Levi's determined effort succeeds: 'The examination is going well. As I gradually realize it, I seem to grow in stature' (p. 112). The final part of the examination requires the greatest effort as Levi excavates the memory of his degree thesis:

> I have to make a violent effort to recall that sequence of memories, so deeply buried away: it is as if I was trying to remember the events of a previous incarnation. (p. 112)

This final effort requires all his strength. As in 'The Canto of Ulysses' the revelation which Levi achieves through sheer determination issues as a triumphant and transcendent climax to his feat of memory. But in the instant which follows, Levi is returned to his *Zugang* role. 'Dull and flat' he watches, without autonomy or status, as Pannwitz records 'my fate on the white page in incomprehensible symbols' (p. 113). Again, as in 'The Canto of Ulysses', the first sign of Levi's return to Auschwitz is linguistic. Alex orders him, '*Los, ab!*' and Levi becomes aware that he does not know how to take his leave of Pannwitz. The transition back to Auschwitz is painful after the astonishing sense of restored identity. It is as though the insults to which Levi had become somewhat inured are revitalized with all their potential for harm. As Levi and Alex return to Bude, Alex dirties his hand on a cable. 'Without hatred and without sneering' (p. 113) Alex wipes his hand on Levi's shoulder. 'He would be amazed, the poor brute Alex, if someone told him that today, on the basis of this action, I judge him' (p. 114).

'THE CANTO OF ULYSSES'

It seems significant that 'Chemical Examination' is followed immediately by 'The Canto of Ulysses'; the two chapters are not only closely related by their form and content but they provide access to related aspects of Levi. It is as though the one reminded Levi of the other. In both chapters Levi is compelled, by external and internal pressures, to perform a feat of memory in inauspicious circumstances and it is those things which he has 'learnt by heart' which aid his survival by restoring his sense of self. In 'Chemical Examination' he remembers himself as a chemist, 'the B.Sc. of Turin'; in 'The Canto of Ulysses' he remembers himself as an educated Italian, perfectly at home in the language of Dante. Together these chapters represent Levi's essential characteristics and provide the reader with a view of him which is whole rather than partial; in the midst of the Auschwitzian project to dehumanize and make anonymous, they depict Levi's acts of resistance and his assertion of individuality.

'The Canto of Ulysses' (p. 115) opens with a description of the task, 'scraping and cleaning the inside of an underground petrol tank', on which Levi is engaged. Though it is 'a luxury job because no one supervised us' it is still 'cold and damp. The powder of the rust burnt under our eyelids and coated our throats and mouths with a taste almost like blood' (p. 115). Pikolo, that is 'the messenger-clerk', takes Levi away from the task to collect the soup. The ever-present potential for memory of life before and outside of the camp is signalled instantly to the reader. As soon as Levi climbs from the underground tank to discover the pleasant day outside, he encounters a fragment of his past. 'The sun drew a faint smell of paint and tar from the greasy earth, which made me think of a holiday beach of my infancy' (p. 117). His memory transforms this prosaic trigger into an evocation of a happy time; the 'holiday beach of my infancy' supplies the epitome of a secure past. As Jean and Levi walk, each recites his past and memories return slowly, perhaps carefully. After Levi has been given the opportunity to move away from the present, the past returns tentatively, for there is a negotiation to be accomplished between the present of the underground tank in Auschwitz and the past of the person Levi 'was'. Like warming-up before exercise, the mundane recollections which Jean and Levi share prepare Levi to perform his feat of memory and permit the ferocity of his determined recollection to rescue Dante's poetry for Jean: 'We spoke of our houses, of Strasbourg and Turin, of the books we had read, of what we had studied, of our mothers' (p. 117). That memory has not quite consolidated its hold is signalled by the way in which Auschwitz and its reality still manages to break in at this point to their recital of the past: 'An SS man passed on a bicycle' (p. 117). Instantly Jean and Levi revert to the behaviour required to negotiate their Auschwitz reality. The constructive power of their memories is taking over from that reality and they are able to return quickly and easily to the 'reality' they are modelling together.

There is another brief interruption and, as Levi and Limentani talk, 'Pikolo listens carefully, picks up a few words of our conversation and repeats them smiling: "Zup-pa, cam-po, acqua"' (p. 118). He is memorizing and reciting, practising and strengthening his memory. The reader may assume that this moment provides an opportunity to witness the learning of Jean's memories of Auschwitz, the ones Jean will 'recite' when he returns to the world outside.

After a final reminder of Auschwitz as 'Frenkl the spy passes' (p. 118), Jean and Levi embark together upon the project of recovering and remembering Dante's words. This raises the question: would Levi have rescued Dante's poetry without the presence of Jean? It is unlikely that, had his companion been Null Achtzehn, Levi would have been induced to embark upon the test. This implies that this act of memory requires two people: the rememberer and the one for whom matters are remembered. Perhaps even where the act of memory is taking place in solitude – for example when the memories are written – there must be a putative listener.[13] Once they are embarked upon Levi's translation of Dante, Auschwitz does not impinge again. It is as if, for that brief time, it has no power over them.

Levi's recital begins but he soon encounters problems. Having begun his recollection well with six complete lines of verse, he encounters 'a hole in my memory' then 'another hole' (p. 118). These holes reveal the vagaries of memory and its uncontrollability. What had been fixed as part of his memory has disappeared, whether because it was not properly learned in the first place or because of the damage inflicted upon memory by intervening time and injuries. Levi knows that 'open sea' and 'left me' rhyme with one another but the fact that they rhyme tells him nothing about which comes first. The power of rhyme, so robustly asserted in 'Rhyming on the Counterattack', is not infallible.

> I have only rescued two lines, but they are worth stopping for:
> '... that none should prove so hardy
> To venture the uncharted distances ...' (p. 119)

Levi is only able to recover two lines from out of his forgetfulness, the rest of this part of the poem he renders reluctantly in prose. That he characterizes this as rescue is significant for it reflects the great importance to him of the poetry he is recalling. His rescue of these lines prompts him to reflect upon an existential matter. 'How many things there are to say, and the sun is already high, mid-day is near. I am in a hurry, a terrible hurry' (p. 119). Levi is referring literally to the reality in which he is recalling these words. It is true that he and Jean have little time for their task before the hour which Jean has 'organized' for them runs out. But the phrasing and its proximity to a contemplation of art tends to reinforce the more philosophical sense in Levi's observation, the *carpe diem* sense. Memory does succeed, and restores some portions of the poetry Levi is translating with such immediacy and vitality that not only for Jean but also for Levi it is 'as if I was hearing it for the first time: like the blast of a trumpet, like the voice of God' (p. 119). The recovered memory of those few lines is so powerful that it overwhelms the present: 'For a moment I forget who I am and where I am' (p. 119). There is a paradox here, one which Levi might have elaborated, that remembering is provoking or permitting forgetfulness. And that forgetfulness in this context is a positive good.

'Pikolo begs me to repeat it' (p. 119). The process of remembering has been made possible for Levi by his repeating these lines in the past. Jean mimics that process by asking Levi to repeat the lines, perhaps wishing to make them his own through the force of repetition. Levi explains Jean's actions as a sign of virtue, a gift which he is giving to Levi. But Levi is also aware of the reciprocal nature of this gift. The recital

which is taking place between them is of benefit to both, it is an assertion
of their humanity, for they 'dare to reason of these things with the poles
for the soup on our shoulders' (p. 120). As Levi recites the lines:

> ... When at last hove up a mountain, grey
> With distance, and so lofty and so steep,
> I never had seen the like on any day. (p. 120)

the memory of Dante's poetry performs two seemingly incompatible
functions. On the one hand the recollection of the poem's lines brings
Levi dangerously close to bitter remembrance:

> The mountains ... oh, Pikolo, Pikolo, say something, speak, do
> not let me think of my mountains which used to show up
> against the dusk of evening as I returned by train from Milan
> to Turin! (p. 120)

On the other, art mediates that memory and others affording Levi a
measure of protection from the full impact of such recollections. He
asserts the cost and the value of poetry, prepared on this occasion to
give up soup for its sake: 'I would give today's soup to know how to
connect "the like on any day" to the last lines' (p. 120).[14]

Memory fails. As Levi tries to make the connection – 'I try to
reconstruct it through the rhymes' (p. 120) – they reach their
destination. In one last urgent bid to speak to Jean in a manner that he
will understand (and prefiguring Levi's Ancient Mariner persona?),
Levi detains Jean. The matter that Levi is recollecting and attempting
to convey coheres around the phrase 'as pleased Another' (p. 121). As
he struggles with memory, Levi suddenly finds himself overflowing
with ideas to be communicated to Jean. He is caught up, enraptured to
discover that his recital has revealed something otherwise ineffable:

> I must explain to him about the Middle Ages, about the so
> human and so necessary and yet unexpected anachronism, but
> still more, something gigantic that I myself have only just seen,
> in a flash of intuition, perhaps the reason for our fate, for our
> being here today ... (p. 121)

That Levi does not share this revelation with the reader suggests either
that it never arrived or that he was unable to express it to Jean and so it
escaped from his memory of that perception, it was not fixed. As with
'Chemical Examination' the end of this chapter is also dismaying. From
the blissful recapitulation of Dante's words, Levi and Jean are returned

to the world of '*Kraut und Rüben*'. There is horror and poignancy in the last line, 'And over our heads the hollow seas closed up' (p. 121), especially as Levi's intended meanings are unclear. Is this the extent of Levi's insight into 'the reason for our fate, for our being here today'? Has he recognized the ability of art to render the terrible truths about human life? Is he succumbing to despair? Is it, in spite of all the good rendered to him and to Jean by their study of Dante, just as Améry says: 'The poem no longer transcended reality'?[15] Are Dante's words unable to mitigate '*Kraut und Rüben*'? The reader is left with the recognition that even after all his striving and his achievement in remembering Dante's poetry, Levi was unable to avoid the conclusion that the human beings in Auschwitz did not survive, that their pre-Auschwitz identities were swallowed up as though they had never been.

I have suggested that as Jean repeated the Italian words of Levi and Limentani the reader witnesses the preparation of memory for the time when Jean would tell his Auschwitz experience. Levi wrote much later: 'Strange as it may seem [Jean] has forgotten much of his year in Monowitz' (p. 393). This does present a shock to the reader and must seem strange to a rememberer such as Levi, but it is explicable. Jean did not have to remember Auschwitz: Levi did it for him. In a sense, Levi is Jean's poem about Auschwitz, Levi provided the rhythm and the rhyme which assisted Jean's memory. After Levi's death, Jean found remembering more difficult: 'I could always turn to him. He had such a memory. He remembered everything about himself, about others, about me. Ever since, [Levi's death] I have felt lost.'[16] Possibly Levi acted as the rhyme for many survivors. Another survivor, Lidia Rolfi says: 'As memory fades, it is always necessary to check it . . . to compare it with someone else . . . who remembers and understands the camps in the same way.'[17]

MEMORY AND *THE MIRROR MAKER*

Levi's memory of the offence is not confined to *If This is a Man* and *The Drowned and the Saved*. It surfaces throughout his writing and informs many of his stories and poems which are not explicitly about the Shoah. I wish to consider here two short works from *The Mirror Maker* which exemplify the way in which Levi's meditations upon his experiences found a variety of expressions. Often in his writing this articulation is faint, like the slight accent or intonation which might remain even years after another language has been adopted and which speaks of a life lived elsewhere. The presence of the Shoah is explicitly signalled, though without apparent disturbance, in the 'Premise' to *The Mirror Maker*. Levi refers to falling into 'a maelstrom' which he 'got out of … more by luck than by virtue' (pp. 3–4) which led him to 'a certain curiosity about maelstroms large and small, metaphorical and actual' (p. 4). This rational, almost dismissive, opening is reminiscent of his 'Preface' to *If This is a Man*. Here too, the apparent calm is undermined and queried by a poem which introduces the selection of stories. In contrast with the frequently jaunty and mainly untroubled tone of many of the stories, 'The Thaw' (p. 9) is brimful of poignancy, nostalgia and loss; it is suffused with memory, its imperatives and its burdens. In spite of conjuring ideas of spring and fertility, the poem is not hopeful about human potential, there is a deadness implicit in its tone. It opens with a reference to a place that is also a past.

> The Thaw
>
> When the snow will all have melted
> We shall search for the old path,
> The one that is being covered by brambles
> Behind the monastery's walls;
> Everything will be as it once was.

This search for 'the old path' invites thoughts of an old way – of life? of behaviour? of observance? – which is being obscured and obstructed. The assertion 'Everything will be as it once was' seems to contain more hope than realism as few things can be again what they once were. The suggestion that the past may be regained or remade in its entirety may constitute a form of reassurance, though whether this is for the benefit of the speaker or for those to whom he speaks is not clear. 'The old path' is not only 'being covered by brambles' but is 'behind the monastery's walls', suggesting that the path might have been there before the walls were erected. If 'the old path' has any connection with Jewish observance and culture, the close proximity of a Christian community seems to have contributed to its falling into disuse. There is nothing explicitly malign about the close proximity of the 'walls' and the 'path', yet there seems to be an implicit potential for conflict.

> On either side, amid the thick heather
> We shall again find certain frail herbs
> Whose name I would not know how to say:
> I read up on it every Friday,
> But every Saturday it leaves my mind:
> I've been told that they are rare
> And good for curing melancholy.

Plant life, without displaying anything as conscious as malice, seems to occupy two distinct positions. The neutral or indifferent brambles, heather and ferns proceed with being what they are, but in the process cover the 'old path', obscure or threaten to overwhelm 'the frail herbs', or mock human uncertainties with their burgeoning growth. By contrast 'the frail herbs' which are beneficial to human existence – 'I've been told that they are … good for curing melancholy' – are also 'rare' and easily overgrown by the more vigorous brambles, heather, ferns. The speaker's search for the herbs is made additionally poignant by the odd admission that the speaker 'would not know how to say' their names. He tries to familiarize himself with these elusive names: 'I read up on it every Friday,/ But every Saturday it leaves my mind'. The allusion to Friday as a time for study and of potential discovery may or may not be an allusion to the customs and preparations associated with the Jewish Shabbat. If it is, there is an additional element of distress implied as the longed-for names resist the speaker so that he is left bereft each Saturday. There is also the question of the 'it' to which the speaker refers. Is he still thinking only of the lost, unsayable, unnameable names of the herbs, or is he referring to a lost, unsayable, unnameable people or culture? And why does the speaker imagine searching for the 'frail herbs' which are 'good for curing melancholy' unless melancholy is the condition from which he requires relief? Perhaps Levi is articulating here, via a speaker who is and is not himself, the loss and grief which are frequently absent from his other essays and stories.

> The ferns bordering the road
> Are like tender creatures:
> They barely push up from the ground,
> Curled in a spiral, and yet
> Right now they are ready for their loves
> Alternate and green, more intricate than ours.
>
> Their germs chafe at the bit,
> Tiny males and tiny females,
> In the rusty sporangium.
> They will erupt at the first rain,
> Swimming in the first drop,
> Eager and agile: long live the bride and groom!

Morbidity is apparent in the distinctions which are drawn between the possibilities which exist for plant as opposed to human life. So the 'old path' made by the presence of humans 'is being covered by brambles' whilst the whole of the third and fourth stanzas is given over to a description of the ferns' burgeoning procreativity, their unfurling and fecundity. But the emphasis is upon the ferns as different; their existence is neither comparable with nor representative of the life of the human observer. The ferns are emphatically 'They': they have 'their loves ... more intricate than ours' and 'Their germs' which 'chafe at the bit'. There is no similar eagerness or joyful expectancy in the human apprehension of spring:

> We are tired of winter. The bite
> Of frost has left its mark
> On flesh, minds, mud, and wood.
> Let the thaw come and melt the memory
> Of last year's snow.

This has an ambiguous tone which combines a longing for spring, usually associated with liveliness and potential, with a longing for forgetfulness, perhaps even for oblivion. 'We are tired of winter' suggests a negative desire to escape from winter rather than a positive welcome for spring. And it is difficult to be positive about the future/spring, when

> ... The bite
> Of frost has left its mark
> On flesh, minds, mud, and wood.

Winter has led to a frozenness, a fixedness and a tendency to immutability which share many similarities with death and will be hard for the speaker to escape. The awareness of approaching spring leads the speaker to make a shocking request:

> Let the thaw come and melt the memory
> Of last year's snow.

What is shocking here, especially for the reader whose perceptions of Levi have been shaped by the voice of *If This is a Man*, is that whilst the speaker is not Levi, yet the speaker and Levi do have kinship and it is difficult in the extreme to imagine Levi requesting that memory be melted, that the past be allowed to trickle away or dry up. This poem contains a burden. In the face of spring's potential, the memory of winter is tiring, it 'has left its mark' (like a scar certainly, but possibly also like a tattoo?) and the speaker is ready and willing to give up memory if that would enable him to enter the future unburdened. The speaker lives by a hopeful but unfounded assertion: 'Everything will be as it once was.'

But after the persecution experienced by Levi, as Améry asserts, nothing can be 'as it once was'. A kind of coded articulation of Levi's altered perceptions after the Holocaust also appears in 'Force Majeure' (p. 62). In this story Levi depicts, in what may be taken as an allegorized self-portrait, the effects wreaked upon an educated and civilized man, M., when he comes face to face with seemingly random and unprovoked aggression and humiliation. Levi gives the narrator no name. Nor does M. have any identifiable traits or attributes which could operate legitimately as provocation to his persecutor. All that the reader knows of M. is that he is hurrying to 'an important appointment with the manager of a library'; that he is 'slim' and wears glasses; that he is well-read and familiar with a range of literature and films. 'M.' is his mark of anonymity and is perhaps equivalent to the number tattooed on the arm of the camp inmate. Yet, in spite of M.'s compromised or non-existent identity in terms of the reader, still the reader is able to perceive the dire injustice of his treatment. A young man, whose own anonymity does not seem to invite humiliation or betray vulnerability but instead affords protection, 'a husky lad in a T-shirt, perhaps a sailor' (p. 62), blocks M.'s path as M. makes his way down a narrow alley. M. attempts to make himself unobtrusive, 'M. moved close to the wall to free the passage'; he is prepared to reduce himself and would disappear through the bricks if that were possible. The other man makes no such concessions.

> He did not have a threatening expression; he seemed to be calmly waiting, [M.] took a step forward, and at that the man put his hands against the walls. There was a brief pause, then the sailor made a gesture with both his palms turned down, as though he were stroking a long back or calming the waters. (pp. 62–3)

M. attempts to defuse the threat with a Levi-like question:

> 'Why don't you let me go through?' But the other answered by repeating the gesture. Perhaps he was mute, or deaf, or did not understand Italian: but he should have been able to understand, the question was not that complex. (p. 63)

The question is no more, nor less, complex than Levi's '*Warum?*', which suggests that the sailor's answer would echo the guard's '*Hier ist kein warum*' (*If This is a Man* p. 35). Suddenly, the sailor punches M., who, though taken by surprise, discovers that he has, in some part of himself, been expecting just such an attack all his life. Though there is no suggestion that M. has any knowledge of the camps which would explain such a wariness yet his cultural references, which are quintessentially Western and of the twentieth century, have suggested to him that this kind of thing happens, and that, as Margaret Atwood puts it, 'We are not exempt'.[18] Whilst there is no attempt to explain what lies behind the seeming randomness of the attack nor M.'s expectations of it, there is still a demand made upon the reader to consider these events and their repercussions. Such a demand brings to mind Améry's stunning dissections of the effects of violence and his assertion that, as a consequence of his experiences, his 'trust in the world' was destroyed. It is also reminiscent of his painful and precise analysis of 'the first blow' and 'the expectation of help'.[19] For M., there is an understanding of the way in which the events of the past have changed his perceptions of possible futures so that he expresses a kind of 'expectation' of persecution. M. already knows, though not through his own direct experience, that he is not exempt. He would have gone on knowing this even if he never met with *force majeure*. Perhaps Levi is suggesting here that this expectation or lack of exemption has become a feature of twentieth-century life to a degree not discovered in earlier times and other cultures. The attack which M. experiences is marked as a specific outcome of twentieth-century mores and philosophies, which had been, for M., presaged and recollected by other artistic forms in films and books. M.'s response is an almost reflex action of looking back, as though the past will help him understand this present. He

> had never found himself in a similar situation, not even as a boy, but he remembered Martin Eden and his encounter with Cheese Face ... he had seen *The Quiet Man*, *High Noon*, and a hundred other films, and so he knew that sooner or later, for him too, the moment would come: it comes for everyone. (p. 63)

A young woman passes. Exhibiting behaviour usually associated in Holocaust memoirs and literature with bystanders, she acts 'as though she did not see them' (p. 64). Her passing in this manner provokes a desperate response in M.:

> M., who until then had lived a normal life strewn with joys, irritations and sorrows, successes and failures, perceived a sensation he had never experienced before, that of persecution, *force majeure*, absolute impotence, without escape or remedy, to which one can react only by submission. Or with death: but was there any sense in dying just to pass through an alleyway? (p. 64)[20]

The woman has 'gaudy clothes,' she is 'perhaps a prostitute' yet the potential of her passing, something which might be considered a more legitimate focus of the sailor's attention, neither attracts the sailor to her, nor distracts him from his determination to continue his casual humiliation of M. Though M. makes a vain attempt to counterattack, he is swiftly overpowered and thrown to the floor. With a deliberation made the more sickening by its calmness, the sailor walks all over M, then continues on his passage along the alley. M.'s response is instantly composed of an attempt at reasonableness, displaying the rational man's need to make this event comprehensible.

> M. got to his feet, put on his glasses, and straightened his clothes. He made a rapid inventory: were there side advantages, advantages that someone trampled on derived from his condition? Compassion, sympathy, greater attention, less responsibility? No, because M. lived alone. There weren't any, nor would there be any; or, if so, they would be minimal. The duel had not resembled its models: it had been unbalanced, unfair, dirty, and had dirtied him. The models, even the most violent, are chivalrous; life is not. He set out for his appointment, knowing that he would never be the same man as before. (p. 65)

M. quickly recognizes that he is changed forever, that he will 'never be the same man as before'. He also discovers, as he reviews his status as a 'someone' who has been 'trampled on' that there are no 'advantages' to victimization. His attempts to make the best of his injury, which does not seem to have any lasting physical effects, are fruitless; he discovers that what he has experienced has no comparable precedent, no adequate 'model' which might help him to make sense of the attack. M. is left with a terrible awareness that there has been nothing of value to be extracted from his experience. The sailor has passed on, undiminished, unscathed, perhaps even confirmed in his sense of his own worth. It is his victim who is left, bereft of himself, humiliated and 'dirtied'. The shock for M. is his discovery of the discrepancy between what, until this moment, he has been led to assume about the nature of 'injury' and 'meaning', and what he now discovers to be the real effects of the attack he has experienced. His imperative, to find meaning, swiftly reveals to him that his experience has in no respect 'resembled its models'. It offers him no meaning and no benefit, but leaves him with an inescapable sense of having been shamed and sullied.

M.'s final conclusion is desolate. He has learnt that the memory of the offence falls only upon the survivor and not at all upon the perpetrator. This insight signals or prepares the way for Levi's very similar conclusions in *The Drowned and the Saved*.

MEMORY AND *THE DROWNED AND THE SAVED*

Thirty years after Auschwitz, Levi began a collection of essays, written over a period of ten years and published as *I sommersi e i salvati*. In these essays he revisited the *univers concentrationnaire* and reconsidered memory, morality and the nature of survival. They were published in Britain, a year after Levi's death, as *The Drowned and the Saved* (1988).

Levi's first concern, articulated in the 'Preface', was what might have happened to the memory of the offence if the Germans had won the war. It is certain that the memory would not have survived in anything like its present form, for the German project was antipathetic to that memory; as the likely outcome of the war became apparent, the Germans attempted to conceal their crime; they blew up crematoria, disposed of remains, destroyed records. The Germans understood that for memory to survive it would require factual corroboration, that remembering and reciting would not be enough. They taunted prisoners with the fact that even if they survived to tell their story they would not be believed. Levi cites Simon Wiesenthal's recollections of such a taunt, 'Even if someone were to survive, he would not be believed' (p. 1). These thoughts and concerns seem to have compelled Levi to consider in detail what had changed about memory in the time between the end of the war and the time at which he was writing. In the intervening period Levi's focus had changed. *If This is a Man* spoke of Levi's memories as a survivor; *The Drowned and the Saved* examines the memories of the perpetrator. The memory with which Levi engages in *The Drowned and the Saved* is no longer 'The Memory' or 'A

Memory', that is, something singular and collective but has become changeable, plural and fragmented:

> Human memory is a marvellous but fallacious instrument...
> The memories which lie within us are not carved in stone; not
> only do they tend to become erased as the years go by, but
> often they change, or even increase by incorporating
> extraneous features ... This scant reliability of our memory
> will be satisfactorily explained only when we know in what
> language, in what alphabet they are written, on what material,
> and with what pen: to this day we are still far from this goal.
> Some mechanisms are known which falsify memory under
> particular conditions: ... Nevertheless, even under normal
> conditions a slow degradation is at work, an obfuscation of
> outlines, a, so-to-speak, physiological oblivion, which few
> memories resist ... It is certain that practice (in this case,
> frequent re-evocation) keeps memories fresh and alive ... but
> it is also true that a memory evoked too often, and expressed in
> the form of a story, tends to become fixed in a stereotype, in a
> form tested by experience, crystallised, perfected, adorned,
> which installs itself in the place of raw memory and grows at
> its expense. (pp. 11–12)

Levi's characterization and description of memory seem to distinguish between a number of memory forms. One is like mineral, 'crystallized', which, though vulnerable to attrition, presents an increasingly obdurate and unacceptably stylized aspect. Levi suggests that this kind of memory develops out of a too frequent repetition which allows it to substitute itself for 'raw memory'. In addition to the fact that this kind of memory is 'evoked too often' it is also 'expressed in the form of a story'. Both attributes seem to draw an implied censure from Levi and it is as if he has specific examples in mind, although he does not cite them. It is difficult to determine exactly what Levi means and though Levi seems to be drawing a clear distinction between 'raw memory' and mineral memory, he does not provide any suitable test for the reader which would aid their identification.

Levi also describes a form of memory which is not mineral, 'the memories which lie within us are not carved in stone'. These memories 'tend to become erased as the years go by, but often they change, or even increase by incorporating extraneous features'. This memory form is not 'crystallised, perfected, adorned', it does not become

polished with too frequent recital and seems to have attributes more
like a text for, in connection with this memory, Levi employs words
like 'erased', 'language', 'written', 'alphabet', 'material', 'pen'. These
memories seem not to provoke his criticism to the same extent as the
mineral memories, yet both forms of memory have elements in
common, their correspondence to and dependence upon narrative.
Another group of memories seems to possess organic as opposed to
mineral tendencies; they are prey to a 'physiological oblivion'.

As a whole, this passage seems to propose a number of distinct
forms of memory which, on closer examination, collapse and merge in
a confusing manner. In the very process of drawing distinctions and
identifying differences, Levi seems to be affirming that memory is so
changeable that it might not be possible to assign it to different
categories, that it will always escape one to reappear in another. This
view is reinforced by the way in which Levi suggests that memory is a
matter of balance. On the one hand memory must be practised for
'practice ... keeps memories fresh and alive'; on the other, any memory
'evoked too often ... tends to become fixed in a stereotype'. Levi does
not make it clear how one would judge whether a memory belonged to
the first or second category and his discussion here seems to lead the
reader around in circles, mimicking the way in which one kind of
memory so easily becomes another. These observations raise a number
of questions regarding Levi's own memories so that the reader
wonders to what extent, if at all, Levi would have applied these
categories to his own memory and whether or not he reached these
conclusions as a result of observing their changes.

Amongst such potential for memory's inconstancy, what does
remain fixed is the fact of the injury to which the victim has been
subjected:

> The injury cannot be healed: it extends through time and the
> Furies, in whose existence we are forced to believe, not only
> wrack the tormentor (if they do wrack him, assisted or not by
> human punishment), but they perpetuate the tormentor's
> work by denying peace to the tormented. (p. 12)

Memory remembers the injury whether or not a suitable means of
expression is found. Levi seems, by the time he writes *The Drowned and
the Saved*, to have a more problematic relationship with memory, he is
more aware of and more self-conscious about remembering. The
urgent need which drives *If This is a Man* is not present in *The Drowned*

and the Saved which is altogether a more reflective body of work; this
engagement with remembering seems to demand of Levi the need to
enter into a discourse of morality. As a consequence, Levi became as
intrigued by perpetrator memory, as he was by survivor memory. In *If
This is a Man* the memories recorded are almost entirely his own and he
is concerned with survivor memory for the greater part, whereas *The
Drowned and the Saved* picks again and again at the question: what do the
perpetrators remember? *The Drowned and the Saved* comes to the
conclusion that whatever 'benefit' there is for survivors in
remembering the insult and the offence, there is no comparable benefit
to the perpetrators in having similar recollections. Levi is left with the
recognition of a one-sided act of memory, where the survivor is
reduced to remembering in a vacuum as perpetrators remember a
different set of events, shaping their memories in order to put aside or
hide the Shoah from themselves.

Survivors have no choice but to remember the terrible events that
they experienced and witnessed; perpetrators do seem to retain the
power to make choices about what they will remember. Even outside
the Lager, the same dynamic of choiceless choice applies and is still
imposed upon the survivors. When Levi writes 'The Furies ...
perpetuate the tormentor's work by denying peace to the tormented'
(p. 12), he seems to be suggesting that the memory of the offence
became something mythical and inhumanly terrible, turning from
something which he often asserted must be preserved into something
malign. It seems that finally memory presents a much greater threat to
the survivor, one which the perpetrator never experiences.

Levi's reference to 'The Furies' is uncharacteristically irrational; he
seems to be suggesting a belief in an outside agency which punishes the
victim through the medium of memory. The view which he develops
in *The Drowned and the Saved* is devoid of justice for the survivor. Levi
might have imagined as he wrote *If This is a Man* that the perpetrators
would also come to suffer the wounds of memory when they realized
the disgraceful nature of the regime with which they had colluded.
After all, if Levi, an innocent man, could be so aware of the possibilities
for shame, then how much more should they be ashamed? But as he
was writing *The Drowned and the Saved*, Levi would no longer have been
able to ignore the fact that the only sufferers were the victims; the
survivors went on suffering whilst the perpetrators did not. Levi came
to recognize that for the oppressor, the memory of the injury is not the
same. As in 'Force Majeure' survivor and perpetrator exist on either
side of a defining event but their perspectives remain entirely distinct

and different, so that there is little correspondence between what each one knows of the event. For Levi, the perpetrators seemed to disappear after the Shoah; they were able to 'weigh anchor, move off, momentarily or forever, from genuine memories, and fabricate for themselves a convenient reality' (p. 14).

Levi acknowledges that there is a potential for pain, that, 'the past is a burden' (p. 14) to the perpetrators as it is for the survivors, but survivors are unable to escape from their past with the perpetrator's impunity. The past becomes the survivor, it holds him or her more tightly than it does the perpetrator. For the perpetrator there is significant room for manœuvre:

> They feel repugnance for the things done or suffered, and tend to replace them with others. The substitution may begin in full awareness, with an invented scenario, mendacious, restored, but less painful than the real one; in repeating its description to others but also to themselves, the distinction between true and false progressively loses its contours, and man ends by fully believing the story he has told so many times and still continues to tell, polishing and retouching here and there the details which are least credible or incongruous or incompatible with the acquired picture of historically accepted events: initial bad faith has become good faith. The silent transition from falsehood to self-deception is useful: anyone who lies in good faith is better off, he recites his part better, is more easily believed by the judge, the historian, the reader, his wife and his children. (p. 14)

This description may go some way towards explaining the tendency to Holocaust denial. Perpetrators must deny what had happened to themselves, but for as long as the world insists upon its truth the perpetrator is in grave danger of 'remembering' what really happened. There arises a disjunction between perpetrator truth and survivor truth: more than a disjunction, an abyss. The perpetrator must convince in order to be convinced that these events did not take place. A convinced liar, as Levi suggests, may be more believable than those telling the truth for their very conviction convinces the listener. Levi's description is very familiar; if it is applied to 'ordinary' criminals the same process appears to be at work again and again. The danger lies in any move towards accepting the 'modifications' of perpetrators and deniers for, 'The further events fade into the past, the more the construction of convenient truth grows and is perfected' (p. 14).

This is one of Levi's greatest achievements; he draws the reader's attention to the ongoing relationship between the survivor and the perpetrator, he brings the reader closer to the oppressor and encourages the reader to query the form and content of perpetrator memory. As we read *The Drowned and the Saved* it is impossible to avoid the conclusion that Levi's memories became more painful with the passage of time. There seems to be a correlation here between his perception of what memory left him to carry and what it left perpetrators to carry. For any individual with a sense of justice, it would have been disturbing and almost intolerable to discover that there was no justice. Not only were perpetrators (with a few exceptions) free after the war (and 'free' in this context meant something different for survivors and perpetrators), to pursue their own lives without punishment, they were also free of the burden of memory. There was no revenge (although Levi does not seem to have desired revenge), but nor was there any equivalence between his life as a survivor and the lives of perpetrators. This explains his impatience with Liliana Cavani's assertion that 'we are all victims or murderers, and we accept these roles voluntarily' (p. 32). 'I do not know, and it does not much interest me to know, whether in my depths there lurks a murderer, but I do know that I was a guiltless victim and I was not a murderer' (p. 32) is Levi's understandable response. Both perpetrator and survivor were in the same place, on either side of acts which defined them as perpetrator or survivor but it was only the victim, the injured one, who is condemned to a life of remembrance. It becomes less surprising in such iniquitous circumstances that Levi may have wished at times for memory to leave him alone.

Levi insists that the reader should recognize the essential differences which exist between the memories of the perpetrator and of the survivor.

> Behind the 'I don't know' and the 'I don't remember' that one hears in courtrooms there is sometimes the precise intent to lie, but at other times it is a fossilised lie, rigidified in a formula. The rememberer has decided not to remember, and has succeeded: by dint of denying its existence, he has expelled the harmful memory as one expels an excretion or a parasite. Lawyers for the defence know very well that the memory gap, or the putative truth, which they suggest to their clients, tends to become forgetfulness and actual truth ... Supposing,

absurdly, that the liar should for one instant become truthful, he himself would not know how to answer the dilemma; in the act of lying he is an actor totally fused with his part, he is no longer distinguishable from it. (p. 17)

'The rememberer has decided not to remember and has succeeded'. That there could be such choice for a rememberer may have seemed astonishing to Levi who had come to know that not all memory is benign or helpful, that there is painful memory.[21] Levi's description of the process by which perpetrators construct and then assimilate a fictional past is completely convincing. For the perpetrator 'the act of lying', that is, remembering a past that was not, became part of such a closely observed 'role' that like 'an actor totally fused with his part, he is no longer distinguishable from it'. This is like the process which fuses the survivor to the memory he or she carries. What makes the difference, and it is all the difference in the world, is that the survivor can only remember the offence; the perpetrator can only 'remember' the 'absence' of the offence. In this particular equation it is lies, rather than forgetfulness, which are the enemy and antithesis of memory, which make 'forgetting' possible. This emphasizes too the extent to which remembering must be a willed act. The memory which Levi describes seems to be both absolutely necessary and shockingly debilitating, and the insistence upon remembering comes increasingly to represent and contain a potential for damage to the rememberer. In such pernicious circumstances it is not surprising that perpetrators refuse to remember and choose to forget whatever may possibly be forgotten. As Levi recognizes:

> The best way to defend oneself against the invasion of burdensome memories is to impede their entry, to extend a *cordon sanitaire*. It is easier to deny entry to a memory than to free oneself from it after it has been recorded. (pp. 17–18)

There is no evidence that Levi had himself in mind here, but these writings problematize the reader's relationship with Levi. It becomes difficult to evade the thought that these observations may apply to Levi himself, especially given his role as one of the earliest chroniclers of the Shoah. If Levi was writing, however obliquely, of his own experience with memory, this raises the possibility that he might have come to regret having let memory take hold to the extent that it did as a consequence of recording it so assiduously. This brings the reader back to the concept of the choiceless choice because, clearly, Levi had no choice but to remember.

So far, Levi's discussion is specifically about perpetrator memory, though there seem to be perceptions which he reaches in the process which, by illuminating perpetrator memory, offer a vital perspective on survivor memory. At this point in the chapter he re-focuses upon survivor memory.

> In the vaster field of the victim, one also observes a drifting of memory, but here, evidently, fraud is not involved. Anyone who receives an injustice or an injury does not need to elaborate lies to exculpate himself of a guilt he does not have (even though, due to a paradoxical mechanism of which we shall speak, it can happen that he feels ashamed of it); but this does not exclude the fact that his memories may also be altered. It has been noticed, for instance, that many survivors of wars or other complex and traumatic experiences tend unconsciously to filter their memory: summoning them up among themselves, or telling them to third persons, they prefer to dwell on moments of respite, on grotesque, strange or relaxed intermezzos, and to skim over the most painful episodes which are not called up willingly from the reservoir of memory, and therefore with time tend to mist over, lose their contours. (p. 19)

'Tend unconsciously . . . prefer to dwell on moments of respite . . . skim over the most painful episodes'; these descriptions of survivor memory are intriguing as Levi suggests that the rememberer is likely to try not to remember or recite memories of injury. This is true, to an extent. But whether it is that survivors choose to remember the 'moments of respite' or are not permitted by listeners to articulate their other, more disturbing memories, is debatable. Increasingly, as discussed in Chapter 2, there is evidence that survivors were discouraged from telling the stories they wished to tell, and so told the stories that would be tolerated. Choiceless choices, again. Yet Levi also suggests that, 'For the purpose of defence, reality can be distorted not only in memory but in the very act of its taking place' (p. 19). Levi goes on to describe Alberto's change in perspective following his father's selection (p. 20) which led him to allow himself to believe comforting rumours whereas before he had been an assiduous seeker of truth. Similarly, Alberto's mother avoids the truth Levi brings her; she prefers her own 'lie' (p. 20). It is ironic that part of the 'memory' Alberto's mother constructed about her son required that Alberto should have lost his memory. As in survivor–perpetrator memories, where the recollections which two sets of memories contain are incompatible, in order for one memory to exist untroubled, another memory must be erased. This is an image of the potential for conflict between memories and describes in microcosm the dilemma of having memories which act in opposition. Either Alberto did not lose his memory, in which case his mother knows from the evidence of his absence that he is dead, or he has lost his memory in which case his absence proves his existence and potential for presence.

So convinced is Alberto's mother of the soundness of her construction that she directs Levi, 'Would I please change the subject, and tell her how I myself had survived' (p. 20). Alberto's mother demands a different narrative from the one that Levi offers. Her request to 'change the subject' echoes the request survivors frequently encountered. Her response is understandable and pitiable; it suggests that the failure of listeners to listen and their insistence upon the hopeful tale of survival were not always ill-meant or insensitive but were the means listeners employed in an attempt to protect themselves. The need to hear that survival is possible is essential for Alberto's mother in the construction of the narrative which she is telling to herself about Alberto's return. Possibly, she is not so convinced by her own tale, and cannot allow it to be tested by any truth she might hear from Levi.

In the light of the rest of 'The Memory of the Offence', Levi's concluding paragraph is problematic and disorienting for the reader:

> An apology is in order. This very book is drenched in memory; what's more, a distant memory. Thus it draws from a suspect source, and must be protected against itself. So here then: it contains more considerations than memories ... As for my personal memories, and the few unpublished anecdotes I have mentioned and will mention, I have diligently examined all of them: time has somewhat faded them, but they are in good consonance with their background and seem to me unaffected by the drifting I have described. (p. 21)

What appears to be a reassuring conclusion intended to secure the reader's trust in Levi's memory actually operates to query that trust.

Like the earlier 'Human memory' paragraph, this paragraph is full of conflicting intents and assertions. Levi has made it clear that 'drifting' of memory is unavoidable, that 'Human memory is a marvellous but fallacious instrument' (p. 11). Yet he claims here that his memories are 'unaffected'. He knows that 'memories . . . are not carved in stone' (p. 11) yet his are immune from the processes which afflict others. Memories 'tend to become erased as the years go by' (p. 11) whilst his are only 'somewhat faded'. *The Drowned and the Saved* 'draws from a suspect source' that is, memory, yet having 'diligently examined all of them' Levi comes to the conclusion that his memories are to be trusted. These conflicts compromise the status of this paragraph as a guarantee for the reader so that, rather than confirming Levi's memory of the offence as something immutable, it seems to challenge its own apparent assertions. Finally, Levi's 'apology' for memory, especially 'distant memory' which is 'a suspect source' problematizes not only 'The Memory of the Offence' but all of his writings associated with memory. Levi's intention in making this apology is not discernible; perhaps it is no more nor less than a caveat, addressed to himself as much as to his reader, a reminder, to check his memories.

MEMORY AT LAST

Levi remembered. He remembered on a grand scale. When, after an interval of nearly 50 years, he saw a photograph of Gerhard Goldbaum, a man whom he had barely known in Auschwitz, Levi wrote:

> I experienced a kind of bedazzlement . . . That was the face, it coincided perfectly with the one that I, without knowing it, bore imprinted in the pathological memory I preserve of that period: at times, but only for what concerns Auschwitz, I feel I am the brother of Ireneo Funes, '*el memorioso*' described by Borges.[22]

The Preface to *Moments of Reprieve* which opens this chapter concentrates and draws attention to Levi's most frequently considered themes in relation to memory. There is Levi's preoccupation with the intensity of his memories – 'as if at that time my mind had gone through a period of exalted receptivity' – which remained (unbearably?) acute after 35 years. Alongside this determined accuracy there is an insistence upon completeness. It is not merely that Levi remembers a handful of moments or smells or sights which burn vividly through a fog of undifferentiated experience. Levi asserts that he remembers it all: 'I have not forgotten a single thing', 'not a detail was lost'. Each detail rescued and recovered is a triumph in the face of the Holocaust's 'organized amnesia'.[23] Nor does Levi have to struggle for this precise recall. He remembers 'without any deliberate effort'. The Preface also refers to Levi's belief that the attention to detail which he practised in Auschwitz aided his 'spiritual and physical salvation'. Levi suggests that the constant observation of himself and his surroundings, the 'research' he conducted, the 'taking of notes' with which he engaged himself, his preparation and rehearsal of 'the story' which he repeated again and again, contributed to his survival. Levi imposed purpose and meaning in Auschwitz, the place which was constructed as a denial of purpose and meaning.

Yet, the ease with which he remembers, his representation of himself as a 'parrot', or a 'tape recorder', and the phrase 'pathological memory' to describe his astonishing facility, hint at the dark side of this prodigious memory. This kind of total recall does not seem entirely unproblematic, there is something here of the automaton which suggests that, even had he wished to do so, Levi could not have evaded his memories. His purpose, to record and to tell, was not an unalloyed benefit wholly benign in its effects. It imposed upon him a burden which, contrary to many of his assertions, was clearly, at times, intolerable. Once Levi had acceded to his role as a witness, or even The Witness, a role which he undertook apparently willingly, he was not able to abdicate. As I have shown, there are comparisons to be made here with the lack of choice he encountered in Auschwitz, or the 'choiceless choices' of Langer's terminology.

Levi's readers and critics applaud the memory and the memory of this man. He has become an object of reverence. In ever growing numbers of essays, monographs, articles, books, Levi is hoisted onto the pedestal reserved for Chief Rememberer. There are themes apparent in the kind of homage for which Levi and his writing are the focus. Commentators refer to the full and eminently successful life Levi led after Auschwitz. For many, this life 'proves' that it was possible to survive and to survive well. There is a life after that death, hope springs from that despair. Levi himself referred at times in positive terms to the 'benefits' he accrued and lessons he learned in Auschwitz. Yet, Mirna Cicioni records the never-ending requests for Levi to attend and speak at all manner of engagements. Her chapter

'Do not Call us Teachers' catalogues the gruelling round of talks, visits, and writing in which Levi was required to play a central role. The reader is left with the image of a man worn out by those who demanded access to his memory, perhaps even worn out by the memories themselves.[24] And Levi's ideas of witness come to a painful conclusion in the *The Drowned and the Saved* when he wrote, 'we the survivors are not the true witnesses' (p. 63).

Levi's writing makes a way in to these events which, perhaps because of his insistence upon rationality, protects the reader from the worst effects of what is being read.[25] Paradoxically, the techniques which Levi employed in *If This is a Man* in his determination to render his Auschwitz experiences accurately may serve as shields for the reader. It is as though we need a Levi, a writer of discrimination and tact through whom we may approach the offence safely. The fact that, as the writer of *If This is a Man*, Levi is frequently characterized as a Dante to that Inferno locates his work in a place of educated civility and of comparative safety. It also reveals the emphasis upon that text as literature. This emphasis may serve as a distancing technique which protects the reader or critic from the full impact of Levi's memories, for there is safety in a response to these texts as 'literature' to be dissected and analysed.[26]

The dismay which inflects reactions to *The Drowned and the Saved*, suggests that this text does not offer any similar protection to the reader. In spite of Levi's specific quarrel with Améry's critique of Auschwitz and its meanings, *The Drowned and the Saved* does suggest that Levi was, after 40 years, angrier about the Shoah (and especially the ease with which perpetrators and bystanders evaded its memory) than he had been in *If This is a Man*. The needs of many readers for Levi to continue to provide a testimony of enlightenment and hope are not satisfied by *The Drowned and the Saved*.[27]

RICORDATI: 'CARRIED IN THE HEART'. OR CARVED IN THE HEART?

I will end by drawing attention to one final example of the matter of memorizing. Levi is insistent that memory has to be memorized and ritualized. One must practise remembering as one might practise an instrument. To remember is not a passive act but a vigorous engagement with the present in order that what rapidly becomes the past may be remembered for the future. Repetition is essential. This applies whether what is to be remembered are chemical formulae, lines from Dante, or experiences in Auschwitz. There is a duty to remember which attains for Levi ritual and quasi-religious characteristics. His determined insistence upon the commandment to remember is made with ferocity in his poem, 'Shemá'. It is both significant and appropriate that Levi took the *Shema* as his model.

> The *Shema* is not a 'prayer' in the strict sense: It is not addressed *to* God, but *by* Him to us. It contains the basic declaration of the Jewish faith, to be reaffirmed every morning and every evening.[28]

The *Shema*, with its fixed text and words which are memorized, recited, repeated and have been memorized, recited, repeated for nearly 6,000 years, is the central 'poem' of Judaism. It is injunction and command.

> Hear, O Israel, the Lord our God, the Lord is One
> Blessed be the name of His glorious kingdom for ever and ever
>
> You shall love the Lord your God with all your heart, with all your soul, and with all your might. And these words which I command you this day shall be in your heart. You shall impress them upon your children, and you shall speak of them when you sit at home, and when you go on a journey, when you lie down, and when you rise up. And you shall bind them for a sign on your hand, and they shall be as ornaments between your eyes. And you shall write them on the door-posts of your house, and upon your gates. (Deuteronomy, 6: 4–9)

Levi's 'Shemá' is also injunction and command:

> You who live safe
> In your warm houses,
> You who find, returning in the evening,
> Hot food and friendly faces:
>> Consider if this is a man,
>> Who works in the mud
>> Who does not know peace
>> Who fights for a scrap of bread
>> Who dies because of a yes or a no.
>> Consider if this is a woman,

Without hair and without name
With no more strength to remember
Her eyes empty and her womb cold
Like a frog in winter.
Meditate that this came about:
I commend these words to you.
Carve them in your hearts
At home, in the street,
Going to bed, rising;
Repeat them to your children.
   Or may your house fall apart,
   May illness impede you,
   May your children turn their faces from you.

NOTES

1. Primo Levi, *Moments of Reprieve*, trans. Ruth Feldman (London: Abacus, 1987), p.11.
2. Primo Levi, *If This is a Man* and *The Truce* (London: Abacus, 1987) and *The Drowned and the Saved* (London: Abacus, 1988). Further references are taken from these editions and page numbers will be given in the text. *If This is a Man* was first published in Italy as *Se questo è un uomo* (Turin: De Silva, 1947) and reprinted under the same title in 1958 by Einaudi. *The Drowned and the Saved* was first published as *I sommersi e i salvati* (Turin: Einaudi, 1986).
3. Primo Levi, *The Mirror Maker* (London: Minerva, 1991). Further references are taken from this edition and page numbers will be given in the text.
4. George Steiner, speaking on *Desert Island Discs*, broadcast BBC Radio 4 (23 February 1996).
5. Jorge Luis Borges, 'The Secret Miracle', *Labyrinths* (London: Penguin, 1971), p. 124.
6. Levi's conclusion is very like Améry's on this point. The two men are often closer in their analyses of Auschwitz and its effects than is at first apparent.
7. Birger Gerhardsson, *Memory and Manuscript: Oral Tradition and Written Transmission in Rabbinic Judaism and Early Christianity* (Lund: Gleerup, 1961), pp. 166–7.
8. This is a point which Steiner made very forcefully in the broadcast cited above.
9. Charlotte Delbo, *Auschwitz and After*, trans. Rosette C. Lamont (New York: Yale University Press, 1995), pp. 186–7.

10. For example in *Holocaust Poetry*, compiled and introduced by Hilda Schiff (London: HarperCollins, 1995), p. 205, where it stands as the 'last word' in the anthology.

11. For discussion of Pikolo and his role see *If This is a Man* p. 115. For significance of Levi in Pikolo/Jean's survival see discussion at pp. 106–8 below.

12. Art Spiegelman, *Maus II* (London: Penguin, 1992), p. 28. Vladek is encouraged by a Polish priest's 'reading' of his number, 175113, because it adds up to 18 and is therefore considered to be auspicious.

13. It is illuminating to compare Jean Améry's view which problematizes these matters:

> I recall a winter evening when after work we were dragging ourselves ... back into the camp ... when – for God-knows-what reason – a flag waving in front of a half-finished building caught my eye. 'The walls stand speechless and cold, the flags clank in the wind', I muttered to myself, in mechanical association. Then I repeated the stanza somewhat louder, listened to the words sound, tried to track the rhythm, and expected that the emotional and mental response that for years this Hölderlin poem had awakened in me would emerge. But nothing happened. The poem no longer transcended reality... Perhaps the Hölderlin feeling, ... would have surfaced if a comrade had been present whose mood would have been somewhat similar and to whom I could have recited the stanza.

Jean Améry, *At the Mind's Limits: Contemplations by a Survivor on Auschwitz and its Realities*, trans. Sidney Rosenfeld and Stella P. Rosenfeld (New York: Schocken, 1986), p. 7.

14. Compare with Delbo relinquishing bread for *Le Misanthrope*.

15. Améry, *At the Mind's Limits*, p. 7.

16. Jean Samuel speaking in a documentary on Levi broadcast in 1987 by BBC Television.

17. Ibid.

18. Margaret Atwood, *Bodily Harm* (London: Virago, 1983).

19. See 'Torture', John K. Roth and Michael Berenbaum (eds), in *Holocaust: Religious and Philosophical Implications* (New York: Paragon House, 1989) and Améry, *At The Mind's Limits*, p. 7.

20. This passage is very like Améry. See for example 'Torture', pp. 177–8:

> The expectation of help, the certainty of help, is indeed one of the fundamental experiences of human beings, ... as much a constitutional psychic element as is the struggle for existence ... In almost all situations in life where there is bodily injury there is also the expectation of help: the former is compensated by the latter. But with the first blow from a policeman's fist ... a part of our life ends and it can never again be revived.

21. With this in mind Langer's memory classifications – for example,

anguished, tainted and humiliated memory – come to seem more admissible.

22. 'A Mystery in the Lager', *The Mirror Maker*, p. 69. Also see Borges, *Labyrinths*, especially 'Funes the Memorious', p. 87; 'The Secret Miracle', p. 118; and 'The Witness', p. 279.

23. I have borrowed this useful phrase from Steiner, see note 4.

24. Mirna Cicioni, *Primo Levi: Bridges of Knowledge* (Oxford: Berg, 1995).

25. In contrast see Améry's *At the Mind's Limits*. Whilst Améry is eminently 'rational' his conclusions are much more difficult to tolerate and may partly explain his comparative lack of wider popularity. Also, the fact that *The Truce* is published together with *If This is a Man*, tends to mitigate the impact of Levi's experiences. Not all commentators would agree with my view: see for example Ferdinando Camon, *Conversations with Primo Levi*, trans. John Shepley (Vermont: The Marlboro Press, 1989), p. 74.

26. I do not exempt myself from this observation but hope that having recognized the tendency I may have counteracted it to some extent.

27. In the literature which discusses Levi's work there are frequent references which emphasize his mildness and lack of anger as though Levi, like his work, must be calm and quiet if we are to tolerate him and it. See again Camon, *Conversations with Primo Levi*.

28. *The Authorised Daily Prayer Book of the United Hebrew Congregations of the Commonwealth* (Enlarged Centenary Edition; Cambridge: Press Syndicate of the University of Cambridge, 1992), p. 65.

5

ART SPIEGELMAN

'REALITY IS TOO COMPLEX FOR COMICS'

In his essay 'Art Spiegelman's *Maus*: Graphic Art and the Holocaust'
Thomas Doherty refers to the problems encountered by the Pulitzer
Prize committee in 1992 when they were considering *Maus* for an
award.[1] *Maus* was clearly 'a project whose merit they could not deny
but whose medium they could not quite categorize' (p. 69). The
dilemma was resolved when the committee 'decided to finesse the issue
of genre', presenting a 'Special Award' to Spiegelman for *Maus*.
Doherty also describes similar difficulties encountered by the *New York
Times*. *Maus* first appeared in their Fiction Bestsellers List but when
Spiegelman expressed concern about this, *Maus* was moved: 'In a tiny
but telling blip on the cultural radar, the *Times* obligingly moved the
volume from the Fiction to Non-Fiction Best Seller List. The veracity
of the image – even the comic book image – had attained parity with
the word' (p. 69).

This last observation 'The veracity of the image – even the comic
book image – had attained parity with the word' is helpful in
approaching these texts. It confirms what the reader discovers in *Maus
I* and *II*. For, whilst the comic-book would seem to be an inappropriate
or even unacceptably flippant medium for representing the Holocaust
there is a degree of authority in Spiegelman's representations which
confounds expectations and which more usually attaches to words than
to comic-book images.

If one measures these matters in terms of Pulitzer prizes, it seems
that *Maus I* and *II* have been judged to provide an entirely appropriate
and serious approach to the memory of the Holocaust in general and to
the memories of Vladek, Art and Spiegelman in particular. One of the
most striking elements of this format is the ease with which the
memories of events become contemporary for the reader. The depicted
events do not look as though they took place more than 50 years ago,
as often happens when photographic images are used. There is an
immediacy which attaches or is attached to graphic images of this kind

and which mitigates the tendency to locate these events in an historical past which barely impinges on our modern present. In spite of their wide use as educational tools, comic-books and their close relations, cartoons, are most frequently used to represent the present or the future; they are less often used to depict the past.[2] It is also intriguing that this medium, which is usually employed to depict fantastic and incredible events, has here been successfully employed to represent real occurrences, emphasizing the extent to which the Holocaust bears a uniquely paradoxical nature, being, for many, unimaginable, unbelievable, yet true.

There is a significant degree of believability intrinsic to this representation. Spiegelman writes and tapes his father's words, and the reader is able to witness this act of transcription, so that it seems as though its veracity cannot be doubted. The drawings serve to corroborate the words in the most convincing manner and the reader is able to believe in Vladek's tale partly because we 'see' him in the situations which he describes. Though Vladek may have forgotten or misremembered past details, the form which Spiegelman gives to them reconstitutes their veracity for the reader. He worries that 'Reality is too complex for comics' (*Maus II*, p. 16), but no medium may adequately contain the uncontainable or represent the unrepresentable. In fact the form, by acknowledging the gap between itself and reality, actually communicates across the gap.

The techniques of the comic-book permit Spiegelman to draw the reader's attention to discontinuities and connections which are difficult to render in prose, whilst the flexibility of the format means that the structure can be set aside whenever necessary in order to provide emphasis or to manage material which may not otherwise be easily managed. Spiegelman is able to represent the magnitude of Vladek and Anja's arrival at the gates of Auschwitz quite simply by allowing his drawing of Auschwitz to escape the page boundaries (*Maus I*, p. 157; reproduced here on p. 172). Similarly, when Vladek shows Art the photographs which are 'all what is left' of Anja's family, Spiegelman depicts them falling in a flurry from Vladek's knees and off the page (*II*, p. 115).

This medium also encourages and enables the reader to recognize more fully that for survivors the Shoah was never over or safely consigned to the past. Vladek's memories possess the awful power to be as real in the present where he speaks with Art as the events they recollect were in the past. The two images of Vladek (*I*, p. 122, ix and x) which Spiegelman draws side by side are sufficiently alike that, though Vladek is more than 30 years older, the visual emphasis is upon the fact that he is the same man who witnessed the events which he recalls for Art. This is reinforced by the way in which, as he recollects Anja's despair, the older Vladek speaks in the present tense with the younger Vladek's voice. Vladek is not referring to the past at this point, he is reliving it. There is no gap between the Vladek of the war and the Vladek of the 'present' and the memory of the older Vladek conjures up the younger until the memory of the past becomes as vivid and lively as present-day events. Vladek later refers to this process of reconstruction with pain, 'All such things of the war, I tried to put out from my mind once for all ... until you rebuild me all this from your questions' (*II*, p. 98, v).

In the same way that Spiegelman is able to represent the simultaneity of past and present for Vladek, he is also able to use this medium to represent different accounts of the same events. During Vladek's descriptions of camp life, Spiegelman depicts the camp orchestra playing as prisoners go out through the gates to work (*II*, p. 54, i). He then draws Art referring to the orchestra, of which Vladek has no knowledge or recollection. In the next frame, Spiegelman corrects his first assumption and depicts Vladek's recollections which are solely of marching out through the gates without the accompaniment of the orchestra (*II*, p. 54, iii). But the medium, unlike prose, allows Spiegelman to represent both versions of this particular memory and whilst representing Vladek's story accurately he is also able to allude to the alternative version as the conductor's ears and baton, the neck of the double bass and the horn are still visible over the heads of the marchers (*II*, p. 54, iii).

The images reinforce and often have a more powerful effect than words alone; to read the description of Mandelbaum's struggle for survival is not as disturbing as being able to witness a representation of the difficulties he experiences (*II*, p. 29, ii). The medium also permits diagrammatic representation of material which is awkward to convey in prose, for example Vladek's description of 'moving mountains' in the work camp (*I*, p. 56), maps of territory (*I*, p. 60), hiding places (*I*, p. 86), the bunkers in Srodula (*I*, pp. 110 and 112), shoemaking (*II*, p. 60), the 'currency' of the camps (*II*, p. 64), the plan of the crematorium (*II*, p. 70). Spiegelman is able to include other documentary evidence: 'facsimiles' of work cards, evacuation notices, photographs, and Vladek himself sketches the plans of their hiding places for Art saying that 'it's good to know ... just in case' (*I*, p. 110). The plan drawing of Auschwitz and Birkenau (*II*, p. 51) aids the reader's visualization more than words alone; Spiegelman is able to dramatize its significance in the lives of Art

and Vladek for the plan occupies the centre of the page and the frames
in which Art and Vladek speak revolve around it.

Spiegelman is also able to employ a variety of line weights and
widths which impart subtlety and nuance to his drawings and words
which cannot be satisfactorily reproduced here. Capital letters are
always used for Vladek's story, they are the norm throughout *Maus I*
and distinguish it from Art's story where the more usual upper- and
lower-case forms appear. After all, Vladek has experienced a larger,
more emphatic reality than Art, for Vladek survived Auschwitz –
though as Pavel points out, Art survived Rego Park (*II*, p. 44, v, vii). In
Maus II, where Art's story is more urgently expressed, lower case
letters are increasingly used. Emphases in *Maus* are represented by
thicker upper- or lower-case letters; I have attempted to reproduce
them in quotations by the use of bold font forms, as in, 'It was so . . .
so **personal**! (*I*, p. 104, iii).

Discussion of this medium gives rise to more complications in
terminology than is the case with the works of either Schulz or Levi. For
example, the relationship between the individuals, Vladek and Art, and
their representations is not easily described or fixed. In order to
distinguish between Art Spiegelman the writer and draughtsman of
these texts and the Art Spiegelman who is his construction, I have
referred to the former as 'Spiegelman' and the latter as 'Art'. Vladek is
Vladek throughout, though he should not be confused with the 'real'
Vladek Spiegelman who does not appear in *Maus*.

There was also the problem of whether to refer to a 'reader' or a
'viewer'; I have tended to use the word 'reader' partly because it is
more viable to think in terms of reading an image than of viewing prose
but this word should also be taken to contain the acknowledgement
that *Maus* is as much about viewing as it is about reading. Words like
'past' and 'present' have also been problematic; *Maus* often confounds
linear time and emphasizes the way in which memory has a layering
effect upon chronology so that pasts and presents frequently appear
alongside one another. For simplicity's sake, I have tended to restrict
my discussions to Vladek's past, that is the story he is telling to Art; his
present which he shares with Art where they encounter Vladek's
recital of the past; and Art's other and later present, which is the time
after Vladek has died but during which he continues to work on *Maus
II* and Vladek's memories.

MAUS I: 'NO ONE WANTS ANYWAY TO HEAR SUCH STORIES'

Maus I opens with a kind of prologue (reproduced at pp. 173 and 174).
The first two pages introduce a range of issues and ideas which will be
encountered in both texts. Whilst the initial impact and awareness of
the story arrive in terms of images – the reader opens the book and
there are three rollerskating mice – yet the process of reading begins
almost immediately so that words and images sit alongside, almost
attaining simultaneity and sharing equal status. The first words are a
statement of time and place, 'Rego Park, N.Y. c. 1958'. That 'circa' is
very noticeable. Spiegelman is signalling to the reader that this is not
History with a capital H with its insistence on precise, verifiable times,
dates and locations but an approximation to or with history. Also, the
use of the word 'circa' signals the fallibility or unfixedness of his own
memory, which prepares the reader for the encounter with Vladek's
memories. This approximation is also reassuring as it suggests that it
does not matter that Art is unable to say, 'It was on the 23 May 1958 at
10.32 a.m.' What does matter in the recollection and recital of this
incident is its meaning.

Art's first words refer immediately to memory: 'It was summer, I
remember' (p. 5). This illustrates the impact upon Art of Vladek's
experiences and consequent view of the world and of the primacy for
Art of the memory of his childhood. The reader sees Art, aged ten or
eleven, rollerskating and racing to school with his friends Howie and
Steve: 'Last one to the schoolyard is a rotten egg' (p. 5, i) says one. Art's
skate comes loose, he calls to his friends to wait for him but they
respond with laughter and call him 'rotten egg'. It is the ordinary stuff
of childhood, the petty insults, humiliations and disappointments
which any reader will be able to recall. But for Spiegelman this event
has a deeper resonance. Spiegelman has chosen to draw this particular
incident as an introduction to what comes later. This memory is of
significance for the adult Spiegelman as he is able to look back and
recognize how, even in such ordinary circumstances, the extraordinary,
that is his father's experiences of the Holocaust, intruded into his life.
It also introduces the relationship which Art has with Vladek and
through Vladek, with the Holocaust and the way in which Vladek's
relationship with his own experiences of the Holocaust were
detrimental to his behaviour towards his young son.

The crying child turns to his father for solace; Vladek is working in
front of the house 'fixing something' (p. 5, v) but Art encounters no
sympathy. Vladek calls, 'Artie! Come to hold this a minute while I saw'
(p. 6, i)', asks, 'Why do you cry, Artie?' (p. 6, ii) but then continues

speaking, impatiently, without waiting for an answer, 'Hold better on
the wood.' Art, still crying, says, 'I-I fell, and my friends skated away
w-without me' (p. 6, ii). At this point, the reader is likely to recognize
that the usual response of a parent to the distress of a child would be an
attempt to calm or reassure. But not Vladek. He stops sawing and
responds, '**Friends**? Your friends?' (p. 6, iii) then, whilst apparently able
to continue with his humdrum task, says, 'If you lock them together in
a room with no food for a week . . . ' and finishes his sentence in the final
frame '. . . **Then** you could see what it is, friends! . . . ' (p. 6, v). Vladek
seems incapable of or unwilling to recognize and acknowledge the hurt
that Art has felt, specifically because, after the experiences which
Vladek has survived, friendship has taken on a completely different
meaning for him. Vladek knows something about human behaviour
which is not available as direct experience to Art. He has
accommodated this knowledge in a way that is difficult to imagine.
Vladek carries on sawing as though what he has seen in the past and
what he knows of human cruelty are not heart-breaking. That the first
encounter with Vladek takes place when he is engaged in a practical task
is also significant; this is a man who has been and continues to be a fixer,
an organizer, a pragmatist. Vladek has got on with life, in a manner and
to an extent of which Spiegelman/Art has been incapable. Spiegelman's
'prologue' suggests that the impact of the Holocaust may have fallen
more heavily on the son of the survivor than on the survivor.

Spiegelman develops the feeling of menace and the pervasive sense
of a growing threat to the mice/Jews almost subliminally by using
simple images repetitively until they accrue meaning and nuance. In
both texts, the image of a light which may be a spotlight or searchlight
recurs. In some cases it is empty, in others it is filled with a swastika
and a representation of the Führer. This repetition of an image which
does not at first have any perceptibly threatening content comes to
express quite precisely the dangerous position of Jews in Europe in the
years just before the war. Through its use Spiegelman is able to allude
to the signs of a threat which were there but which impinged so little
that it was possible to continue everyday existence without becoming
unduly alarmed. The spotlight/searchlight appears on the cover of
Maus I and on the endpapers which depict Vladek and Anja cowering,
caught in the glare of Hitler's murderous intentions. This same circle
of light reappears on the contents page as Anja and Vladek dance
happily, under the title 'My father bleeds history (mid-1930s to winter
1944)', in an image reminiscent of a film poster. The light could be read
as unthreatening; it might simply represent the lighting in the
ballroom where they dance. But it does seem to hint at the future,

unheeded by Anja and Vladek, when a different spotlight will fall upon
them. This image of Anja and Vladek is an enlarged version of images
which depict their visit to the sanatorium when Anja was recovering
from postnatal depression following Richieu's birth (p. 35).

The fact that the spotlight has already fallen upon the Jews, even as
Anja and Vladek dance together, is alluded to during their journey to
the sanatorium when they have their first encounter with fascist
antisemitism (reproduced at pp. 175–7). They see a swastika flag
displayed prominently over a town and suddenly the evidence is
before them of the effects of Nazi authority and propaganda upon the
population of Czechoslovakia. Vladek says: 'I remember when we were
almost arrived, we passed a small town. Everybody – every Jew from
the train – got very excited and frightened' (p. 32, ii). In that moment,
as they see the flag, a great change is wrought and Vladek has to amend
his own words and perceptions as 'Everybody' becomes 'every Jew'.
The existence and sight of the flag and all that it represents make
Vladek and the others into Jews by removing them from the category
of 'Everybody' and constructing them as not-Everybody and therefore
Other. It is a moment of realization and Vladek acknowledges its
memorable significance, 'Here was the first time I saw, with my own
eyes, the swastika' (p. 32, iii). The reader also witnesses the effect this
moment has on the other passengers. In the first panel, Anja sleeps, her
head resting on Vladek's shoulder, in the next she is wide awake and
staring out of the window. The mouse who draws the attention of the
others to the swastika is represented with wide-eyed shock and the
exclamations, 'Oi!' and 'Look!' The bottom half of the page contains
one image and the reader's point of view shifts. Having been
positioned as an observer who looks into the carriage and sees the
reactions of the mice, the reader is allowed to adopt the point of view
of the mice and to see what they see.

The title of this chapter is 'The Honeymoon'. At first, the reader
accepts this uncritically as a reference to the relationship between Anja
and Vladek. But Anja and Vladek have been married in Chapter 1 and
Richieu is already born; their honeymoon must be over. Perhaps
'honeymoon' refers ironically to the period between Hitler's takeover
of power in Germany and the effects upon the population in Poland of
German policies towards the Jews. The traveller who has drawn their
attention to the swastika tells them of recent events in Germany where
the 'honeymoon' is already over for the Jews. The searchlight and
swastika image, minus the Führer's face, appears with sinister effect in
four consecutive panels. Its position in the first and last is like that of a

sun, rising and setting and as the light 'sets' behind the 'Jew-free' town of the fourth panel of the sequence it is both omnipresent and highly suggestive of a perverted image of romantic happiness. The little houses and the empty street rest quietly in the 'glow' bestowed by the swastika/sun. As the traveller describes events, the image of the swastika is 'behind' everything that is happening in Germany; it is the backdrop to events (p. 33). When Anja and Vladek are depicted on the following page (35), their pleasure and happiness are compromised for the reader by the presence of the spotlight upon them. Although empty of the swastika menace, the void looks as though it is waiting to be filled and the threat from the previous page seems to bleed through to this one, so that they do not dance in unambiguous security. Given the dramatic and theatrical resonance of a following spot, these images also call up phrases like 'waiting in the wings', 'the stage is set', the 'theatre of war'. Adding to the imminence of threat, the tales Vladek tells Anja 'to keep her busy' are tales of insecurity and flight (p. 35).[3]

It is noticeable that in *Maus I* and *II* every chapter begins and ends in the 'present', that is the present which was the time and place where Vladek was recounting his story to Spiegelman/Art. This makes the chapters into something rather like therapeutic interventions or sessions with a psychoanalyst during which the survivor, his son and the reader are taken back to the time of pain and difficulty but then returned, safely, to the present. This contributes to the recognition of the significant psychological elements to the dynamics which exist between Art and Vladek. The first session between Art and Vladek acts as a model for all their later encounters; Vladek sits peddling on his exercise bike which seems almost the equivalent of the psychiatrist's couch. Art takes notes, first by hand, then in later sessions with the aid of a tape recorder. The matter they are engaged upon investigating is memory. Each session opens with a brief exchange of pleasantries or mundane information (though there is more insight into the relationship that exists between Art and Vladek in these banalities than in any other part of their exchange). Art then guides or prompts his father to start talking about the past, often by reminding him what stage they had reached in the last 'session'. Vladek embarks upon his recollections, possibly for an hour or so: when one or other of them will break out of the narrative. Vladek will then put away his memories and return to the present. The session closes, usually with the exchange of further trivial information or comments. Art rarely interrupts once his father has begun his recollections, though occasionally, like a psychiatrist, he may comment upon or clarify a point or bring Vladek back to the matter in hand when he digresses. Vladek displays no reluctance to talk, but nor is he eager or compelled to speak of the past. In this respect, the sessions are a reversal of the usual therapeutic model because they seem to be more for the benefit of the one who listens than for the one who speaks. The compulsion to engage in these encounters is all Art's and though Vladek does benefit by having his son visit more frequently than he would do otherwise, his memories of the Shoah are more like 'bait' with which he entices Art than necessary outpourings. Art seems to have adopted the role of neutral recorder yet it is his compulsion to hear which is motivating the sessions. In the earlier sessions, Vladek seems to be unmoved by the memories he recounts; later he finds the material more distressing and seems to be troubled by what he is remembering.

The opening frame (p. 11, i; reproduced here at p. 178) depicts Art and Vladek greeting one another; Vladek in particular seems very pleased to see Art as he rushes forward, arms outstretched. But there is instantly tension in the scene as Vladek first says that Art is late and then expresses disappointment that Françoise has not come too. The tension is heightened by Vladek's disapproval of Mala as she is about to use a wire rather than wooden hanger for Art's coat, and there is an insight into Vladek's construction of the world where respect may be signified by a coat-hanger. Art has already made it clear that he and Vladek 'weren't that close', and Vladek uses the hanger incident as an opportunity to point out that they have not seen each other in two years. The tension and sense of distance which the three are experiencing is completed when Art reveals that Vladek and Mala 'didn't get along' (p. 11, vi).

Vladek's recollections begin in 1935, giving them a context which, as Art recognizes, 'makes everything more **real** – more human' (p. 23, iii). Art visits Vladek specifically to find out about his experiences because, as he openly admits 'I still want to draw that book about you' (p. 12, ii). Vladek seems reluctant at first, and expresses two conflicting views of the project. On the one hand, his story may not easily be rendered or communicated: 'It would take **many** books, my life' (p. 12, v). On the other, Vladek suggests that 'No one wants anyway to hear such stories' (p. 12, v). Art offers what he thinks Vladek may like to hear at this point, 'I want to hear it', but then inadvertently betrays the real focus of his attention when he encourages Vladek to begin the story by saying 'Start with Mom' (p. 12, vi).

Vladek is not presented as a saint or a hero. He is shown to be a flawed human being: he is something of an opportunist (p. 12, viii), ready to see Lucia whilst it suited him (p. 15), but prepared to get rid of her when Anja comes along (p. 20, iv). He rummages through Anja's closet to 'see what a housekeeper she was' and finds 'everything is neat and straight just the way I like it' (p. 19, iii). In the course of doing this he discovers pills to which his response is, 'If she was sick, then what did I need it for?' (p. 19, v) but a friend tells him that the pills are 'only because she was so skinny and nervous' (p. 19, vi). Reassured, he marries Anja. In Chapter 2 Spiegelman reveals that Vladek was vehemently anti-communist (p. 27, ii) and when he discovers that Anja has been helping them, orders her, at the risk of losing him, to cease all her involvement (p. 29, i, ii). That Vladek has been prepared to reveal himself in this way seems understandable, but when Spiegelman exposes Vladek, the uses to which Spiegelman is putting this information have to be considered.

Vladek's past, in the form of memories, is represented simultaneously with Art's present, permitting correspondence and negotiation between their very different lives. This format allows dilemmas concerning truthfulness and voyeurism to be recognized, rather than repressed. At the end of the first session Vladek imposes an injunction, 'But this what I just told you – about Lucia and so – I don't want you should write this in your book' (p. 23, i). He feels that this would not be 'respectful'. Art promises not to use the story, but as he has already conveyed the information to the reader, his promise comes too late. It is honest (and wittily postmodern), of Spiegelman to record Vladek's prohibition: it alerts the reader to queries about the extent of the teller's rights over his or her tale, dramatizes questions of voyeurism and of the uses and abuses to which this kind of material might be put, whilst making of the reader a collaborator implicating him or her in the use Spiegelman makes of Vladek's story. This illustrates some of the problems about 'hearing' and 'seeing' this material. It is also clear that Spiegelman/Art visits Vladek 'quite regularly, to hear his story' (p. 26) yet prior to embarking on this project had not visited for two years. By including this information about his motives, Spiegelman acknowledges his own pragmatism and willingness to barter with Vladek; he offers time in return for narrative. This recognizes the dangers inherent in 'translating' the recollections of others, in appropriating their story and making their memories available for consumption. The propriety of what Art is doing is not ignored by Spiegelman, and he allows the reader to engage with the dilemmas involved in telling the story of another, even someone whose story overlaps so much with one's own that permission would seem to be implicit in the degree of proximity involved. Art is visibly shocked by Vladek's assertion of ownership of the story and tries to counter his father's command by cajoling Vladek into releasing the 'rights' to tell it, 'But **Pop** – it's great material. It makes everything more **real** – more human' (p. 23, iii). Art displays ruthlessness in pursuit of Vladek's story which, from Art's perspective, is a story that should be told. But he discloses the gap that exists between one person's life and another's perception of that life. In *Maus I*, Art, no matter how close he is to his father's story, is still able to maintain a degree of separation from it, to the extent that he can see it as 'material'. For Vladek, this is not 'material', it is his life. Art attempts to allay Vladek's concerns, but he lies to him by promising not to disclose what he has already disclosed. This moment dramatizes the choices that Spiegelman/Art has made in relation to this 'material', and the reader is led to wonder whether Spiegelman decided that he would use the story of Lucia even as Art was promising not to or whether the decision to use this 'material' came later, as Spiegelman was working on the book.

The start of the next session reinforces the view that Art is at least as interested in Anja's story as in Vladek's and that to some extent he is using his father's story as a vehicle to gain access to Anja's lost story. This imperative, understated at first and only hinted at or given away by Art by the manner in which he introduces her in these first sessions, becomes inescapable until, at the end of *Maus I*, Art and the reader have become almost obsessed by the quest for Anja's story. Art opens this chapter/session with an 'admission' that he continued to visit his father, 'quite regularly, to hear his story' (p. 26). But this assertion is qualified by his first words to Vladek which are, 'About Mom . . .' (p. 26, i). Vladek is counting tablets and when Art asks what he is doing, he embarks upon a description of his medical régime. Art seems not to be interested in his father as his father, but as the site of a story which must be excavated. He appears not to make notes about the number or purpose of Vladek's tablets for example, though his pen is poised over the pad (p. 26, v). Again he prompts, 'About Mom – ' (p. 26, vii). Yet, Spiegelman must have taken some note of Vladek's concerns about Mala, money, health, for how else could he have represented these matters in *Maus*? Spiegelman's representation of himself as Art and of Art's relationship with Vladek does reveal that he was not especially interested in Vladek's 'now' but only in Vladek's 'then'. So Art dismisses Vladek's interest in and fascination with his health, although, for Vladek, this struggle represents a continuous fight for survival and may hint at the kind of personality he had which helped him survive the camps, 'For my condition I must fight to **save** myself' (p. 26, v). When Vladek offers Art one of the magazines which Vladek regularly reads to find out about 'prevention', Art makes no attempt to feign interest and replies with a brief, 'No thanks' (p. 26, vi). At the end of this session (pp. 39–40) Vladek returns to his present-day concerns, which are as live for him as the past, and talks, over two pages, about his eyes. Spiegelman permits Vladek to communicate these concerns to the reader; Art dismisses them with, 'Uh-huh – you told me about that' (p. 40, vii). And in the final panel which runs across the bottom of the page, they seem to have retreated into their individual concerns entirely. Vladek says 'It's enough for today, yes? I'm tired and I must count still my pills' (p. 40, viii). Art shows no interest in his father's well-being, though he agrees to stop, 'Okay, good idea . . . my hand is sore from writing all this down.' The story that Vladek is reciting and which Art is rendering brings them together only for as long as it is being told and rendered, but does little at other times to mend a relationship which displays many flaws. Art's refusal of or lack of interest in much that concerns his father is frequently evident throughout the text; so Art says, '**Please** Pop! I'd rather not hear all that **again**' (p. 44, iv) when his father complains about Mala. Some of this impatience can be explained as the usual conflicts which exist between parent and child, but it seems more polarized in this case as Art is avid in his desire to hear the story of the war years but dismissive about most of the rest of his father's life.

At the start of Chapter 3, Art's admissions about his intentions become more open, 'I visited my father more often in order to get more information about his past . . .' (p. 43, i). Spiegelman depicts Art arriving to see his father. Behind him is the circle which I have suggested may have a metaphorical relationship with the Holocaust. It is empty of swastika and Hitler but its presence here is troubling. It may represent the continuing impact of the Shoah upon Art, for although the direct threat encountered by his parents has disappeared, the Holocaust still represents a menace to survivors and their children. The spotlight may represent Art's involvement with the story and his growing perception of the impact of the Holocaust upon his own life. There is more evidence of that impact in the brief scene at the start of this chapter where Vladek urges Art to 'finish at least what's on your plate' (p. 43, iii) and Art tells Mala of occasions in his childhood when, 'if I didn't eat **everything** Mom served, Pop and I would argue 'til I ran to my room crying . . .' (p. 43, iv).

Vladek starts to tell the story of being drafted into the Polish army (p. 44). Spiegelman draws the 'present' where Vladek is sitting with Art, reciting the story. Art lies on the floor at his feet in a powerful image; father and son seem relaxed and intimately engaged with one another as Art gives his full attention to Vladek. Vladek recalls his own father teaching him survival tactics, in this case methods of keeping out of the army. Ironically, the tactics which were employed were the opposite of those needed to survive in the camps as they entailed starving oneself and getting as little rest as possible so that when it came to the medical examination Vladek would be considered unfit. Ironic too that in this context, when Vladek is judged unfit, the doctors are rather kindly and send him away, suggesting, 'Build yourself up for a year young man, and we'll review your case again' (p. 46, vii). Art listens to this tale with some interest, perhaps because he can see the relevance it has to Vladek's later experiences, but still shapes the story by bringing Vladek back to the point, 'But let's get back to 1939!' (p. 47, i).

Vladek's memories frequently impinge upon the 'present' to influence his thoughts and actions. The present breaks into the past or the past suffuses the present and this correspondence is represented by the way in which pages are constructed with equal space and weight given to both. Page 52 is equally divided between Vladek's recollections of the Herculean task of cleaning out the stables as a prisoner of war and his present where he sits telling Art about cleaning out the stables. The recollection of cleaning triggers an awareness in him, so that just as he remembers the German officer calling them 'lazy bastards' (p. 52, iv) he realizes that Art is dropping cigarette ash on the floor. He chastises Art and compares the tidy room where they sit with the stable of 40 years earlier. The degree of disturbance which Art's transgression provokes in Vladek is out of all proportion to the offence. It is as though the proximity of the memory of that other, impossible cleaning task ignites the anger, frustration and anxiety in the present which Vladek had to suppress in the past. This exemplifies the extent to which the past is informing, even de-forming the present, and provides an insight into what may have been the psychological effects of that past upon the person Vladek became. Yet there is no simple correspondence between the one and the other, and though it is tempting to explain all the vagaries of Vladek's persona entirely in the terms of his status as survivor, it is clear from comments made by Mala – '**All** our friends went through the camps. **Nobody** is like him' (p. 131) – and Art that Vladek should not be taken as a representative survivor.

It seems likely that those aspects of his character which were already evident before the war were reinforced and to some extent corroborated by his experiences during the war. This question of the impact upon Vladek of his experiences is not resolved in either *Maus I* or *Maus II*.

Examples of the 'preparedness' and determination of Vladek to survive appear during his time in the POW camp. Although it is autumn and already cold, Vladek bathes regularly in the river. He explains this to other incredulous prisoners by saying, even as he shivers in the chilly water, 'I'll be clean! And I'll feel warm **all** day by comparison' (p. 53, v). This is not an assertion comparable with Steinlauf's recognition that 'to survive we must force ourselves to save ... the form of civilization' (Levi, *If This is a Man*, p. 47). At this point, Vladek is not making a statement about dignity or resistance. He is a pragmatist who bathes to stay clean, to avoid frostbite, infection and lice, who 'did gymnastics to keep strong' (p. 54, i). This same pragmatism seems to drive his daily commitment to prayer and religious observance for although he says, 'I was very religious', he also concedes that 'it wasn't else to do' (p. 54, i) and the evidence of his religious observance does not appear before he is in the POW camp. His experience in the POW camp seems to prepare him for his time in Auschwitz so that he learns, or practises, what he already knows, that to 'keep strong' requires determination. The kind of self which Vladek recalls is at odds with the survivor selves Langer identifies in *Holocaust Testimonies*.[4] Vladek never seems to remember a shamed or humiliated self: his recollections of himself are of a resourceful and determined individual, always doing things for the best, making decisions, making choices, acting, rather than being acted upon.[5] Even in Auschwitz, Vladek seems to avoid being made to feel powerless by the presence of 'choiceless choices'; though he says 'it wasn't else to do' he does not mean that he had no choice, he means that, having recognized the need to keep his mind and body active, he took every available opportunity to do so. He never seems to suffer any qualms about his actions. What starts out as pragmatism comes to take a different form, or Vladek begins to express it differently. When volunteers are requested from amongst the Jewish POWs to work on 'labour assignments' many of his fellow prisoners decide to stay where they are, some arguing that, 'If we **have** to die, let's die **here**!' (p. 54, viii). Vladek disagrees and admonishes them, 'I'm not going to die, and I won't die **here**! I want to be treated like a human being!' (p. 54, ix). This is closer to Steinlauf's perceptions, but still the determination to survive which Vladek expresses does not have any testimonial purpose. Vladek is not saying, as Steinlauf does, 'one must want to survive, to tell the story, to bear witness' (*If This is a Man*, p. 47). This discrepancy may be explained by the fact that, though conditions are hard for the Jewish POWs, they are not conscious of a deliberate intention to annihilate them. Yet, even in Auschwitz, when Vladek is aware of the German intentions, his determination to survive is never expressed as a determination 'to tell the story'. Vladek also seems able to accept the losses which he experiences: he displays little emotion as he refers to those POWs who returned to the camp, 'But what happened to them, I don't know' (p. 56, vii), nor to the rabbi who reminds him when the day of Parshas Truma arrives, 'I never heard again from him' (p. 60) and this ability to tolerate loss is even more noticeable in *Maus II*.

When Vladek finally returns to his home in Sosnowiec, there is great joy at the reunion with Anja and Richieu but as they embrace the spotlight reappears behind Anja and Vladek, so that the reader remains fearful for their security (p. 66, iv). This highly charged moment is a precursor of the scene at the end of *Maus II* when Anja and Vladek are reunited after Auschwitz (p. 136, iv) and draws attention to the circularity of these narratives. Spiegelman makes frequent use of repetition in images and emphasizes the form of Vladek's tale so that whilst, in chronological terms, the story remains linear, in psychological terms the feeling of *déjà vu* is constantly being reinforced. Just as the recollections of anger and frustration when he was made to clean out the stables propelled Vladek into the present where Art is dropping ash on the carpet, so it is that the recollected joy of that distant reunion recalls Vladek to his present circumstances. He sits, tired and distressed, missing Anja and wishing she could be with him, believing that she would make life better for him, 'I tell you, if Anja could be alive now, it would be everything different with me!' (p. 67, iii). Art looks at his father but it is impossible to know what he is thinking. Like Vladek, though for different reasons, the reader also longs for Anja. The fracture as Art and Vladek leave the past and return to their present seems to require physical movement. In the first panel, Art is still lying on the floor, where he has been throughout, in a childlike pose which seems to convey a complete engagement with the story his father is narrating. Too big to sit on his knee, this seems to be the next best position for listening to Vladek's tale. But, as soon as Vladek begins to talk about the present, Art shifts. First he adopts a more upright, adult position, then he half kneels but is ready to stand up, finally he stands and walks forward to his father, hand outstretched, staunching the flow of a story he does not wish to hear. This act of refusal, so like his others, is accompanied by Art's familiar complaint in these situations, 'You always tell me the same things' (p. 67, v). Vladek's role is reversed suddenly. No longer the father telling a tale to his enthralled child, he becomes a supplicant as he lifts his hands to Art and begs to be heard, 'But I haven't with whom **else** to talk!' (p. 67, v). Vladek cannot tolerate such an impotent position for long and in the next frame he is pushing himself out of the chair, finger pointing accusingly so that Art lifts his hand in surrender. Vladek wields the only weapon he has: '**And** it's for you I watch out my **money**!' (p. 67, vi) which propels Art towards the door to look for his coat. But his coat is gone. Vladek, in his usual peremptory manner, has thrown it away and offers as a substitute his own coat, first seen in the opening panel of Chapter 1. Art is forced to put it on and, partly because it is too large for him, begins to resemble Vladek. As Art leaves the house, dressed in Vladek's Nauga-hyde windbreaker, the moon is behind him, as it was when he arrived. The confluence of these images, the putting on of Vladek's coat and the appearance of the moon/spotlight is troubling as they seem to suggest that Art is being increasingly influenced by the time spent with his father, he is 'putting on' his father's past and the 'material' Vladek recounts, so that the impact of that past falls to a greater extent upon Art.

The formal structure of each chapter provides a strong underpinning to this narrative, which might otherwise become too diffuse. As Art encourages Vladek's reminiscences, he also has to order them. It is clear, especially from the additional material contained in *The Complete MAUS*,[6] that Vladek is inclined to stray from a purely chronological and linear recounting. Though there are times when Vladek asserts some control over the shape and form of the story, 'Yes. I'll tell you about how it was with him – but now I'm telling here in the prison' (p. 156, vii), there are frequent examples of Art's reordering of Vladek's narrative. Vladek, having talked about the decision not to hide Richieu with another friend's child, goes on to recollect, 'When we were in the ghetto, in 1943, Tosha took all the children to –' (p. 82, i). Art interrupts, '**Wait**! *Please*, Dad. If you don't keep your story chronological, I'll never get it straight . . . Tell me more about 1941 and 1942' (p. 82, i). Vladek, on this occasion, complies, 'So? . . . Okay. I'll make it so how you want it. 1941? . . .' (p. 82, ii). Vladek deals with his memories in a thematic and frequently repetitive manner so that he wants to continue with the story of the children and what happened to them. However, in order to shape the narrative, Art has to impose something more like linear chronology than the natural intermittence and circularity of memory. This suggests that Spiegelman believes that the kind of connections which make sense of his memories for Vladek would not necessarily be legible to others.

Whilst the content of the text is potentially disorienting for the reader as it oscillates between the past and the present which Art and Vladek inhabit, the structure of each chapter is constant, so that each provides a familiar matrix into which Vladek and Art's encounters are slotted. This encourages a comparative approach in the reader which assists in developing the characterizations and strength of the narrative. The reader is easily able to recognize and measure the shifts in the relationships between the characters and especially that between Vladek and Art. The strength of this technique may be illustrated by comparing pp. 11 and 73 (reproduced here at pp. 178 and 179). The content and shape of both pages are very similar. Art arrives at the home of Mala and Vladek, Mala takes his coat, hangs it up, Vladek and Art are about to talk. The repetitive and ritual elements of Art's arrival are emphasized by Spiegelman's use of familiar images. But the relationship between the three has changed from the time of the first visit. The first sign of this is the increase in the number of panels, from six to eight, indicating that there is more 'material' to be conveyed. The small but noticeable sources of tension in p. 11 have matured and realized their potential. So Vladek's 'Oi, Artie. You're late. I was worried' (p. 11, i), spoken with arms outstretched in welcome, has become an accusation **'You're late**!' (p. 73, i), which Vladek speaks with hands on hips, in what is very like a caricature of an angry wife. Other sources of disagreement are brought to the reader's attention as a reminder of the increasing store of difficulties which are building up between the three. Spiegelman's drawing 'points' at the 'wooden hanger' which Mala, having learnt the lesson of p. 11, now uses to hang up Art's coat, and the 'new trench coat' which Art has bought, in defiance of Vladek's attempts to clothe him in his cast-offs. This assertion goes deeper than a refusal to be dressed like a child to suit the father, and seems symptomatic of a struggle Art is conducting not only with Vladek but also with Vladek's 'material'. The struggle between Art and Vladek is becoming polarized, developing explicit demands and areas of conflict. Art has come as late as suits him, and has not arrived in time for dinner. Any pretence about socializing has been done away with, there is no suggestion that Françoise will accompany Art; Art is visiting Vladek in order to get the story. But Vladek, apparently prepared to give up the dinner, already identified as a source of conflict (p. 43), is not prepared to concede the potential for usefulness which Art represents. This is the first occasion when Vladek makes a specific demand of Art; he wants Art's visit to bestow a tangible benefit. Clearly, for Vladek, telling his story to Art is not beneficial, or he does not count it so, and there must be an almost monetary reciprocity in the transaction. Art is required to pay for the story somehow and Vladek increasingly expects Art to perform practical 'fixing' tasks around the house. The matter of money and Vladek's 'carefulness' in relation to it, are also signalled here; again, these become increasingly potent sources of disagreement and discomfort between the three. The old discrepancies between what Vladek expects of Art and what Art is able or willing to deliver are more visible with each meeting. Vladek wants a son who will be a 'fixer' like himself; Art admits, with something like pride, 'I'm no good at fixing that kind of stuff' (p. 73, iii); he has managed to refuse a part of Vladek's legacy. In this context, being able to say to Vladek 'If you want, I'll pay for the handyman' (p. 73, v) is indisputable evidence of Art's status as an independent adult and another aspect to Art's defiant difference; he knows that his father can afford to pay but that the point, for Vladek, is to get the job done without anyone paying.[7] Art and Vladek are about to continue with the story when Vladek notices Art's new tape recorder and cannot avoid asking, 'So, how much you paid?' (p. 73, vii). Art is pleased with himself; he has a bargain and can show to his father more evidence of his maturity. But Vladek cannot allow this and has to undermine Art's achievement, 'Pssh, at **Korvettes** you could find it for – maximum – $35.00' (p. 73, viii). Art almost falls into the trap and is about to remonstrate with Vladek when he realizes that he is embarked upon a pointless and unwinnable debate, though one which Vladek would be delighted to conduct.

This medium significantly affects the way the reader reads; it demands that the reader develop a relationship with each page that is interactive and encourages a tendency to cross-refer and to make comparisons that is more pronounced than where there are no images and only words. These techniques also allow the related medium of film to be referred to or implied. This is very apparent on p. 74 (reproduced here at p. 180). The top half of the page is composed of one image. The observer looks in through the window of a room and sees Anja's family at dinner. This is so like a frame from a film that the reader imbues the view with liveliness, animating the drawing to a remarkable degree. The view 'zooms' in and picks out the individuals who sit around the table and they are held for an instant in 'freeze frame'. It is as though the family has been made motionless for the purpose of the explanations and introductions which Vladek is making but that they will start to move again at any moment. The poignancy of this is intense; of those seated around the table, only Vladek, Anja and Lolek survive. They are only frozen for a moment in time whilst Vladek explains to Art who they are; on the following page each person continues upon his or her intended course of action. So Anja's mother takes the book from Lolek who is reading at the table; Richieu tips up his plate and is smacked by Anja; Lonia takes her place at the table. The reader's point of view, quite distant in the half-page frame perhaps to match Vladek's own distance from the event in terms of time, draws closer. Vladek is framed at the top left of the larger scene; he is describing it but not a part of it. At the end of the page Vladek, still on his bike, has a larger presence in relation to the events he depicts; perhaps this exemplifies his re-entry into that time via the medium of memory. Vladek's presence at the beginning and end of the page acts as a boundary; the events that are being described are contained in Vladek's memory. Later in *Maus I*, there is a terrible echo of this scene where the reader looks in through a window. The final frame of p. 115 depicts Anja's father standing at the window of the building where the family have been imprisoned. Anja, Lolek and Vladek have already escaped by bribing Vladek's cousin, Haskel, but Anja's parents are too old to get past the guards and though Haskel accepts their jewels, he makes no attempt to save them. As the vans arrive which will take the Zylberbergs to Auschwitz, Anja's father is depicted standing at the window, his hands held up, his mouth open in what looks like a cry of despair. Vladek stands here too, alongside this frame, just as he appears alongside the final frame of p. 74. The point of view which allows the reader to look up at the window to see Anja's father is also his: 'Anja and I saw her father at the window. He was tearing his hair and crying' (p. 115, vi). Some of Vladek's seeming dispassion is conveyed by his physical 'separation' from the image; this separation is reinforced by his words, 'He was a millionaire, but even this didn't save him his life' (p. 115, vi).[8]

As *Maus I* approaches its close, Spiegelman depicts a series of unendings. Anja and Vladek find themselves increasingly marginalized as they face an extremely precarious existence. They survive each dangerous incident through a combination of luck, Vladek's resourcefulness, and outside help. Around them friends and family disappear; again and again Anja and Vladek escape the narrative that leads others to Auschwitz. Often they have nowhere to hide (p. 125, v) or are refused assistance (p. 136, iv) and Anja is driven to articulate her sense of 'this is the end' a number of times (pp. 122, 143, viii), but until they enter the gates at Auschwitz, Vladek resolutely refuses the end which seems to be approaching them. Narrative tension increases as Spiegelman represents these unendings, any of which could have had a significantly different outcome, and as the impossibility of Anja and Vladek's survival becomes more apparent. As the narrative approaches the moment of the Spiegelmans' entry into Auschwitz, fact and fiction collide. The plot's 'cliff-hangers' and dilemmas, staple ingredients of any adventure story, add to the fictional quality of the text; the paradox of *Maus* is that these apparently fantastic events actually happened.

Inexorably, and in spite of the many escapes and avoidances, the narrative and Spiegelman approach Auschwitz. This is a cliff-hanger of massive proportions, for Anja and Vladek enter Auschwitz just as *Maus I* ends. The enormity of their arrival is represented visually as Auschwitz overwhelms the framing techniques of Spiegelman's format (p. 157; reproduced here at p. 172). The largest panel in either *Maus I* or *II*, and too large to be contained, Spiegelman's representation of Auschwitz's infamous gates spills out across a whole page and it is apparent from the absence of page margins that Auschwitz has burst the boundaries of the page. This escape from the confines of text and image dramatizes the extent to which the Holocaust does not obey formal rules and allows Spiegelman to go some way towards representing the unrepresentable. Vladek's recital of his story is proof that he lived, yet the reader is left with an acute sense of anxiety; the certain knowledge that Vladek and Anja survived is not sufficient to offset the usual meaning of Auschwitz, which is non-survival. Vladek recognizes this too; he articulates his own belief in his death as he enters the gates of Auschwitz, 'And we came here to the concentration camp Auschwitz, and we knew that from here we will not come out anymore ...' (p. 157). This almost biblical assertion of The End is entirely consonant with the reader's perceptions, so that it is possible to believe that Vladek and Anja did not 'come out anymore'.

In the face of that potential for ending, to turn the page and be reminded of Vladek's continued existence is shocking. Vladek and Art sit safely in the garden; of the two, Vladek appears to be the least troubled by what he has just 'witnessed'. Art seems exhausted by the experience of hearing about and visualizing his parents' arrival at Auschwitz, and this is one of the rare occasions when he responds with an expression of emotion to what Vladek has been telling him as he comments, 'My God' (p. 158, i). This might have heralded a moment when Art and Vladek could, at last, have shared a degree of mutual understanding and sympathy. Vladek seems frail and vulnerable and Art looks at him (p. 158, iv) with something like affection. But the moment is lost; Art returns to the subject of Anja's lost diaries, which increasingly represent for him something other and more than Vladek's reminiscences. Art has imbued Anja's diaries with an aura of near-sanctity; for him they hold out the hope of an answer or resolution which otherwise eludes him. He speaks pragmatically about them, 'This is where Mom's diaries will be **especially** useful. They'll give me some idea of what she went through while you were apart' (p. 158, iv) but it is clear that the diaries will be much more than 'useful' to Art; they represent Anja herself and will connect him with her in a way that escapes Vladek's mediation. Vladek, solipsistic as ever, cannot acknowledge the real meaning of Art's need for the diaries and believes that he is capable of telling Anja's story satisfactorily, 'I can tell you ... she went through the same what me: **terrible**!' (p. 158, iv). Art's passionate need for the diaries becomes so urgent that he is no longer able to wait for them and he suggests that he and Vladek should look for them immediately. At last Vladek has to admit that they no longer exist, 'These notebooks, and other really nice things of mother ... one time I had a very bad day ... and all of these things I **destroyed**' (p. 158, viii). Art's shock is registered visually; his cigarette falls from his mouth and he looks, for the space of two frames (p. 159, i, ii), as though he might faint. He clutches his head and speaks at first with astonishment and then with increasing anger until he curses Vladek, 'God **damn** you! You – you murderer! How the hell could you do such a thing!!' (p. 159, iv). His speech balloon also represents the intensity of the negative emotion he directs against Vladek, like those used elsewhere as Poles or Germans denounce, threaten or insult Jews (p. 136, iii; p. 137, ii; *Maus II*, p. 25, vii) its edges are spiked rather than smooth.

The proximity of the two events, Vladek's story's arrival at Auschwitz and the discovery that Anja's notebooks are no longer in existence, seems to draw together all of the potential for Art's conflicting emotions in relation to his parents' experience. The expectation that he might feel gentler or more forgiving towards Vladek at this point in the narrative has been entirely confounded and instead Art expresses a fury and anger which is at odds with his quiet, tired response to Auschwitz. To curse Vladek and to call him a murderer for burning notebooks within minutes of having been visualizing Auschwitz and its unique capacity for murder seems out of all proportion and there is an echo here of Vladek's unwarranted anger with Art for dropping cigarette ash (p. 52). For the reader, the proximity of the two events serves to distinguish between expected and unexpected outcomes. The arrival of Anja and Vladek at Auschwitz is not unexpected; it is remarkable that they avoided that end for so long. The destruction of Anja's notebooks is, and the reader is able to experience something like Art's acute disappointment; Anja's diaries were something to hope for and it is clear that it was not only Art who imbued them with a special significance. Art calls Vladek a 'murderer' because, by the end of *Maus I*, Anja and her story have become one.

Maus I ends as it began, with a reference to friends. Vladek is not silenced or shamed by Art's anger, instead he points out the impropriety of Art's outburst and chastises Art like a child, 'To your **father** you yell in this way? . . . even to your **friends** you should never yell this way!' (p. 159, v). Yet Vladek has been telling Art a story in which the meaning of words like 'family' and 'friends' was utterly changed, 'At that time it **wasn't** anymore families. It was everybody to take care for **himself**!' (p. 114). As Vladek has said in the Prologue, '**Friends**? Your friends? . . . If you lock them together in a room with no food for a week . . . **Then** you could see what it is, friends! . . . ' (p. 6).

MAUS II: 'MORE I DON'T NEED TO TELL YOU'

The shift in perspective which *Maus II* represents dramatizes the potential for a significant change to the memory of the offence. In this text, it is not only Vladek's past which is being narrated; increasingly Art is compelled to examine his own relationship with Vladek's story. Art's ambivalent responses to his parents' past and the impact upon him of being the child of survivors impinge more insistently in this text than in *Maus I*, whilst the difficulties Art faces in relating to, as well as relating, his father's tale become more urgent. The memory of the offence has entered a new phase, one in which it is non-survivors and especially the children of survivors, who are, or feel themselves to be, increasingly responsible for the carriage and transmission of survivor stories.

Art's relationship with Vladek, Anja and the Holocaust comes into clearer focus in *Maus II*. Art is more visible and voluble than in *Maus I*, perhaps reflecting Spiegelman's growing need to give form and voice to the internal dialogue which takes place as he investigates his own part of the story. And, although the reader has been aware from *Maus*

I, especially in 'The Prisoner from Hell Planet' episode (pp. 100–3), that Art is not unscathed by his parents' story, his distress is more apparent and more vehemently expressed in *Maus II*. This change and sense of increasing urgency may have been provoked by the fact that, though Spiegelman continues to depict Art visiting his father and transcribing his story, Vladek is dead by the time *Maus II* is being drawn. And, in *Maus II*, Spiegelman/Art also knows that Anja's story is lost, destroyed by Vladek in his vain attempts to escape the painful memories of the past.

There is greater access to Art's and Françoise's story in *Maus II*; other characters also become significant and, although this does not mitigate Art's sense of claustrophobia, it demonstrates the way in which Vladek's story is moving out into the world, touching more and more people, becoming less enclosed and self-contained than in *Maus I*. This movement may reflect the changing response and increasing willingness to listen to survivor testimony which have been evident in the last 20 or 25 years, and it certainly reflects the critical attention which *Maus I* had already received. The story moves inexorably closer to the 'present' which the reader inhabits and as Art tells his father's story, he tells more of his own story so that details of Art's life accumulate. This leakage from the texts into the world outside them seems more pronounced in *Maus II* than in *Maus I* as it becomes increasingly difficult to contain or to own this material. Seeing into Art's life also raises a query about the amount of time and energy that Art expends upon Vladek's story. What becomes clear in *Maus II* is that in many respects, Art has no alternative, he is compelled to tell Vladek's story with something like a survivor's compulsion. Whereas in *Maus I*, it is possible to form a view that Art's relationship with Vladek's story is as controlled as his relationship with Vladek himself, such a view is not sustainable on reading *Maus II*. Vladek's story is with Art all the time, it has become Art's story too.[9]

Maus II opens with Art's recollections and remembrances, his discussions with Françoise, his 'presumption' and feelings of inadequacy about trying to 'make any sense out of Auschwitz' (p. 14, vi), his guilt and confusion about his parents' ordeal, the troubled relationship he has with his dead brother Richieu, his own nightmares as a child about the SS, the impossibility of representing the Holocaust adequately. Chapter 1 begins with Françoise and Art debating which animal Art should use to represent Françoise. Françoise insists that it should be a mouse, Art is concerned because this does not adequately represent her Frenchness, and he has been drawing her as a moose, a

poodle, a frog or a rabbit. The discussion between them ends abruptly
when the friend with whom they are staying comes to report that
Vladek has had a heart attack and Art must ring him immediately. But
Vladek is not ill; he is simply guaranteeing that Art will ring as Mala
has left and he needs Art and Françoise to visit. Spiegelman uses their
journey to be with Vladek as an opportunity to examine a number of
essential elements in Art's perceptions of himself as he ponders the
nature of his relationships with his parents, Richieu, and the
Holocaust.

As Art talks to Françoise, he articulates many of the frequently
expressed concerns of survivors' children, and pp. 14, 15 and 16
provide the lengthiest and most focused depiction of Art's
preoccupations yet encountered. The drive begins with Art expressing
his ambivalent relationship with Vladek. On the one hand he can agree
with Françoise when she says, 'Poor guy ... I feel so sorry for him'
(p. 14, ii). But his agreement is qualified, 'Yeah, me too ... 'til I have to
spend any time with him – then he drives me **crazy**!' (p. 14, iii). This
statement is immediately followed by a frame in which the reader is
able to look straight into the car. Françoise drives, her attention on the
road ahead, whilst Art sits, head down, silent apart from a sigh. There
is no way of knowing how long they drive in silence before Françoise
asks, 'Depressed again?' (p. 14, v). Her question provokes a speech
from Art about the book he is working on. He is clearly very troubled
by the implications of the project: 'It's so **presumptuous** of me. I mean,
I can't even make any sense out of my relationship with my father...
How am I supposed to make any sense out of **Auschwitz**? ... of the
Holocaust? ...' (p. 14, v and vi). This thought about the difficulty of
making sense leads Art to disclose the kind of concerns he had as a
child: 'When I was a kid I used to think about which of my parents I'd
let the Nazis take to the ovens if I could only save one of them ...
Usually I saved my mother. Do you think that's normal?' (p. 14, vii and
viii). Françoise's answer, '**Nobody's** normal' (p. 14, viii), is not entirely
satisfactory. Whilst it properly acknowledges the absence of objective
measures of 'normality' it does not give due weight to the quite
different experience of childhood to which survivors' children were
exposed.[10] It flattens out that experience and seems to suggest that the
concerns of survivors' children are common to all children, that they
are not at all inflected by the Shoah. Art's statement, 'usually I saved
my mother' (p. 14) is much more like a confession; it is as though he is
seeking approval for having made an impossible decision and this
moment emphasizes the way in which survivors' children, like their

parents, also know the concept of choiceless choices, even if only theoretically. Art's confession is not surprising; in *Maus I*, it has been made clear that Anja was the more significant parent. Nor is Art's troubled relationship with his dead brother, Richieu, surprising: the presence of a perfect child, a '**ghost**-brother' who 'never threw tantrums or got in any kind of trouble ... an ideal kid' (p. 15, vi) would be a difficult sibling with whom to compete. Art knew the extent to which his parents had gone in their hope that Richieu had survived, 'After the war my parents traced down the vaguest rumors, and went to orphanages all over Europe. They couldn't believe he was dead' (p. 15, iii). Richieu dead was always potentially more valuable than Art alive, or at least, that was what the child Art understood. This perception, that aliveness represents a particular kind of inadequacy, reflects another constant theme in survivor testimony, the view that 'the best all died'. Art's relationship with the photograph of his absent brother operated as 'a kind of reproach'; though Anja and Vladek 'didn't **talk** about Richieu' (p. 15, vii) their silence spoke more loudly of their loss and massive disappointment. Art is left with the hardest tasks: not only has he had to compete with a flawless sibling, he also has to deal with Vladek.

Art tells Françoise too about his nightmares of persecution and his imaginings about 'Zyklon B coming out of our shower instead of water' (p. 16, ii). Though he asserts, 'I wasn't **obsessed** with this stuff ...' (p. 16, ii), as he talks the reader builds up a picture of the Holocaust acting as a constant point of reference in the young Art's psychological terrain. The sense of having been excluded from an experience of unusual proportions results in what seems to be a bizarre wish, 'I know this is insane, but I somehow wish I had been in Auschwitz **with** my parents so I could really know what they lived through!' (p. 16, iii). The fulfilment of such a wish would not have had the desired outcome: if Art had been in Auschwitz, the likelihood is that he would not have survived. Whilst Art does not recognize any sense of guilt in relation to Richieu, he does in relation to Anja and Vladek. Part of the wish to have been in Auschwitz is concerned with neutralizing the 'guilt about having had an easier life than they did' (p. 16, iii). The bottom half of this page is devoted to an expression of Art's almost overwhelming sense of incapacity in the face of the Holocaust. The task he has set himself seems impossible.

Art's conclusion, 'Reality is too **complex** for comics ... so much has to be left out or distorted' (p. 16, vi), is true for any representation of Holocaust reality, and Spiegelman expresses through Art the recurrent dilemma for writers and artists when faced with 'a reality that was worse than my darkest dreams' (p. 16, iv). Art's dilemmas about representation are presented to the reader just before he draws the scenes in Auschwitz. It is as though he knows what he is about to face and represent, and that knowledge provokes disturbance in him. In some respects the actual, physical drawing of Auschwitz will be the first time that Art has apprehended this material and expressed it in this particular and, for him, highly significant mode. Spiegelman's disturbance is made available to the reader; he does not ignore the implications of what he is doing, and this struggle with the medium and the project help to keep the outcome honest. Of course, Spiegelman will have managed and shaped this material; the proximity of his qualms to the representations of Auschwitz may be fictional. It is not necessarily the case that he really experienced these qualms just before he spoke to Vladek about Auschwitz. It seems more likely that his qualms will have surfaced at different times throughout the project and been more or less dismaying. Spiegelman neatly reminds the reader that what he or she is encountering is not necessarily the way Spiegelman encountered his father's story. As Art comes to his conclusions about the impossibility of adequate representation, Françoise says, 'Just keep it honest, honey' (p. 16, vi). Art replies, 'See what I mean ... in real life you'd **never** have let me talk this long without interrupting' (p. 16, vii). Spiegelman's willingness to undermine his own and Art's narrative authority is beneficial as it signals the possibilities for manipulation that exist in relation to the shaping of any story.

Once with Vladek in the Catskills, Art seems to need to reinforce his difference and separateness from Vladek. Vladek is very tidy; Art is not. Vladek puts a great deal of effort into keeping well by exercising, eating a healthy diet, monitoring the drugs and supplements he takes; Art smokes, drinks lots of strong coffee, takes no exercise. Vladek has a very intricate relationship with objects and possessions; he becomes angry when Art uses wooden matches because he has worked out how many are needed and his carefulness borders on the obsessive (p. 20). Françoise discovers that, as gas is included in his rent and in order to save matches, Vladek leaves a gas burner lit all the time. Françoise observes, 'It's so **claustrophobic** being around Vladek. He straightens everything you touch – he's so **anxious**' (p. 22). Yet Vladek's perception is that it is Art who is the troubled one, 'Always Artie is nervous – so like his mother – she also was **nervous**' (p. 20, viii). Françoise wonders, 'Maybe Auschwitz made [Vladek] like that', but Art asserts what Mala also repeats, 'Maybe. But lots of people up here are survivors … if they're whacked up it's in a **different** way from Vladek' (p. 22, vi). Vladek is always very aware of his physical needs, 'For my legs I could **use** now that we walk a little' (p. 23, viii). This is perhaps not so different from many people, survivors or not, but almost everything Vladek says or does is couched in these solipsistic terms. He does not say that it would please him to walk with Art, nor does he accept Françoise's offer to check his accounts very graciously. And Art, in spite of his insistence upon their differences, displays similar attributes. He agrees reluctantly to walk with Vladek and gets his tape recorder so that 'today isn't a **total** loss' (p. 23).

Spiegelman represents Art's dilemma in marrying his own and Vladek's conflicting demands. Vladek needs to have Art (and Françoise) with him and he makes assumptions about their willingness to put aside their own plans for his sake; he expects them to remain on holiday then to move in with him when he returns to New York. Art needs to perform a balancing act: to keep a distance from Vladek who would subsume him entirely, whilst remaining close enough to get the story. Having refused to stay with Vladek in Queen's, Art is necessarily hesitant when he broaches the question, 'Um – can I ask you more about your past . . . about **Auschwitz**?' (p. 24, vii). Art is not really interested in Vladek's past in its entirety but only in that part of the past which has come to have meaning for Art. Vladek's wholehearted and warm response, 'Of course, darling. To me you can ask **anything**!' (p. 24, vii), is at odds with Art's wariness. Having brought up the subject of Auschwitz, Art also refers to Anja though his reference explicitly calls up her absence, 'What happened when you and Mom arrived there and were separated?' (p. 24, viii). As Art poses these questions, Spiegelman depicts him holding a large microphone between himself and Vladek. This act keeps Vladek at a distance and is echoed later in the frames on page 42 when Art is himself besieged by questions from reporters and journalists. Possibly Spiegelman is signalling his recognition of or discomfort with his own approach to Vladek and his appropriation of Vladek's story, and he may be aware that Vladek found his questions intrusive or troubling. Vladek describes their arrival in Auschwitz, but then asserts, '**Never** Anja and I were separated!' (p. 25, i). He is querying Art's use of the word 'separated' which Vladek applies to his estrangement from Mala and in doing so draws a distinction between the fact that though he and Anja were set apart in Auschwitz, they were still 'together'. Art's attempts to get back to Auschwitz are often threatened by Vladek's

preoccupation with the present and the mention of Anja reminds
Vladek of his problems with Mala, causing him to draw unfavourable
comparisons. Art's insistence upon 'Auschwitz, Pop. Tell me about
Auschwitz' (p. 25, iii) begins to take on unpleasant aspects as the reader
witnesses Vladek's need to talk about his present dilemmas and Art's
refusal to permit that need to be satisfied. Spiegelman allows the reader
to draw an analogy here between Art's interview technique and that of
the journalists.

Vladek's description of Auschwitz mirrors that of most survivors'
recollections: there are the dealing and strategies, his good fortune, the
skills which made him valuable and saved his life, the selections, the
hanging of the conspirators, the dreams of food. This is a feature of
survivors' stories; the material overlaps, they provide corroboration for
one another, whilst each set of memories adds, uniquely, to the overall
picture. Vladek describes 'the demolition of a man' in precisely the
same terms used by Levi: 'They took from us our papers, our clothes,
and our hair' (p. 25, vi); 'they took from us our names' (p. 26, vi).
Unlike Levi, Vladek does not record the dream of telling his story for
it is Spiegelman/Art who 'draws' the story out of him rather than
Vladek who volunteers it. As Vladek enters Auschwitz the strength
and flexibility of this form of representation becomes apparent. Visual
representations of these events are always problematic and open to
criticism. It is difficult to divorce the pleasures of looking and seeing
from the material that is being shown, and reconstructions run the risk
of offending the viewer or of making the spectator into a voyeur.
Spiegelman's images enable the reader to visualize what was happening
whilst avoiding such dangers, for these images demand a different kind
of work and involvement. It is also helpful that the reader has
witnessed Art having qualms about what he is doing and has been
alerted to the potential for offence and the dangers of impropriety
connected with representing Auschwitz.

Auschwitz is terribly present from the moment of Vladek's arrival
and the medium allows the reader to 'witness' key elements in the
processing of the Jews. They arrive (p. 25, v), are stripped (p. 25, vi),
sent into showers (p. 26, i), and tattooed (p. 26, v). Vladek meets
Abraham again and as Abraham rushes up to Vladek, the reader is
conscious of a tiny, featureless figure calling 'Uncle' (p. 27, i) across a
desolate and brutal expanse (reproduced here at p. 181). This sense of
the vastness and ruthlessness of Auschwitz is reinforced in frame vi.
Abraham has just finished explaining that he was forced to write the
postcard which tricked his uncle into believing that he was safe in

Hungary. The tiny mice figures clustered at the bottom of the frame are indistinguishable from one another, only the German cats can be identified as they raise their batons to lash out at the mice. The group which is composed of Vladek, Abraham and Mandelbaum are at the back of the crowd and their features have disappeared completely; they are represented as almost-shapeless black figures. Their voices are the only indicators of their presence, but their speech balloons are placed at the top of the frame, as though even this mark of identity is vulnerable. The scene is dominated by the buildings which hem them in, and by the chimney in the distance. The smoke which rises out of the chimney is the antithesis of the speech balloons and the silencing power of that smoke is reinforced by the words of Vladek's group, 'Well . . . so here's our Hungary . . .' 'And there's only one way out of here for all of us . . . through those chimneys' (p. 27, vi). In the 'present', Vladek confirms Abraham's words, 'Abraham I didn't see again . . . I think he came out the chimney' (p. 27, vi). The terrible effect of Auschwitz and its chimneys is not contained in the past but also taints the present. In the next frame (vii), Spiegelman depicts Vladek telling Art that the Poles who had tricked him and Mandelbaum 'finished also in Auschwitz' (p. 27, vii). Neither Vladek nor Art look quite like themselves, their bodies are blackened and featureless; though they are still recognizable, they have some of the characteristics of the mice (p. 26, v) who stand in line waiting for their tattoos.

As with Levi, knowledge aids Vladek's survival. By teaching English to the Kapo, Vladek is able to help himself and exerts his influence to save Mandelbaum. Vladek keeps him close by during the selections (p. 32, i); gets him a belt, a spoon and a pair of shoes (p. 33). Vladek too recognizes the power of the name, 'Everyone they called by number but me, [the Kapo] called by name' (p. 32, ii). His name plus food, clothing and status reconstitute Vladek, 'Always I was handsome . . . but with everything fitted, I looked like a million!' (p. 33). This does not seem to be an attempt at satire; Vladek was really able to see himself looking good even in Auschwitz, though as he stands proudly displaying his properly fitting uniform and leather shoes, he cannot escape the spotlight (p. 33, v). In spite of Vladek's aid, Mandelbaum does not survive, 'How long I could, I kept him. But a few days later the Germans chose him to take away to work . . . **Nobody** could help this. So. It was finished with Mandelbaum. I never saw him more again' (p. 34, viii). There is no suggestion that Vladek feels guilty about his impotence in the face of these events. He seems to have accepted that he did what he could: 'nobody' could have done more and there is a fatalistic element to his use of the word 'so' which also has a sense of 'thus', as though in Auschwitz certain equations were bound to have certain conclusions. Vladek's acceptance of loss seems to be almost calm and he shows little distress in what becomes a familiar refrain, 'Abraham I didn't see again' (p. 27, vi); 'I never saw him again' (p. 28, ix); 'I never saw him more again' (p. 34, viii).

Vladek not only remembers those events which happened, he recollects events as they might have happened. When he tells Art about Mandelbaum, he refers to a number of possible deaths; Spiegelman draws one of them (p. 35, ii and iii), but the rest are described solely in Vladek's words (p. 35, iv and v). This recollection of another's end reminds Vladek of his own state of mind at the time, 'And I had it still **happy** there. For **me** it was not yet the end' (p. 35, v). Vladek describes his ability in Auschwitz to take advantage of any opportunity to save himself and his willingness to attempt anything which might work to preserve him longer. His survival in Auschwitz rests on being very practical and therefore useful to the regime. Even as Vladek is describing himself and his abilities in the past, the reader is shown evidence of these traits in the present. As he and Art walk along, Vladek suddenly slips into 'The Pines' which is for 'guests only' (p. 36, vi), where he takes advantage of the benefits intended for guests. Vladek does not obey rules, unless they are to his advantage. Once inside 'The Pines', Vladek begins triumphantly to describe his past escapades at the hotel and in particular the story of an occasion when he won at bingo. Unable to claim the prize himself and unwilling to disclose his non-resident status, Vladek turned the incident to his advantage. By giving his winning ticket to a real resident he was able simultaneously to appear magnanimous and avoid any embarrassment.

Art allows Vladek his head with this story and, perhaps because he is taking the time to 'put in a new tape' (p. 37, iv), does not cut it short as quickly as usual. Buried in this scene at 'The Pines', and almost lost in it, is an allusion to Art's one constant concern, which is his mother's story. As Vladek begins to tell Art about tin-smithing, Art interrupts with 'Uh-huh. You told me. What I wanted to ask you about though, is what happened to Mom while you ...' (p. 36, v). But Art is interrupted in turn by Vladek's dash into 'The Pines'. There is a suggestion that this is the story Art had intended to get out of Vladek when he first asked about his separation from Anja at Auschwitz (p. 24) and that Art has been waiting since then to bring Vladek back to this matter. Both he and Vladek become committed to telling and hearing the story of Vladek in Auschwitz, although when Art says, 'You told me' (p. 36, v) it is not clear whether he is referring to all Vladek's experiences in Auschwitz or to the final part about the tin-smithing.

The opening pages of Chapter 2 (pp. 41–6) recapitulate the themes of Chapter 1 though, whilst they mirror and repeat Art's concerns, they achieve a greater depth and are more revealing of Art's distress as he struggles to assimilate conflicting views and emotions. These pages encapsulate and represent many of the responses to the Holocaust experienced by non-survivors. The dilemmas Art faces are provoked by his layered identity as the child of survivors, a Jew, and an artist trying to represent the Holocaust.

As the child of survivors and the brother of a victim, Art's proximity to the memory of the offence is as close as can be without his actually having lived through the Shoah. Art has experience of a range of losses. He never knew his grandparents; his wider family are few and dispersed; his mother committed suicide when he was 20 years old; his father's personality traits have been exaggerated by his experiences; his brother died in the Holocaust.

Art's Jewishness presents him with other dilemmas. It is not as seamlessly a part of himself as it is for Vladek, Anja and the Polish Jews represented in *Maus I*. The mouse-mask Art wears is very clearly a mask (p. 41, i), and behind the mask is a man with a man's ears, hair and unshaven appearance. Whenever masks are put on in *Maus I*, for example when Vladek talks about deceiving the train guard, he masquerades as a Pole (*I*, p. 64).[11] Yet, though he puts on a pig-mask, Vladek remains a mouse behind the mask. The appearance of human features in Spiegelman's representation of Art is surprising and it continues to be a noticeable element of his images of Americans. These characters are often identifiably human and their masks sit on top of their common humanity to confer additional characteristics and identities which they present, apparently unproblematically, to the world. This representation suggests that there is a tolerance of diversity in postwar America which was not present in prewar eastern Europe. In each of the images on page 42, Spiegelman represents these characters as people first; their masks act as representations of their points of view and allegiances. They are human, though with dog, cat or mouse-like propensities.

As an artist representing the Holocaust, Art faces the dilemmas of any individual working with this 'material' and Spiegelman depicts Art querying the propriety of what he is doing, perhaps voicing his own dilemmas through Art. The effectiveness, significance and outcome of Art's creative life and work are all queried and tested when set alongside the Holocaust. It is highly significant that even Spiegelman, whose 'credentials' would not seem to be open to any viable challenge or criticism seems to be fretting about the nature and extent of his rights in relation to Vladek's story.

The chapter's title page opens with an horrific example of this medium's attempts to represent the unrepresentable. Under the words 'Auschwitz (time flies)', naked, skeletal mice, their mouths wide open in silent screams (a repetition of *Maus I*, p. 115, vi) are being consumed by flames. The phrase 'time flies' is problematic; it begs its usual (British) conclusion, 'when you're having fun'. This image sits centrally on a white page which is bare except for the words, 'Chapter Two' and the presence of six flies which seem to be escaping the flames.

These flies reappear on the following page (41; reproduced here at p. 182). Art sits at a drawing board. Two or three flies buzz around him. Frames i and ii depict Art's head and shoulders, part of the board and his hand drawing. As the focus pulls back, more of Art is revealed (*II*, p. 41, iii and iv); he sits hunched over the board, an image of dejection or weariness. The flies still buzz around and their meaning is not immediately apparent; they could easily be an unproblematic sign of a hot summer's day. Their significance is revealed in the last frame which fills the lower half of the page.

Art is still hunched, head down on the drawing board as he speaks, 'Lately I've been feeling depressed' (p. 41, v). At his feet and threatening to inundate the drawing board and Art is a mass of skeletal mice corpses. The bodies lie where they have been thrown, stretched out or twisted in their final death throes and the presence of the flies is explained. Art's words come at the end of a litany composed of significant dates and events so that a correlation between the litany and his depression is suggested. The dates and events he recites are both joyful and sad but it seems as if their consequences are all the same to Art. His relationship with the mound of corpses qualifies the pleasure he could feel about the imminence of his first child's birth, especially as he makes an explicit connection between, 'In May 1987 Françoise and I are expecting a baby' and, 'Between May 16, 1944, and May 24, 1944 over 100,000 Hungarian Jews were gassed in Auschwitz' (p. 41, iii); the massive incompetence of one fact to mitigate the other is palpable.

Similarly, Art's recollection that 'Vladek started working as a tinman in Auschwitz in the spring of 1944', provokes, then problematizes, Art's reference to his own work and the very notion of 'work' itself, 'I started working on this page at the very end of February 1987' (p. 41, ii). Art's work has achieved 'critical and commercial success' (p. 41, iv) with 'At least fifteen foreign editions [and] four serious offers to turn my book into a T.V. special or movie' (p. 41, v), but there is the implication of an adverse criticism of the worth of this 'work' when compared with Vladek's. Art's success is also tainted by his statement that, 'In May 1968 my mother killed herself. (She left no note.)' (p. 41, v). The fact of his mother's suicide, more than any of the other facts he recites, seems most closely related to his state of mind, 'Lately I've been feeling depressed', and Art later acknowledges to his therapist, Pavel, that although 'things couldn't be going better with my "career" or at home ... mostly I feel like crying' (p. 43, vi).

The reader assumes that he or she is witnessing Art's solitary distress, that, apart from the reader's presence, he is alone with his anxieties. But in the final frame a disembodied voice appears, coming from a speaker who is outside the frame and therefore possibly outside or divorced from the text. The voice says, 'Alright Mr. Spiegelman ... We're ready to shoot! ...' (p. 41). In this context, 'shoot' is not a neutral verb, especially as the voice balloon hangs over the pile of corpses. The voice's jaunty indifference to Art's revelation about his feelings of depression and the causes which might be underlying or provoking that pain is reinforced on the following page, as journalists and TV reporters clamber over the bodies, ignoring what it is that they are standing upon, in order to get to Art (reproduced here at p. 183). They pose a representative set of typically clichéd questions: 'Tell our viewers what message you want them to get from your book?'; 'Why should **they** [young Germans] feel guilty?'; 'If your book was about **Israeli** Jews what kind of animal would you draw?' (p. 42, i, iii, v).

Art responds as well as he is able to in this intimidating setting, though all his answers speak of an incapacity to answer, 'A message? I dunno ...'; 'Who am I to say? ...'; 'I have no idea ... porcupines?' (p. 42, i, iii, v). He displays growing bewilderment and a sense of harassment is evident from his facial expressions. As the frames progress Art becomes smaller, as though the questions are attacking and diminishing him. In the penultimate frame an agent who is negotiating 'a licensing deal' for a Maus vest takes Art's reluctance as a sign that Art is merely attempting to drive a hard bargain and responds, 'So, whaddya **want** – a bigger percentage? Hey, we can talk' (p. 42, vii). His question is the final straw for Art's already compromised sense of security, 'I want ... **absolution**. No ... No ... I want ... I want ... my **Mommy**!' (p. 42, vii). Art sits in his chair, now no bigger than a toddler. The reporters are not put off by his distress; instead they draw closer, greedily recording his responses. One takes advantage of this moment to try out a different approach to the *Maus* story and asks, 'Could you tell our audience if drawing *Maus* was cathartic? Do you feel better now?' (p. 42, viii). Art's reaction to this is to lapse into incoherence as he wails at the top of his voice. This pseudo-psychoanalytic approach is revealed as trite and insulting when it is contrasted with Art's visit to Pavel on the facing page (p. 43, reproduced here at p. 184). Once the journalists have left, the childlike Art clambers down from his chair. His fragility and need for protection are expressed visually in the representation of him as an infant and reinforced by his words, 'I can't believe I'm gonna be a father in a couple of months. My father's ghost still hangs over me' (p. 43, ii). In an aside to this speech, Spiegelman records the birth of his daughter, 'Nadja Mouly Spiegelman. Born 5/13/87'.[12]

Art's studio is not only full of corpses but the view from his window is of watch-towers and barbed wire (p. 43, iii). Even when he leaves the studio for his visit to Pavel, he cannot leave the Holocaust behind. The streets are littered with corpses; the watch-tower's searchlight seems to follow him; the death's head insignia of the SS is visible on the walls. However, the Shoah is not simply the cause of his distress; it also contains the key for the amelioration of his pain. Pavel, his therapist, is also 'A Czech Jew, a survivor of Terezin and Auschwitz' (p. 43, iv). Paradoxically, it is only by approaching his experiences as a child of survivors with the aid of another survivor that Art has any hope of accommodating the Holocaust. As the tiny Art arrives he is welcomed by Pavel, a man who seems to be the antithesis of Vladek. Art tells the reader that Pavel is a refuge for 'stray dogs and cats' (p. 43, v), whilst Spiegelman questions the reader directly, 'Can I mention this, or does it completely louse up my metaphor?' (p. 43, v). Such infrequent but direct dialogue, when Spiegelman speaks to the reader out of the frame, creates a sense of intimacy and immediacy. This transparency in relation to Spiegelman's creative processes, dilemmas and queries encourages the reader to accept that there is a dialogue taking place between Spiegelman and the reader and emphasizes the reader's responsibility to engage with the story actively, to take nothing for granted or at face value. It is too late for Spiegelman/Art to be asking this question; once again, as in *Maus I* (p. 23) the reader has already read and any damage which may be done to the viability of the metaphor has already been sustained. Art's reference to the stray cats and dogs does draw attention to the fact that the animals which Spiegelman is using symbolically to represent extreme antagonisms may be capable of peaceful cohabitation. The 'framed photo of a pet cat' (p. 43, viii) to which Spiegelman draws the reader's attention reinforces this perception and encourages a recognition that there are flaws in the metaphor. Using mice and cats to represent Jews and Germans may be taken wrongly as a suggestion that the antipathy expressed by Germans towards Jews is as natural and as morally neutral as a cat's propensity to hunt and kill a mouse. That Poles are represented as pigs also presents problems as the relationship between mice and pigs does not seem to contain any natural potential for antagonism.

Art's visit to Pavel mirrors Art's visits to Vladek. Art's need for a recognition of the psychological content and impact of his experience is more explicit in this relationship; Art visits Pavel in order to talk about the experience of the Shoah which he has inherited from Vladek and Anja. He catalogues its deleterious effects, he is 'completely messed up' (p. 43, vi); 'feel[s] like crying' (vi); 'can't work' (vii); has demands made of him which he 'can't deal with' (vii), but even when he is given time to work he finds himself 'totally **blocked**. Instead of working ... I just lie on my couch for hours and stare at a small grease spot on the upholstery' (viii). In the circumstances, Art's emotional state seems unsurprising, yet it serves to dramatize the apparent absence of any comparable disturbance in Vladek. The image of Art lying 'on my couch for hours' is the antithesis of Vladek's vigorous and implacable exertions; the reader might expect Vladek to have complained of the ills which Art experiences. In a sense, Art is not only the conduit of Vladek's story, but also perhaps of the emotions which Vladek has, of necessity, had to repress; Art is Vladek's proxy and *Maus II* is Art's story of the Holocaust. Even its title, *Maus II*, whilst referring to its nature as a sequel may also be read as an allusion to Spiegelman's/Art's growing recognition of his own survivor status; Spiegelman/Art is 'mouse too'.

This ambiguous network of responses to survivor status, especially for a child like Art who is the child of survivors, is represented by pp. 44–5. Page 44 concentrates on Art's relationship with Vladek's relationship with the Holocaust and what effects that has had upon them. Together they represent a specific individual-sized aspect of the Shoah. Page 45 develops these themes into a discussion which refers to all survivors. Pavel asks Art, 'Do you **admire** your father for surviving?' (p. 45, i). Art shows by his response that 'admire' is problematic and does not exactly express the ambiguities of his feelings towards Vladek. 'Well ... sure. I know there was a lot of **luck** involved, but he was

amazingly present-minded and resourceful . . .' (p. 45, i). Pavel reveals
the inherent difficulty which might arise here as there are possible
implications for the status of those who did not survive, 'Then you
think it's admirable to survive. Does that mean it's **not** admirable to **not**
survive?' (p. 45, ii). Art is shocked by this suggestion, but it does seem
to be a logical corollary of their earlier exchange. Pavel, in what may be
read as a direct response to Levi's 'the best all died' (*The Drowned and
the Saved*, p. 63) articulates the fracture between the two statements,
'Life always takes the side of life, and somehow the victims are blamed'
and 'It wasn't the **best** people who survived, nor did the best ones die'
(p. 45, ii). Pavel's statement of these discontinuities, 'It was **random**!',
is helpful and appropriate here because it removes a moral judgement
from the equations with which Art is grappling. Survival was random
and no matter how 'present-minded and resourceful' Vladek was, he
could still have been killed. These matters are not only necessary for
Art to resolve but are essential to Pavel and the reader.

Pavel grapples with the implications for the future of the past and
comes to the disturbing conclusion in relation to books about the
Holocaust, 'What's the point? People haven't changed . . . Maybe they
need a newer, bigger Holocaust' (p. 45, iv). Pavel suggests that, as the
stories of those who died will always be absent from Holocaust
literature, it may be better to stop telling stories altogether. Art cites
Samuel Beckett in agreement, 'Every word is like an unnecessary stain
on silence and nothingness' (p. 45, vi). Frame vii shows Art and Pavel
enacting a contemplative, maybe stunned, silence, one of the few
frames in either *Maus I* or *II* without words. It seems that they have
argued themselves into a position of speechlessness in relation to the
Shoah and that the huge emotional content of their earlier discourse
may finally only be articulated by silence. But Art breaks out of the
silence, which, if it were to continue, would leave Spiegelman and the
reader with a dilemma. Art points out that Samuel Beckett was not
innocent of staining 'silence and nothingness' because 'On the other
hand, he **said** it' (p. 45, viii). The dilemma is resolved; for the time
being Art has reached the conclusion that the response to the
Holocaust may not be only silence. Pavel approves Art's conclusion by
encouraging him to continue with his own project of breaking the
silence, 'He was right. Maybe you can include it in your book' (p. 45,
viii). But Art remains troubled by his own lack of willingness and
ability to engage fully with the Shoah, which for him is represented
always by the word 'Auschwitz'. He complains, 'My book? Hah! What
book?? Some part of me doesn't want to draw or think about

Auschwitz. I can't visualize it clearly, and I can't **begin** to imagine what it felt like' (p. 46, i).

The most significant aspect of the aid which Pavel extends to Art consists of helping him to realize Auschwitz as well as he may and for himself. Vladek could not do this and was only ever able to articulate an Auschwitz which was entirely his own experience; he was unable to imagine that others had similar but different apprehensions of Auschwitz and that each story would be unique.[13] Pavel shouts 'Boo' (p. 46, ii) at Art and as a measure of the force with which he does this, and the shock which it entails for Art, Spiegelman uses larger than usual capital letters. Pavel explains, 'It felt a little like **that**. But **always**! From the moment you got to the gate until the very end' (p. 46, iii). Pavel is able to offer practical as well as psychological help to Art, he tells him what tools might have been used in the tin shop (p. 46, v), and is able to share his experiences of Auschwitz with Art in a beneficial way, in a way which is not like Vladek's. He helps Art to recover his self-confidence.

Throughout the session Art has remained child-sized, but as he walks away (p. 46) he seems to be resuming his adult dimensions and he muses, 'Gee, I don't understand exactly why ...' (p. 46, viii) 'but these sessions with Pavel somehow make me feel better ...' (p. 46, ix). There is a contrast here between his leaving Pavel's and his father's; often after his sessions with Vladek, Art leaves in a very troubled state. In the final frame (p. 46, x) Art seems to be completely restored to himself as an adult; this is signalled by his reference to his work which he is ready and able to begin again. But the therapy session is not a quick-fix solution, as it might be if this text was fictional. Pavel's restorative influence does not last long and cannot undo the years of distress which Art has experienced. Back at his drawing board (the flies are gone), Art switches on the tape recorder and listens to Vladek's voice. The tape takes up the tale as Vladek is continuing his complaints about Mala. As Art listens to himself struggling with his dead father in an attempt to get him to talk about Auschwitz, he begins to lose his hold on his newly reconstituted self and slips back into the insecurities of the child. Listening to his father's voice recalls his own ambivalence and returns Art to his childlike mode; his regression is signalled again by a physical diminution.

The closing page of Chapter 2 reuses two images which have already appeared within the chapter. The first is the large, capitalized AAWOOWWAH! (p. 74, iv) which unnerves Françoise as she and Art sit outside on the verandah discussing Vladek. Françoise has said, 'It's

amazing how hard it is to spend a whole day with him. He just radiates
so much tension' (p. 74, iv) and she asks if Mala and Vladek will 'get
back together' (p. 74, iii). Art says, 'I sure **hope** so. Otherwise he's **our**
responsibility, and I don't think I can take him for too much longer'
(p. 74, iii). Just at this moment, the noise appears, without a speech
bubble and hangs over them like a cloud. Françoise is clearly afraid as
she asks, 'Wh-what's that noise?' but Art is unmoved, he continues to
light a cigarette as he answers, 'Oh, nothing – just Vladek ...' (p. 74, iv).
He explains to Françoise that Vladek has always moaned in his sleep,
'When I was a kid I thought that was the noise **all** grown-ups made
while they slept' (p. 74, v). The representation of the sound Vladek
makes is almost identical to – it is slightly smaller than – the sound
made by the Belgian boy, Felix, after he failed the second selection in
Vladek's Block (p. 59, iv). Spiegelman is drawing an analogy between
the articulation of distress expressed by Felix in Auschwitz when he
knew that he had been selected to die and the noise Vladek made after
and outside Auschwitz.

The second image is of the flies which had appeared on the title
page and opening pages of the chapter. Whilst Art and Françoise sit, the
flies hover around them; as Art explains the noise which has its origins
in Auschwitz to Françoise, their numbers increase. Françoise, soothed
by her surroundings and reassured by Art's explanation of the noise,
which has stopped, is able to relax, 'It's so peaceful here at night. It's
almost impossible to believe Auschwitz ever happened' (p. 74, vi). Art
is beginning to agree with her, 'Uh – huh' when he suddenly shouts
'**Ouch**!' and slaps at his body (p. 74, vi); the sound of the SLAP is
drawn in the same form as Vladek's AAWOOWWAH. Art jumps up
with a spray can of insecticide as he explains, 'But these damn bugs are
eating me alive!' (p. 74, vii); the PSHT of the spray is also like the
AAWOOWWAH and SLAP images. Françoise is also being bitten so
they decide to go inside. The 'damn bugs' are dead; two lie within the
final frame (p. 74, viii), another lies on the page, outside of the story. It
seems that, at the end of this long and demanding chapter, Art is able
to brush aside the concerns which are 'eating me alive' for a while.

This respite is brief and largely illusory; the next morning, as Art,
Françoise and Vladek drive to the shops, Vladek recounts the story of
the death march which went out from Auschwitz. As usual, it is Art
who prompts Vladek to begin his recollections again when he says,
'Last night I was reading about Auschwitz' (p. 79, v). There is never
any suggestion that Vladek allocates any time to reading or thinking
about the Shoah, other than the time he spends with Art. It is Art's

relationship with the memory of the offence which is constantly provoking Vladek's investigation and expression of his own memories. For Vladek, Art and Françoise the memory of the past and the actuality of the present are contiguous territory. The road on which they drive passes through trees from which hang the bodies of 'the four young girls' (p. 79, vii) who assisted those who 'blew up a crematorium' (p. 79, vi); there is no frame dividing that past from the present. Françoise finds Vladek's story of the death march and the arrival in Dachau especially harrowing (she is not often depicted as party to Vladek's recollections), and it leads Art to a disturbing conclusion about the nature of survival. As they sit outside the supermarket where Vladek is exchanging half-opened packets of groceries, Françoise expresses her response in extreme terms, 'I'd rather **kill** myself than live through all that' (p. 90, i) which suggests that Françoise has not, at this point, grasped the imperatives which drive the desire to survive and which later left survivors feeling ashamed or tainted. Art's joking response, 'What? Returning groceries?' (p. 90, i) does nothing to alleviate her distress and Françoise replies, 'No. Everything Vladek went through. It's a miracle he survived' (p. 90, ii). Art's response articulates an essential recognition in regard to Vladek's life after Auschwitz, 'But in some ways he **didn't** survive' (p. 90, ii). Art is able to reach this conclusion as a result of an intense period of time spent listening to and considering the implications of Vladek's story. When Vladek said, 'And we knew that from here we will not come out anymore' (*Maus I*, p. 157) he was expressing a certainty which was true in a way; he and Anja survived physically but the Anja and Vladek who went in through the gates at Auschwitz were not the same Anja and Vladek who came out. Art has finally articulated what writers like Langer and Améry also assert: Auschwitz could not be survived and the Shoah is never over for survivors.

Art's painful conclusion is not undone by anything he encounters as Vladek's story continues and it remains, unchallenged, at the end of *Maus II*. In one of the final frames (p. 136, iv), Spiegelman depicts the desired ending, the reunion between Anja and Vladek after the end of the war (reproduced at p. 185). The two of them embrace and Vladek is able to do no more than repeat Anja's name, 'Anja, Anja, my Anja', as they hold one another. Vladek, describing the scene to Art says, 'More I don't need to tell you. We were both very happy, and lived happy, happy ever after' (p. 136, iv). Art and the reader know that this fairy-tale ending is a construction of Vladek's, a necessary gloss on the facts which has enabled him to continue to live, after a fashion. After the war Vladek and Anja searched for Richieu until they were convinced that he was dead; they discovered the extent of the family losses they had sustained; they were forced to leave their homes and to become refugees in Sweden and then in the United States, where Anja suffered episodes of depression until she killed herself. This was their 'happy ever after'. Spiegelman signals the difficulties contained in Vladek's memory/rendition of an unproblematic reunion; behind the ecstatic couple the spotlight/searchlight remains. The triumphant image of the longed-for ending of Anja and Vladek's story – so like The End of any conventional literary romance when, in spite of outrageous trials and tribulations, the hero and heroine are alive and together are able to live 'happy ever after' – is undermined by the frames which follow. Spiegelman might have chosen to leave the image of Vladek and Anja's embrace as his final frame; that he did not confirms the fact that 'real' lives end differently outside literature's representations of them. This depiction of Vladek's recollection of their happiness is also marred by its close proximity to the image of Vladek, apparently bedridden, asking Art, 'So ... let's stop, please, your tape recorder' (p. 135, v).

It is as though Vladek's request signals his death; when his story ends, so does Vladek. This is a difficult moment, full of a potential for acute grief, as Art silently obeys and, like switching off a life-support machine, switches off the tape recorder. Vladek has gone, he is no longer in the present which Art inhabits and at the end of his life he believes himself to be back with Richieu in his remembered past, where he is finally exhausted by his role as story-teller, 'I'm **tired** from talking, Richieu, and it's **enough** stories for now ...' (p. 135, vi).

As *Maus I* opened with its reference to the genesis of Art's memories of the Shoah, 'It was summer, I remember' (*I*, p. 5, i) it is entirely appropriate that the penultimate image of *Maus II* reflects the unquestionable significance of willed acts of remembrance. This image, which appears underneath and beyond the page's frames, is of a memorial stone to Anja and Vladek; it represents another, truer end to their stories than the romantic image of their reunion. On the stone, beneath the name Spiegelman, the names of Vladek and Anja, inseparably reunited at last, sit side by side above their dates of birth and of death. Beneath the memorial is inscribed *Maus*'s final image; the name 'Art Spiegelman' and another set of dates '1978–1991'. This image, by mirroring the one immediately above, suggests that these are Art Spiegelman's dates of birth and of death; that the life of the Art Spiegelman depicted in these texts was synonymous with the time when that Art was writing *Maus*. Spiegelman has illustrated recollections which, though not his own, still formed and defined his existence; for him the act of telling the tale and inscribing that memory became as vital, as inescapable as Levi's witness.

Illustration 1
Maus I, p. 157

Illustration 2
Maus I, p. 5

Illustration 3
Maus I, p. 6

Illustration 4
Maus I, p. 32

Illustration 5
Maus I, p.33

33

Illustration 6
Maus I, p. 35

Illustration 7
Maus I, p. 11

Illustration 8
Maus I, p. 73

73

Illustration 9
Maus I, p. 74

Illustration 10
Maus II, p. 27

27

Illustration 11
Maus II, p. 41

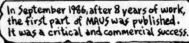

Illustration 12
Maus II, p. 42

Illustration 13
Maus II, p. 43

Illustration 14
Maus II, p. 136

NOTES

1. Art Spiegelman, *Maus I: A Survivor's Tale* (London: Penguin, 1987) and *Maus II: A Survivor's Tale* (London: Penguin, 1992). *American Literature*, 68: 1 (March 1996), pp. 69–84.

2. Joseph Witek's *Comic Books as History: The Narrative Art of Jack Jackson, Art Spiegelman, and Harvey Pekar* (Jackson: University of Mississippi, 1989), discusses the educational uses of comic books.

3. The spotlight never disappears and continues to be present in the closing pages of *Maus II*.

4. Lawrence Langer, *Holocaust Testimonies: The Ruins of Memory* (New Haven: Yale University Press, 1991).

5. Vladek's greatest achievement in this context occurs in *Maus II*, when he 'organizes' for Anja to be moved to new barracks close to where he is being kept (pp. 62–4).

6. Art Spiegelman, *The Complete MAUS* (New York: The Voyager Company, 1994).

7. In *Maus II*, Art's insistence upon his unlikeness assumes even greater proportions (pp. 18–20).

8. Compare *Maus II*, p. 42 viii and *II*, p. 72, v for similar images of despair.

9. The position of survivors' children is succinctly illustrated in the phrase, which I imagine will be used with increasing frequency, 'second-generation Holocaust survivor'; see for example, *The Jewish Quarterly*, 166 (summer 1997), p. 68, where a discussion of the work of artist Lily Markiewicz uses and explains the use of this term.

10. For a revealing fictional representation of such a childhood see David Grossman, *See Under: Love* (London: Picador, 1991). The literature on and by survivors' children grows and includes psychological as well as memoir material. The effects of the Holocaust upon those children have been and continue to be massive; even where they are not the explicit subject of a particular text the repercussions of those years continue to be felt in a myriad of ways. I would suggest, for example, that Daniel Goldhagen's remarkable book, *Hitler's Willing Executioners: Ordinary Germans and the Holocaust* (London: Little, Brown, 1996), though very different is still as much a response to his father Erich's experiences during the Shoah as *Maus* is Spiegelman's response to Vladek's; both men simply did what they could with the material that had been with them since birth. Consider also David Helfgott's story as represented in *Shine* (Hicks, 1996); Anne Karpf, *The War After: Living with the Holocaust* (London: Heinemann, 1996); Helen Epstein, *Children of the Holocaust: Conversations with Sons and Daughters of Survivors* (London: Penguin, 1988); Martin S. Bergman and Milton E. Jucovy (eds), *Generations of the Holocaust* (New York: Columbia University Press, 1990).

11. There is something odd about this matter of the masquerading Jews

because, of course, they *were* Poles, so to represent themselves as such is hardly a masquerade.

12. Will Nadja and Dashiell Spiegelman also have their stories to tell of being the children of the child of a survivor?

13. His response to Art's desire for Anja's story makes this plain, *Maus I* (p. 158, iv).

6

CONCLUSION:
REMEMBERING IN FUTURE

'Good God! To think they rake it all up again.'

There is no such object as the Memory of the Offence. That is, there is no single, finite, easily transmittable Memory of one describable Offence. Instead there are uncountable memories of a catalogue of offences. Even for Levi, who was at the centre of the Shoah vortex, there was a spectrum of recollections which ranged from what seemed to be an inadvertent and unintended injury like the wiping of an oily hand upon the 'rag' of a demolished man to the deliberate and cynical murder and cremation of people on an unprecedented scale. Yet, whilst they resist codification or capture, loose groupings of Shoah memories constituting a hierarchy of remembrance are discernible.

At the heart of the memories of the offences are the significant numbers of survivors' testimonies. Some, like Levi's, are mediated to the extent that those to whom they belong have been compelled to form them into objects which may be transmitted to non-survivors, as memoirs, novels, poetry, testimony. Others, like Vladek Spiegelman's, are handed on through the mediation and compulsion of non-survivors. In both cases there is an unquestionable authority attached to such memories which is partly bestowed by the survivors' proximity to the Shoah.

There are also those memories which once existed but which will never, no matter how assiduous and determined the researcher, be recovered. These are the memories which may only be read between the lines of available texts. I have dealt specifically with Schulz's inklings, those fantastic 'memories' of an event which had not yet taken place. But, of course, Schulz would also have been a source of memories of actual events, for example, of his time in the ghetto at Drohobycz; these invaluable memories are lost. Levi's readers are unavoidably aware of individuals like Null Achtzehn who left behind nothing more tangible than an oblique impression upon another's memories. Still, the shadowy, apparently ephemeral, presence of the memory of Null Achtzehn in Levi's writing will endure; there are millions whose lives and memories have not left even this limited mark.

The memories of, and belonging to, those unrecorded people become increasingly significant and compelling; what is apparently tangential in and for memory gradually becomes central. Rosette Lamont, the translator of Charlotte Delbo's trilogy, comments succinctly upon this process.[1]

> The presence of 'presence' is not too hard to understand. When memory imprints on us the meaning of the presence of 'absence' and animates the ghost that such a burden has imposed on our lives, then the heritage of the Holocaust will have begun to acquire some authenticity in our postwar culture.

The recognition of Anja's lost narrative and the longing to hear or read it impinges more and more upon Spiegelman's readers; as with Schulz, it is only by reading between the lines that Anja's and Richieu's stories may be (unsatisfactorily) deduced. Anja's untold story exerts such a powerful narrative imperative that the reader finds him or herself compelled to piece it together from the hints and allusions discovered in Vladek's narrative. Similarly, Art's frequently repeated lamentation, 'I wish I got Mom's story while she was alive' (*Maus II*, p. 132) becomes the reader's; as the reader longs for and laments for what is lost, memory seems to be back where it started, with inklings only.

There also exists a massive repository of memories of these offences which has often been resisted or forbidden. It is located with the forgetters, that is the people who were there when the offences were committed but have since absented themselves from that place; who saw, but have lived as though they did not; who knew, but now take refuge in not knowing. Levi recognized and described them in *The Drowned and the Saved*; they could still fill in many of the gaps if they wished.[2] A documentary broadcast by the BBC in 1997 contained an interview with a woman, Resi Kraus, who played a minuscule part in the Shoah; whilst she could not be called a perpetrator, she was more deliberate in her actions than is conveyed by the term 'bystander'.[3] In 1938 Resi Kraus was 20 years old and lived in Würzburg, next door to another young woman, Ilse Totzke, who became the object of denunciations from her neighbours and was finally deported to

Ravensbrück, where she died. Ilse's crime was, 'simple: she didn't fit in; she avoided her neighbours and had Jewish friends.' Resi Kraus was one of the many neighbours who made a statement against Ilse to the Gestapo.[4] She is an example of the resisters and deniers of memory; now a woman in her early seventies, the interview with her provides an insight into the mechanisms of the Shoah.

As the interviewer begins to read out the signed statement in which she denounced Ilse, Resi insists, 'That is rubbish. That is rubbish.' 'So none of this is true?' asks the interviewer. 'No, this is not true', responds Resi. The interviewer, with Resi's agreement, reads the statement to the end. Resi laughs indulgently at her own reference to the German Reich as though she is being reminded of the harmless indiscretions of youth, but does not interrupt again. As the interviewer comes to the end of the statement and reads, 'Read and signed: Resi Kraus', she acknowledges, 'That is my name' and 'That is my signature.' Resi then makes three stunning statements: 'I can't understand this. I don't know. I can't tell you.' In answer to the interviewer's question, 'So, how do you explain this document?' Resi repeats, 'I cannot understand'. The interviewer provides her with a possible explanation, 'The Gestapo did question a lot of people at the time', to which she responds, 'Yes. Yes.' but then she says, 'Well, I can't remember.'

'You can't remember', the interviewer repeats, to which Resi replies, 'I don't know. The address is correct. My signature is correct. But where it comes from I don't know.' Then she says, 'You're grinning. All this incriminates me.' 'Yes, well, it is a rather curious document', the interviewer observes. Resi is galvanized by this:

> Yes, but I was talking to a friend of mine – she said, 'Good God! To think they rake it all up again after 50 or 51 years.' . . . But it is you who is starting it . . . I mean, I didn't kill anybody, didn't murder anyone. I didn't even join the BDM, the Hitler Youth for girls. My father said to me, 'BDM – I will not have you travel into town twice a week when it is dark.' I told you how strictly I was brought up . . . Now it's starting to rain.

There are a number of elements to this interview which are both illuminating and compelling. Resi Kraus represents the tens of thousands of ordinary people who have resisted and repressed their memories. She looks like any middle-class woman in her early seventies; she is an absolutely ordinary woman, one of the ordinary people. Faced with the evidence of her crime – which was certainly not the most heinous in that time of despicable inhumanity – she took refuge in expressions of disbelief, then incomprehension, and finally forgetfulness. For the viewer the recognition of the rarity of such interviews was striking. Given the massively disproportionate ratio of surviving perpetrators and bystanders to survivors of the Holocaust it is astonishing to realize how infrequently their memories are recounted or made available. The reasons for this reticence are not difficult to fathom, but such reticence is culpable as an element in the forces of attrition to which memories of the Shoah are subjected. What was most troubling was Resi's perception that these matters should be left to lie, that to 'rake it all up again' was the truly blameworthy act. Such a view not only challenges memory but also justice; there may be no statute of limitation on the recital of Shoah memories.

When Levi wrote, 'We the survivors are not the true witnesses', he was clearly referring to his recognition that it was the 'submerged' and not the 'saved' who were best qualified to bear witness. His insight was a way of perceiving, and honouring, the *sommersi* and the power of their lost stories. But there is another possible gloss on this assertion which relates to Western ideas concerning justice and legality. As a survivor victim, Levi should not have been called on to stand as witness to his own demolition and to the crimes committed against him. The witnesses should have been the bystanders. Their refusal to witness at the time – and 'to witness' in this context must surely have implied a duty 'to prevent' – and subsequently, left survivors with terrible burdens: they were both the victims of the offences they suffered and the witnesses to those same offences. In such circumstances survivors were compelled to witness; without their testimonies there would have been only silence. Those who should have testified to the events of the Shoah turned away and carried on with their lives, refusing to see or speak of what was all around them. Many, like Resi, colluded in innumerable, mundane ways. Even now, as Resi Kraus's response makes clear, when the possibility of any significant punishment is long past, bystanders and perpetrators continue to maintain their incomprehension and shameful amnesia.

Resi Kraus's statements of forgetfulness cannot be allowed to stand here as my last words on the memories of the offences. Finally, there are the vicarious memories of those who have no direct recollections of the events of the Holocaust.[5] This ever-growing group includes, for the time being, individuals such as Art Spiegelman and Daniel Goldhagen who may legitimately claim proximity to, and a kind of memory of, the

Shoah. As the children of survivors, their experience of and response to their parents' memories have significantly shaped their own lives and choices. And there are those who were children during the war and whose first awareness of the Holocaust came via the newsreels shown in cinemas as the death camps were opened up by Allied troops. Their memories reflect a different kind of proximity to the event and many of these individuals speak and write of that shocking revelation as a terrible epiphany, a moment unlike any other before or since, when the possibilities for human cruelty were confirmed. But clearly, as time passes, an increasing majority of those who obey the injunction to remember the Shoah will be 'remembering' something which happened ten, 50, 100 years before they were born. Their 'memories' will arise out of and be composed by various disciplines: history, literature, philosophy, politics, film, and will be informed by survivor testimony and archive material. They will be remembering for all kinds of reasons. Many rememberers will require, even demand, that memories should have locations which may be visited; the 'pilgrimage' proposed by the narrator of Schwarz-Bart's *The Last of the Just* (1962) will not be sufficient for the adequate expression of 'pious memory'.[6] The forms that memories will adopt, the role of remembrance itself, the viability of memories, the tensions between memorials, monuments, museums and the act of remembrance, will continue to provoke debate and criticism. Memories will be misappropriated and misused, and whilst there is little to be done to prevent this happening – attempts at censorship or regulation are as likely to trammel the well-meaning as the exploiter – any potential for damage may be more than mitigated by making room for and paying attention to those memories which tell the truth.[7]

The understandable determination to remember the Shoah seems increasingly to be expressed through the experiential, the tangible and the viewable, as though memory itself is not up to the task of remembering. Of course, remembering requires aid, memories demand props and rehearsal; they must have a theatre. Everyone fortunate enough to live long enough comes to this realization in a small way. The memories of parents, siblings, friends, colleagues, all combine to help compose our own memories and identities. The death of one person, the loss of one element in my memory's repertoire, compromises the viability of the whole; if this is the case for those who have lived in relative safety, how much more debilitating such losses must be for survivors.[8]

The impulse to remember and to memorialize, rather than being eroded, is strengthening. The demand for touchstones and markers, deliberate references to the idea of shared pasts, reveals a different set of imperatives from those usually attributed to the postwar people and societies of Europe and North America. In his commentary on the reappearance of the observance of a two-minute silence at 11 a.m. on the 11th of November in 1996, an event which he characterized as representing 'the undimmable sense of community', Martin Kettle made a number of points which are relevant here. And, whilst he draws attention to what may seem to be inappropriate reasons for these rituals, he asserts the overwhelming message which he discovers in these acts of a desire for a 'shared memory of loss'.

> It is undoubtedly strange that after half a century in which our people have not been engaged in a European war, the impulse to participate in remembrance should have increased rather than diminished. But however strange it may be it is also true. The era in which such remembrance events could be depicted as merely right-wing, nationalistic and private to those who had fought has long gone. The instinct to share these memories is now much wider.
>
> It goes without saying that for many people in Britain such remembrance remains bound up with a nostalgic sense of the end of national greatness and certainty. For some these November ceremonies are, of course, a defiant affirmation of lost power. And they cannot also fail to contribute a meaning within the irresistible public debate about British identity, the stability of our institutions and our place in Europe.
>
> But we also take part in these events because in various ways they continue to affirm something about a shared past, a common inherited memory and a collective present. They speak of the pain of the 20th century.[9]

There is no doubt that the repercussions, whether acknowledged or not, of the Shoah will continue to colour the memories and therefore the behaviour of people and governments not only in Europe but throughout the world. The time approaches when the last survivor will have died. Then the memories of these offences will only be written and spoken of, visualized and 'remembered' by second, third, fourth generations of those who are neither survivors nor the children of survivors. At that point memories will have to depend for their continued expression upon the willingness of individuals, unlike Resi Kraus, to 'rake it all up again'.

> It was only by crushing the dandelions underfoot that I could feel something other than soft-packed dirt. I knelt down and parted the stalks and leaves, brushed away the fuzz of their seedballs. Two inches of grizzled stone appeared, the Hebrew lettering virtually obliterated by heavy growths of tawny and mustard-colored lichen. I could just make out a name, Tet, Bet Yud, Hay, Tevye, Tovye? I sat and swept my arms about in the dandelions like a child making a snow-angel. Another stone appeared and another. Digging down a few inches brought another from the netherworld. I could have spent a day with a shovel and shears and exposed an entire world, the subterranean universe of the Jews of Punsk.[10]

NOTES

1. Charlotte Delbo, *Auschwitz and After*, trans. Rosette C. Lamont (New York: Yale University Press, 1995), p. xviii.
2. Primo Levi, *The Drowned and the Saved*, trans. Raymond Rosenthal (London: Abacus, 1988), pp. 13–18.
3. *Hitler: A Warning from History*. BBC2 broadcast (17 September 1997). The people who practised this kind of deliberate but low-level hostility seem to demand a new term – neither 'perpetrator' nor 'bystander' seem adequately to describe their activities.
4. This statement, along with thousands of others made by neighbours against their neighbours, has recently become accessible in the Gestapo archives in Würzburg. See above reference.
5. I have borrowed this phrase from James Young. See his Introduction, *The Texture of Memory: Holocaust Memorials and Meaning* (New Haven: Yale University Press, 1993), especially pp. 5–7, for discussion of the ways in which memories become the narratives 'shared' by a community which may not have experienced the event or events which gave rise to those memories.
6. André Schwarz-Bart, *The Last of the Just* (London: Reprint Society, 1962), p. 349. The full quotation reads:
   So this story will not finish with some tomb to be visited in pious memory. For the smoke that rises from crematoria obeys physical laws like any other: the particles come together and disperse according to the wind, which propels them. The only pilgrimage, dear reader,

would be to look sadly at a stormy sky now and then.

7. Here I am using the word 'truth' as at p. 10ff. above.

8. Maybe this awareness suggests another gloss on Donne's frequently repeated assertion 'Any mans *death* diminishes *me*', from 'Devotions XVII', in *Complete Verse and Selected Prose*, ed. John Hayward (New York: The Nonesuch Library, 1936), p. 538.

9. *The Guardian* (16 November 1996), p. 21.

10. Simon Schama, *Landscape and Memory* (London: Fontana, 1996), p. 36.

BIBLIOGRAPHY

PRIMARY TEXTS

Levi, Primo, *The Periodic Table*, trans. Raymond Rosenthal, London, Abacus, 1986.

Levi, Primo, *If This is a Man and The Truce*, trans. Stuart Woolf, London, Abacus, 1987.

Levi, Primo, *Moments of Reprieve*, trans. Ruth Feldman, London, Abacus, 1987.

Levi, Primo, *If Not Now, When?*, trans. William Weaver, London, Abacus, 1987.

Levi, Primo, *The Drowned and the Saved*, trans. Raymond Rosenthal, London, Abacus, 1988.

Levi, Primo, *Other People's Trades*, trans. Raymond Rosenthal, London, Abacus, 1990.

Levi, Primo, *The Mirror Maker*, trans. Raymond Rosenthal, London, Minerva, 1991.

Schulz, Bruno, *The Fictions of Bruno Schulz: The Street of Crocodiles and Sanatorium Under the Sign of the Hourglass*, trans. Celina Wieniewska, London, Picador, 1988.

Schulz, Bruno, *Letters and Drawings of Bruno Schulz with Selected Prose*, ed. Jerzy Ficowski, New York, Fromm, 1990.

Spiegelman, Art, *Maus I: A Survivor's Tale*, London, Penguin 1987.

Spiegelman, Art, *Maus II: A Survivor's Tale*, London, Penguin 1992.

Spiegelman, Art, *The Complete MAUS CD-ROM*, New York, The Voyager Company, 1994.

SECONDARY WORKS

Books

Abzug, Robert H., *Inside the Vicious Heart: Americans and the Liberation of Nazi Concentration Camps*, New York, Oxford University Press, 1985.

Alexander, Edward, *The Resonance of Dust: Essays on Holocaust Literature and Jewish Fate*, Columbus, Ohio State University, 1979.

Alexander, Edward, *The Holocaust and the War of Ideas*, New Brunswick, Transaction, 1994.

Améry, Jean, *At the Mind's Limits: Contemplations by a Survivor on Auschwitz and its Realities*, trans. Sidney Rosenfeld and Stella P. Rosenfeld, New York, Schocken, 1986.

Appelfeld, Aharon, *Badenheim 1939*, trans. Dalya Bilu, Boston, Godine, 1980.

Arendt, Hannah, *Eichmann in Jerusalem: A Report on the Banality of Evil*, London, Penguin, 1994.

Atwood, Margaret, *Bodily Harm*, London, Virago, 1983.

Auster, Paul, *The Invention of Solitude*, London, Faber & Faber, 1988.

Authorised Daily Prayer Book of the United Hebrew Congregations of the Commonwealth, Enlarged Centenary Edition, Cambridge, Press Syndicate of the University of Cambridge, 1992.

Avisar, Ilan, *Screening the Holocaust: Cinema's Images of the Unimaginable*, Bloomington, Indiana University Press, 1988.

Bauman, Zygmunt, *Modernity and the Holocaust*, Oxford, Basil Blackwell, 1989.

Begley, Louis, *Wartime Lies*, London, Macmillan, 1991.

Bellow, Saul, *Herzog*, London, Penguin, 1978.

BenGershôm, Ezra, *David: Testimony of a Holocaust Survivor*, Oxford, Berg, 1988.

Benjamin, Walter, *Illuminations*, ed. Hannah Arendt, London, Fontana, 1973.

Bergman, Martin S. and Milton E. Jucovy (eds), *Generations of the Holocaust*, New York, Columbia University Press, 1990.

Berkovits, Eliezer, *Faith after the Holocaust*, New York, Ktav, 1973.

Berkovits, Eliezer, *With God in Hell*, New York, Sanhedrin Press, 1979.

Bernstein, Michael André, *Foregone Conclusions: Against Apocalyptic History*, Los Angeles, University of California Press, 1994.

Bielawski, Shraga Feivel, *The Last Jew from Wegrow: The Memoirs of a Survivor of the Step-by-Step Genocide in Poland*, ed. Louis W. Liebovich, New York, Praeger, 1991.

Bitton Jackson, Livia E., *Elli: Coming of Age in the Holocaust*, London, Grafton, 1984.

Blanchot, Maurice, *The Writing of the Disaster*, trans. Ann Smock, Lincoln, University of Nebraska Press, 1986.

Bloch, Joshua, *On the Apocalyptic in Judaism*, Philadelphia, The Jewish Quarterly Review, 1952.

Block, Gay and Malka Drucker, *Rescuers: Portraits of Moral Courage in the Holocaust*, New York, Holmes & Meier, 1992.

Bohm-Duchen, Monica, *After Auschwitz: Responses to the Holocaust in Contemporary Art*, London, Lund Humphries, 1995.

Borges, Jorge Luis, *Labyrinths*, London, Penguin, 1971.

Borowski, Tadeusz, *This Way for the Gas, Ladies and Gentlemen*, London, Penguin, 1967.

Brecher, Elinor J., *Schindler's Legacy: True Stories of the List Survivors*, London, Hodder & Stoughton, 1994.

Bresheeth, Haim, Stuart Hood and Litza Jansz, *The Holocaust for Beginners*, London, Icon Books, 1994.

Browning, Christopher R., *The Final Solution and the German Foreign Office: A Study of Referat DIII of Abteilung Deutschland 1940–1943*, New York, Holmes & Meier, 1978.

Browning, Christopher R., *Fateful Months: Essays on the Emergence of the Final Solution*, New York, Holmes & Meier, 1985.

Browning, Christopher R., *Ordinary Men: Reserve Police Battalion 101 and the Final Solution in Poland*, New York, HarperCollins, 1992.

Browning, Christopher R., *The Path to Genocide: Essays on Launching the Final Solution*, Cambridge, Cambridge University Press, 1992.

Camon, Ferdinando, *Conversations with Primo Levi*, trans. John Shepley, Vermont, The Marlboro Press, 1989.

Caruth, Cathy (ed.), *Trauma: Explorations in Memory*, Baltimore, Johns Hopkins University Press, 1995.

Cesarani, David (ed.), *The Final Solution: Origins and Implementation*, London, Routledge, 1994.

Cheyette, Bryan, *Constructions of 'the Jew' in English Literature and Society: Racial Representations, 1875–1945*, Cambridge, Cambridge University Press, 1993.

Chmurzynski, Wojciech, *Bruno Schulz 1892–1942, English Supplement of Catalogue-Memoirs of the Exhibition 'Bruno Schulz (1892–1942). Ad Memoriam'*, Warsaw, Andrzej Zielinski Press, 1995.

Cicioni, Mirna, *Primo Levi: Bridges of Knowledge*, Oxford, Berg, 1995.

Cohen, Arthur A. and Paul Mendes-Flohr, *Contemporary Jewish Religious Thought*, New York, Macmillan, 1987.

Coleridge, Samuel Taylor, *The Rime of the Ancient Mariner.*

Delbo, Charlotte, *Auschwitz and After*, trans. Rosette C. Lamont, New York, Yale University Press, 1995.

Des Pres, Terrence, *The Survivor: An Anatomy of Life in the Death Camps*, Oxford, Oxford University Press, 1976.

Donne, John, *Complete Verse and Selected Prose*, ed. John Hayward, New York, The Nonesuch Library, 1936.

Drew, Margaret (ed.), *Facing History and Ourselves: Holocaust and Human Behavior Annotated Bibliography*, New York, Walker, 1988.

Dwork, Deborah, *Children with a Star: Jewish Youth in Nazi Europe*, New Haven, Yale University Press, 1991.

Dyer, Geoff, *The Missing of the Somme*, London, Penguin, 1994.

Eban, Abba, *Heritage: Civilization and the Jews*, London, Weidenfeld & Nicolson, 1984.

Edelheit, Abraham J. and Herschel Edelheit, *History of the Holocaust: A Handbook and Dictionary*, Oxford, Westview Press, 1994.

Eliach, Yaffa, *Hasidic Tales of the Holocaust*, New York, Vintage Books, 1988.

Epstein, Helen, *Children of the Holocaust: Conversations with Sons and Daughters of Survivors*, London, Penguin, 1988.

Ezrahi, Sidra De Koven, *By Words Alone: The Holocaust in Literature*, Chicago, University of Chicago Press, 1980.

Felman, Shoshana and Dori Laub, *Testimony: Crises of Witnessing in Literature, Psychoanalysis, and History*, London, Routledge, 1992.

Ficowski, Jerzy, *Letters and Drawings of Bruno Schulz with Selected Prose*, trans. Walter Arndt, New York, Fromm, 1990.

Ficowski, Jerzy (ed.), *Bruno Schulz: Ilustracje*, Warszaw, Wydawnictwo Reprint, 1992.

Ficowski, Jerzy (ed.), *Le Livre Idolâtre*, Varsovie, Editions Interpress, n.d.

Fink, Ida, *A Scrap of Time*, trans. Madeline Levine and Francine Prose, London, Penguin, 1989.

Friedlander, Albert H., *Out of the Whirlwind: A Reader of Holocaust Literature*, New York, Union of American Hebrew Congregations, 1968.

Friedlander, Albert H., *Riders Towards the Dawn: From Ultimate Suffering to Tempered Hope*, London, Constable, 1993.

Friedlander, Saul (ed.), *Probing the Limits of Representation: Nazism and the 'Final Solution'*, Cambridge, Harvard University Press, 1992.

Fry, Stephen, *Making History*, London, Picador, 1996.

Gerhardsson, Birger, *Memory and Manuscript: Oral Tradition and Written Transmission in Rabbinic Judaism and Early Christianity*, Lund, Gleerup, 1961.

Gilbert, Martin, *The Holocaust: The Jewish Tragedy*, London, Collins, 1986.

Gilbert, Martin, *The Dent Atlas of the Holocaust: The Complete History*, London, Dent, 1993.

Goldberg, David G. and John D. Rayner, *The Jewish People: Their History and their Religion*, London, Viking, 1987.

Goldhagen, Daniel Jonah, *Hitler's Willing Executioners: Ordinary Germans and the Holocaust*, London, Little, Brown, 1996.

Green, Arthur (ed.), *Jewish Spirituality from the Sixteenth-Century Revival to the Present*, New York, Crossroad, 1989.

Grossman, David, *See Under: Love*, trans. Betsy Rosenberg, London, Picador, 1991.

Gruber, Ruth Ellen, *Upon the Doorposts of Thy House: Jewish Life in East-Central Europe, Yesterday and Today*, New York, John Wiley, 1994.

Hartman, Geoffrey H. (ed.), *Holocaust Remembrance: The Shapes of Memory*, Oxford, Basil Blackwell, 1994.

Hayes, Peter (ed.), *Lessons and Legacies: The Meaning of the Holocaust in a Changing World*, Illinois, Northwestern University Press, 1991.

Heinemann, Marlene E., *Gender and Destiny: Women Writers and the Holocaust*, New York and London, Greenwood Press, 1986.

Hilberg, Raul, *Perpetrators, Victims, Bystanders: The Jewish Catastrophe 1933–1945*, New York, HarperCollins, 1992.

Hodes, Tamar (ed.), *Other Rooms*, Keele, Ryburn Publishing, 1994.

Hoffman, Eva, *Lost in Translation: A Life in a New Language*, London, Minerva, 1991.

Hoffman, Eva, *Exit into History: A Journey through the New Eastern Europe*, London, Minerva, 1994.

Huyssen, Andreas, *Twilight Memories: Marking Time in a Culture of Amnesia*, London, Routledge, 1995.

Insdorf, Annette, *Indelible Shadows: Film and the Holocaust*, Cambridge, Cambridge University Press, 1983.

Isler, Alan, *The Prince of West End Avenue*, London, Cape, 1995.

Kampf, Avram, *Chagall to Kitaj: Jewish Experience in 20th-Century Art*, London, Lund Humphries, 1990.

Kantor, Alfred, *The Book of Alfred Kantor: An Artist's Journal of the Holocaust*, New York, Schocken, 1987.

Kaplan, Harold, *Conscience and Memory: Meditations in a Museum of the Holocaust*, Chicago, University of Chicago Press, 1994.

Karpf, Anne, *The War After: Living with the Holocaust*, London, Heinemann, 1996.

Keneally, Thomas, *Schindler's Ark*, London, Hodder & Stoughton, 1982.

Kis, Danilo, *Garden, Ashes*, London, Faber & Faber, 1985 (United States, Harcourt, Brace, Jovanovich, 1978).

Klee, Ernst, Willi Dressen and Volker Riess, *The Good Old Days: The Holocaust as Seen by its Perpetrators and Bystanders*, trans. Deborah Burnstone, New York, Macmillan, 1991.

Kushner, Tony (ed.), *The Jewish Heritage in British History: Englishness and Jewishness*, London, Frank Cass, 1992.

Lang, Berel (ed.), *Writing and the Holocaust*, New York, Holmes & Meier, 1988.

Langer, Lawrence L., *The Holocaust and the Literary Imagination*, New York, Yale University Press, 1975.

Langer, Lawrence L., *Holocaust Testimonies: The Ruins of Memory*, New Haven, Yale University Press, 1991.

Langer, Lawrence L., *Admitting the Holocaust: Collected Essays*, New York, Oxford University Press, 1995.

Lanzmann, Claude, *Shoah: An Oral History of the Holocaust – The Complete Text of the Film*, New York, Pantheon, 1985.

Lerski, George J. and Halina T. Lerski, *Jewish–Polish Existence, 1772–1939: A Topical Bibliography*, New York, Greenwood, 1986.

Levi, Primo and Tullio Regge, *Conversations*, trans. Raymond Rosenthal, London, Penguin, 1992.

Lipstadt, Deborah, *Denying the Holocaust: The Growing Assault on Truth and Memory*, London, Penguin, 1994.

Litvinoff, Emanuel (ed.), *The Penguin Book of Jewish Short Stories*, London, Penguin, 1979.

McEwan, Ian, *Black Dogs*, London, Picador, 1993.

Mendelsohn, John (ed.), *The Holocaust: Selected Documents in 18 vols*, New York, Garland, 1982.

Milosz, Czeslaw, *The History of Polish Literature*, Los Angeles, University of California Press, 1983.

Moore, R. I., *The Formation of a Persecuting Society: Power and Deviance in Western Europe (950–1250)*, Oxford, Basil Blackwell, 1987.

Nehar, André, *They Made their Souls Anew*, trans. David Maisel, New York, University of New York Press, 1990.

Nepomuk, George and Owen John, *Hell's Mouth: Confessions of Count Nepomuk*, London, Peter Davies, 1974.

Ozick, Cynthia, *The Messiah of Stockholm*, London, André Deutsch, 1987.

Ozick, Cynthia, *What Henry James Knew and Other Essays on Writers*, London, Vintage, 1994.

Patai, Raphael, *The Jewish Alchemists: A History and Source Book*, New Jersey, Princeton University Press, 1994.

Rawicz, Piotr, *Blood from the Sky*, London, Secker & Warburg, 1964.

Richmond, Colin, *The Penket Papers*, Gloucester, Alan Sutton Publishing, 1986.

Richmond, Colin, *Annals*, Stoke-on-Trent, Whatland Press, 1994.

Richmond, Colin, *Parkes and I: The Parkes Lecture*, Southampton, University of Southampton Press, 1994.

Roberts, Michèle, *Daughters of the House*, London, Virago, 1993.

Rose, Gillian, *Love's Work*, London, Chatto & Windus, 1995.

Rose, Jacqueline, *The Haunting of Sylvia Plath*, London, Virago, 1991.

Rosenfeld, Alvin H., *A Double Dying: Reflections on Holocaust Literature*, Bloomington, Indiana University Press, 1988.

Roskies, David, *Against the Apocalypse: Responses to Catastrophe in Modern Jewish Culture*, Cambridge, Harvard University Press, 1984.

Roskies, David, *A Bridge of Longing: The Lost Art of Yiddish Storytelling*, Cambridge, Harvard University Press, 1995.

Roth, John K. and Michael Berenbaum (eds), *Holocaust: Religious and Philosophical Implications*, New York, Paragon House, 1989.

Rubenstein, Richard L. and John K. Roth, *Approaches to Auschwitz: The Legacy of the Holocaust*, London, SCM, 1987.

Rudolf, Anthony, *At an Uncertain Hour: Primo Levi's War against Oblivion*, London, Menard Press, 1990.

Rudolf, Anthony, *I'm Not Even a Grown-up: The Diary of Jerzy Feliks Urman*, London, Menard Press, 1991.

Rudolf, Anthony, *Engraved in Flesh: Piotr Rawicz and his Novel Blood from the Sky*, London, Menard Press, 1996.

Sabin, Roger, *Comics, Comix and Graphic Novels: A History of Comic Art*, London, Phaidon, 1996.

Saperstein, Marc, *Moments of Crisis in Jewish–Christian Relations*, London, SCM Press, 1989.

Schama, Simon, *Landscape and Memory*, London, Fontana, 1996.

Schiff, Hilda (ed.), *Holocaust Poetry*, London, HarperCollins, 1995.

Schwarz-Bart, André, *The Last of the Just*, London, Reprint Society, 1962.

Sebald, W. G., *The Emigrants*, trans. Michael Hulse, London, Harvill, 1996.

Segev, Tom, *The Seventh Million: The Israelis and the Holocaust*, trans. Haim Watzman, New York, Hill & Wang, 1993.

Sicher, Efraim, *Beyond Marginality: Anglo-Jewish Literature after the Holocaust*, Albany, State University of New York, 1985.

Tarrow, Susan R. (ed.), *Reason and Light: Essays on Primo Levi*, Cornell, Cornell University Press, 1990.

Tedeschi, Giuliana, *There is a Place on Earth: A Woman in Birkenau*, London, Minerva, 1994.

Thomas, D. M., *The White Hotel*, London, Penguin, 1981.

Vishniac, Roman, *A Vanished World*, London, Penguin, 1986.

Waxman, Meyer, *A History of Jewish Literature*, 5 vols, New Jersey and London, Thomas Yoseloff, 1960.

Weinberg, Jeshajahu and Rina Elieli, *The Holocaust Museum in Washington*, New York, Rizzoli, 1995.

Weiss, Peter, *The Investigation*, trans. Jon Swan and Ulu Grosbard, New York, Atheneum, 1975.

White, Patrick, *Riders in the Chariot*, London, Penguin, 1984.

Wiesel, Elie, *Night*, London, Penguin, 1981.

Wiesel, Elie, *Twilight*, London, Penguin, 1991.

Williams, Val, and Greg Hobson, *The Dead*, Bradford, The National Museum of Photography, Film and Television, 1995.

Witek, Joseph, *Comic Books as History: The Narrative Art of Jack Jackson, Art Spiegelman, and Harvey Pekar*, Jackson, University of Mississippi Press, 1989.

Yerushalmi, Yosef Hayim, *Zakhor: Jewish History and Jewish Memory*, Seattle, University of Washington Press, 1982.

Young, James E., *Writing and Rewriting the Holocaust: Narrative and the Consequences of Interpretation*, Bloomington, Indiana University Press, 1990.
Young, James E., *The Texture of Memory: Holocaust Memorials and Meaning*, New Haven, Yale University Press, 1993.
Yudkin, Leon I. (ed.), *Hebrew Literature in the Wake of the Holocaust*, New Jersey, Associated University Press, 1993.

ARTICLES

Baranczak, Stanislaw, 'The Faces of Mastery', *The New Republic* (2 January 1989), pp. 28–34.
Bernstein, Michael André, 'The Lasting Injury', *The Times Literary Supplement* (7 March 1997), pp. 3–4.
Biasin, Gian Paolo, 'Till My Ghastly Tale is Told: Levi's Moral Discourse from *Se questo è un uomo* to *I sommersi e i salvati*', in *Reason and Light: Essays on Primo Levi*, ed. Susan R. Tarrow, Cornell, Cornell University Press, 1990, pp. 127–47.
Brown, Russell E., 'Metamorphosis in Bruno Schulz', *The Polish Review*, 30 (1985), pp. 373–80.
Brown, Russell E., 'Bruno Schulz: The Myth of Origins', *Russian Literature*, 22 (1987), pp. 195–220.
Brown, Russell E., 'Bruno Schulz and World Literature', *The Slavic and East European Journal*, 34: 2 (1990), pp. 224–46.
Brown, Russell E., 'Joseph Visits his Dead Father: Bruno Schulz's *Sanatorium Pod Klepsydra*', *Canadian–American Slavic Studies*, 24:1 (1990), pp. 47–59.
Budurowycz, Bohdan, 'Galicia in the Works of Bruno Schulz', *Canadian Slavonic Papers*, 28:4 (1986), pp. 359–68.
Cannon, JoAnn, 'Chemistry and Writing in *The Periodic Table*' in *Reason and Light: Essays on Primo Levi*, ed. Susan R. Tarrow, Cornell, Cornell University Press, 1990, pp. 99–111.
Cannon, JoAnn, 'Canon-Formation and Reception in Contemporary Italy: The Case of Primo Levi', *Italica*, 69:1 (1992), pp. 30–44.
Douglas, Lawrence, 'Exhumations of Dreams', *Witness*, 10:1 (1996), pp. 26–33.
Epstein, Adam, 'Primo Levi and the Language of Atrocity', *Bulletin of the Society for Italian Studies*, 20 (1987), pp. 31–8.
Ficowski, Jerzy, 'The Schulzian Tense, or the Mythic Path to Freedom', *Polish Perspectives*, 10:11 (1967), p. 49.
Gilman, Sander, L., 'To Quote Primo Levi: "Redest keyn jiddisch, bist nit kejn jid" ["If you don't speak Yiddish, you're not a Jew"]', *Prooftexts*, 9:2 (1989), pp. 139–60.
Gopnik, Adam, 'Comics and Catastrophe', *New Republic* (22 June 1987), pp. 29–34.
Hansen, Miriam Bratu, '*Schindler's List* is not *Shoah*: The Second Commandment, Popular Modernism, and Public Memory', *Critical Inquiry*, 22 (winter 1996), pp. 292–312.
Harrowitz, Nancy, 'Representations of the Holocaust: Levi, Bassani, and the Commemorative Mode' in *Reason and Light: Essays on Primo Levi*, ed. Susan R. Tarrow, Cornell, Cornell University Press, 1990, pp. 26–39.

Iadonisi, Rick, 'Bleeding History and Owning his [Father's] Story: *Maus* and Collaborative Autobiography', *CEA Critic*, 57:1 (1994), pp. 41–56.

Jarrett, David, 'Bruno Schulz and the Map of Poland', *Chicago Review*, 40:1 (1994), pp. 73–84.

Krystals, Henry, 'Trauma and Aging: A Thirty-Year Follow-up', in *Trauma: Explorations in Memory*, ed. Cathy Caruth, Baltimore, Johns Hopkins University Press, 1995, pp. 76–99.

Lakritz, Andrew, 'Cynthia Ozick at the End of the Modern', *Chicago Review*, 40:1 (1994), pp. 98–117.

Levi, Primo and Gail Soffer, 'Beyond Survival', *Prooftexts*, 4:1 (1984), pp. 9–21.

Myers, Wayne, 'Hyper Torah', *Wired* (April 1996), pp. 60–4.

Milosz, Czeslaw, 'A Few Words on Bruno Schulz', *New Republic* (22 June 1987), pp. 30–1.

Rachwal, Tadeusz, 'A Ticket to Elsewhere', *Chicago Review*, 40:1 (1994), pp. 85–97.

Rachwal, Tadeusz and Andrew Lakritz, 'Bruno Schulz: An Introduction', *Chicago Review*, 40:1 (1994), pp. 62–5.

Richmond, Colin, '*Nachlass*: A Fragment', *Common Knowledge*, 1:3 (winter 1992), pp. 108–22.

Richmond, Colin, 'Remembrance of Things Not Past', *Immigrants & Minorities*, 12:2 (1993), pp. 119–227.

Richmond, Colin, 'Medieval English Jewry: Postmodernism and Marginalization', *Patterns of Prejudice*, 28: 3, 4 (1994), pp. 5–17.

Richmond, Colin, 'Autobibliography: From Sidcup to Prusków, 1942–1992,' *Common Knowledge*, 4:3 (winter 1995), pp. 113–52.

Richmond, Colin, 'Acceptable Atrocity', *Immigrants and Minorities*, 15:3 (November 1996), pp. 270–80.

Richmond, Colin, 'Eastern Atrocities: Three Holocaust Survivor Memoirs', *The Journal of Holocaust Education*, 5:1 (winter 1996), pp. 84–94.

Richmond, Colin, 'Why the University Should Not Be Named after de Montfort (or Why I Don't Drive a Volkswagen)', *Patterns of Prejudice*, 31: 2 (1997), pp. 19–29.

Rothberg, Michael, '"We Were Talking Jewish": Art Spiegelman's *Maus* as "Holocaust" Production', *Contemporary Literature* 35:4 (1994), pp. 661–87.

Scharf, Rafael F., 'A Beloved Teacher: A Vanished Human Landscape', *Judaism Today*, 1 (spring 1995), pp. 31–3.

Schehr, Lawrence R., 'Primo Levi's Strenuous Clarity', *Italica*, 66:4 (1989), pp. 429–43.

Schönle, Andreas, '*Cinnamon Shops* by Bruno Schulz: The Apology of *Tandeta*', *The Polish Review*, 36:2 (1991), pp. 127–44.

Sodi, Risa, 'An Interview with Primo Levi', *Partisan Review*, 54:3 (1987), pp. 355–66.

Taylor, Colleen M., 'Childhood Revisited: The Writings of Bruno Schulz', *The Slavic and East European Journal*, 13:4 (1969), pp. 455–72.

Vital, David, 'From Curiosity to Remorse: The Struggle to Establish the Truth about the Holocaust', *Times Literary Supplement* (7 March 1997).

Wilde-Menozzi, W., 'A Piece You've Touched is a Piece Moved: On Primo Levi', *Tel Aviv Review*, 2 (1989–90), pp. 149–65.

INDEX